Praise for *Gone Boy*

"Gibson is a fine writer whose work rivals the subtleties of Norman Mailer's best fiction."—*Boston* magazine

"Complex, surprising.... This book should be seriously considered by educational professionals, as well as by violence survivors who might benefit from Gibson's singular odyssey."—*Kirkus Reviews*

"Gibson is one of those rare birds whose humanism is a result of his innate curiosity about people. He's not interested in demonizing anyone, and he readily admits how people confound his expectations. To his great credit, Gibson writes about everyone he meets as an irreducibly complex human being."—*Salon*

"*Gone Boy* is not merely a book; it's a journey you experience. You move with Gregory Gibson as he looks down the barrel of the gun that killed his son, stands face to face with the man who sold it, comes to know the killer, comes to know the killer's parents—and comes to know himself. You will never read a more honest book, and honestly, it changed me."—Gavin de Becker, author of *The Gift of Fear*

GONE BOY

A Father's Search for the Truth in His Son's Murder

GREGORY GIBSON

North Atlantic Books
Berkeley, California

Published by
North Atlantic Books   Cover art @ istockphoto.com/chrispecoraro
P.O. Box 12327   Cover and book design by Brad Greene
Berkeley, California 94712

Printed in the United States of America

Gone Boy: A Father's Search for the Truth in His Son's Murder is sponsored by the Society for the Study of Native Arts and Sciences, a nonprofit educational corporation whose goals are to develop an educational and cross-cultural perspective linking various scientific, social, and artistic fields; to nurture a holistic view of arts, sciences, humanities, and healing; and to publish and distribute literature on the relationship of mind, body, and nature.

North Atlantic Books' publications are available through most bookstores. For further information, visit our website at www.northatlanticbooks.com or call 800-733-3000.

Library of Congress Cataloging-in-Publication Data

Gibson, Gregory, 1945–
  Gone boy : a father's search for the truth in his son's murder / Gregory Gibson.
      p. cm.
  "First published by Anchor Books, Garden City, N.Y., [1999]."
  Summary: "In this timeless memoir recounting every parent's worst nightmare, a literary stylist on par with powerhouses such as Raymond Chandler and Norman Maclean offers a balm for the many families who have suffered unthinkable loss. A truthful, coura-geous inquiry into guns, violence, and manhood in America today"—Provided by publisher.
  ISBN 978-1-55643-959-9
  1. Murder—Massachusetts—Great Barrington. 2. Bard College. Simon's Rock. 3. Gun control—Massachusetts—Case studies. 4. Gibson, Gregory, 1945—Family. I. Title.
  HV6534.G73G53 2011
  364.152'3092—dc22
  [B]
                                                        2010050865

1 2 3 4 5 6 7 8 9 UNITED 16 15 14 13 12 11

Galen Crotty Gibson
1974–1992

~

Everything I do now
I do for you, too

It would be a start to a story if this catastrophe were found to have circled around out there somewhere until it could return to itself with explanations of its own mysteries and with the grief it has left behind, not removed, because grief has its own place at or near the end of things, but altered somewhat by the addition of something like wonder ... then what we would be talking about would start to change from catastrophe without a filled-in story to what could be called the story of a tragedy, but tragedy would be only a part of it, as it is of life.

—NORMAN MACLEAN, *Young Men and Fire*

CONTENTS

INTRODUCTION
to the North Atlantic Edition

Gone Boy was published in 1999 and has remained in print ever since. Even now, more than a decade after its initial appearance, I get letters and emails from people to whom something very bad has happened. Invariably they describe the tragedy, then thank me for writing a sort of guidebook to the difficult territory they must traverse. Often they tell me how important it is to know that someone else survived such a journey, because there are times when survival does not seem possible.

As you can imagine, these responses are gratifying. It's good to know that something useful can arise from such a catastrophe. And it's even better to have a sense of the book being out there on its own, doing this necessary work so that my family and I no longer have to. So that we can "move on," as the talk show hosts like to say. With this new edition, North Atlantic Books is continuing to make that possible. I am very grateful to them for doing so.

But what about this matter of moving on, and the healing and forgiveness it implies? There's a lot of grand-sounding mumbo jumbo in circulation, but I've never read a book or seen a talk show that can explain the mystery of a person making a conscious decision not to be defined by a Bad Thing, and simply living life from that point on, day-by-day. Then the Bad Thing becomes just a part of a life, and when we look around at other people we discover that most of them have experienced bad things too, and have made similar decisions. Survival is the rule, not the exception, and I can't understand the "why" of it any more than I can understand why a cut heals over.

The idea of forgiveness is a greater mystery still—one I'll spend the rest of my life attempting to unravel. As it happens, I've got a helper in this endeavor, a strange sort of sidekick. His name is Wayne Lo and he's the man who murdered my son.

Wayne writes to me a few times a year, usually with a small check, which I deposit in the Galen Gibson Scholarship Trust. He earns the money by selling his artwork on the internet. This made the news for a moment in the spring of 2007 when a zealous fellow down in Houston realized that murderers were cashing in on their crimes. He coined the term "murderabilia" and decided to put an end to this practice.

Media people contacted me for an opinion, expecting some juicy murdered-son outrage. I opined that donating money to a scholarship fund in Galen's name was one of the few ways that Wayne Lo, locked in prison for the rest of his life, could try to atone for what he'd done. Society, I told them, has been very efficient about punishment, but backward about reconciliation and rehabilitation. This was not the answer they wanted to hear, so it didn't make the news.

Then, a couple of years ago I got a letter from Wayne telling me that there was a new book on school shootings that plagiarized *Gone Boy*.

I bought a copy of the book and found it to be the work of a hack sociologist who'd appropriated whole chunks of my material, citing fictionalized names and incidents as if they were fact. When I confronted him he confessed his crimes and slunk back into his hole. I then published an unfavorable review of the book, characterizing it as something akin to pornography, and pointing out that it was part of a burgeoning genre of sensationalist school-shooting literature. (Search Amazon under "school shootings" and see how many hundreds of hits you get.)

A few weeks later, I received a long distraught letter from Wayne Lo. He told me he felt terrible. Not only had he damaged so many lives with his shooting, now he was responsible for ruining the reputation of the sociologist. I told Wayne not to worry, that the man had done sloppy work, and that Wayne had been right to call attention to this. Wayne wrote back, greatly relieved, and I returned to my meditations on the mysteries of moving on—this time to ponder the bizarre situation in which I console the murderer of my son.

I never expected to have a murdered son, and I never expected to find myself considering the degree to which—like the old Indian custom someone told me about—I have swapped my son for his killer. That's not exactly what's going on, but sometimes it feels close. Wayne keeps sending his letters and checks, and I keep writing back, and we inch toward whatever deep and inexplicable destination we have in common. Perhaps some day we'll get there. Perhaps we never will. It seems strange to me, and I can only imagine how it must look to others, including my patient and tolerant family.

But that's exactly the point. There are endless branches on this journey, and no two people's experiences are ever the same. I hear a lot about what I "ought" to be doing and feeling and, as was the case with the "murderabilia" issue, I am often confronted by people who expect me to feel a certain way when, in fact, I do not feel that way at all.

Much of the time, I realize that what I'm really dealing with are people's own fears or their overwhelming desire to normalize what for them must be an unthinkable situation. What is there to do but try to be honest with them, and keep on moving? If I've learned anything since Galen's death, it is simply to follow my heart, regardless of the expectations that surround me.

That, as much as anything else, is what this book is about.

The names of some of the characters
in this narrative have been changed
to protect them from the unwarranted
glare of publicity.

PROLOGUE

In 1980 Red Auerbach, presiding genius of the Boston Celtics basketball franchise, orchestrated a series of deals, which enabled him to obtain a gangly rookie named Kevin McHale from the University of Minnesota. This acquisition helped establish the last of the Celtics dynasties, the front court of Bird, Parrish and McHale. The Celtics dominated the league for a decade.

By 1990 the brash and articulate Kevin McHale was an institution in the Boston sports world, with strong ties to his adopted community. One of the people with whom he'd developed a relationship was a Boston College graduate named Robert Durand. At the time Kevin McHale knew him, Durand was serving as a state Representative from the Middlesex and Worcester district in Massachusetts. The two men had much in common. Tall and rangy, with a weathered face, Durand was athletically inclined, and an active participant in outdoor sports. McHale, a native of Hibbing, Minnesota, was an avid outdoorsman. As their schedules permitted, Kevin McHale was a guest at Bob Durand's home in Marlboro, Massachusetts. The two men hiked and hunted together.

In the winter of 1990 McHale and Durand were hunting ducks on Cape Cod when McHale ran out of shotgun shells. He went to a local sporting goods store and was surprised to discover that there was a law in Massachusetts forbidding the sale of longarms or ammunition to non-residents. The only exception this law made was for people who lived in states contiguous to Massachusetts.

McHale was not a particularly vain man, but he wasn't used to being denied things for apparently arbitrary reasons, certainly not a mere box of shotgun shells. He mentioned the incident to Bob Durand who agreed that the law seemed senseless. In Representative Durand's opinion, it presented a conflict between state and national legislation. Under the terms of a federal act signed by President Reagan in 1986, firearms dealers were permitted to sell ammunition and longarms to American citizens who met the legal requirements for purchases in their home states. The Massachusetts law forbade this.

Durand enlisted bi-partisan support for a new gun law, which corrected the inconsistency. It came before the Massachusetts legislature at a time of fierce political battles over school choice and seatbelt laws, and it slid through the House and Senate with hardly a ripple. On June 24, 1991, Governor William F. Weld signed into law AN ACT RELATIVE TO EXEMPTIONS FOR NONRESIDENT PURCHASERS OF CERTAIN FIREARMS AND AMMUNITION. This act made the purchase of a longarm or ammunition legal for, "Any nonresident who is eighteen years of age or older when acquiring a rifle, shotgun or ammunition from a licensed firearms dealer, provided that such nonresident is in compliance with the law of the state where he resides and has the proper firearms license if required..."

The conflict between state and federal law had been efficiently repaired.

A year and a half after the passage of this act, and just three weeks past his eighteenth birthday, Wayne Lo walked into Dave's Sporting Goods in Pittsfield, Massachusetts. He showed the clerk his Montana driver's license, the sole document required for the purchase of a gun in Montana, paid the requisite amount, and walked out the door with an SKS rifle.

He returned to the small New England college where he was a student, took a test, ate dinner, then went on a shooting rampage. He wounded four people and killed two, one of whom was my son, Galen Gibson.

PART ONE

1
SICK OF IT ALL

I always had a knack for making plans. Not long range plans, but an endless supply of existential ones, in an ongoing calculus of strategy. Whenever the situation changed there'd be a new plan. Sometimes there were several in an hour.

So, it was not surprising that, when the dean of my son's college called, late on a Monday night in mid-December of 1992, and told me there'd been a terrible accident at the college, and that my son had been shot and killed, I soon had a plan.

At first I could not speak. I handed the telephone to Annie, my wife, and as I stood there, gasping for breath, the idea came to me. I was going to drive out to the college and bring Galen back. I was going to spread out his old sleeping bag in the back of the van and lay his body on it. I was going to get the body and bring it home so we could clean it up and bury it, so we could wash those bullet holes with our tears. Three hours out and three hours back. I'd be home by dawn. That was the level at which I was capable of planning.

Annie put the telephone down and walked to one end of the hall, then back, a wild, distracted look about her. This was not one of those revelatory moments in which husbands and wives learned deep truths about one another. Shock had driven us down inside ourselves. The truth was more physical, literal. Annie was standing beside me, as she had been for eighteen years.

She picked the phone up again and called her mother, who gently pointed out to me that my proper place during this time of crisis was

3

at home with my family, not at the other end of the state trying to haul the corpse out of a murder investigation. So I stayed home that night, with Annie, and our son Brooks, and our daughter Celia.

Initially, the news of Galen's death was so enormous that we could not assimilate it in any meaningful way. We stumbled woodenly about the house, trying to make the necessary phone calls to relatives and friends. Brooks, a sophomore in high school, went out for a long drive with another boy. We let Celia, our baby, have one last night of untroubled sleep. She was nine years old, the special pet of eighteen-year-old Galen.

We could not cry. We kept telling ourselves that it was a mistake, that it had happened to someone else. We kept thinking, throughout that long and terrible night, that in the morning we'd wake, and it all would have been a dream. But when the morning came, it brought a deluge of news reports. Our waking nightmare became common knowledge; an absurd violation and an inescapable fact. Galen was dead. The radio said so.

Somehow, on the small, sleepy campus of Simon's Rock College, a student had gone crazy. Somehow, he'd ordered bullets through the mail. Then he'd gone to a local gun shop and bought a military-style semi-automatic rifle. Somehow he got the gun back onto school grounds undetected. At about 10:15 on the evening of Monday, December 14, 1992, he began walking through the campus, shooting people. First he shot and seriously wounded the guard at the front gate. Then he murdered a professor driving past. Then he walked to the library where he murdered Galen and wounded another student. Then he wounded two more students. Then, somehow, he surrendered and was arrested, unharmed. His name was Wayne Lo. He'd emigrated from Taiwan six years before.

Beyond establishing the place and time of our son's death, these few stark facts were of little use to Annie and me. We desperately needed an exact account of how this terrible thing had come to pass, but we got no word from anyone on the scene. Our imagining of the event took the form of a grotesque cartoon, drawn from the terse hyperbole of news reports.

Thus, Galen had died in a "campus shooting spree" at his "exclusive Berkshires school." The killer was a "troubled, angry youth ... an outcast." He "proceeded across the snowy paths ... panic in his wake" and "sent a blast into Gibson's chest." Galen "staggered to the front desk ... blood soaking through his shirt, and cried 'I've been shot.'"

The report ended with "steel gray hearses" removing the bodies at dawn, and with Wayne Lo being taken into police custody. His head was shaved, and he was wearing a sweatshirt on which was printed the motto, "Sick of It All."

This version of what had happened raised more questions than it answered, but we were too stunned to ask them.

2

THE MAN OF WORDS

The atmosphere of those first days was remarkable. The air had a particular pearlish luminescence. Space had a palpable texture and time was just a part of that space-stuff. Certainly it was fatigue and extreme distress that made things seem so different, but just as surely it was because suddenly we were right up close to the place where birth and death have their origins.

That place is at the core of this world, after all the superficial covering has been ripped away. It is a place of unthinking cruelty and of absolute understanding. It is a place where things simply happen. It is a holy place, a source place, suffused with that peculiar color and specificity of space and time, and with a vast, compassionate impulse. It was a balm to our hurt, and Annie, Brooks, Celia and I huddled there instinctively, each of us enveloped in loss.

The whole town gathered around us and helped with our burden. Our families and friends showed up out of nowhere, it seemed. On Tuesday morning, Wednesday and Thursday, one after another they appeared in our midst to entertain Celia, to console Brooks. The floors got swept, funeral arrangements got made, newspeople got taken care of, and the endless stream of well-wishers got seated and watered and fed. I remember nothing more vividly than the courage of those visitors, every one of them. I mean the bravery it took to show up at our door, all awkward and pained and stupid, knowing that no matter what food or offers of help they brought, there was really nothing they could do but sit with us.

We buried Galen on Thursday, three days after the shooting, and there was a huge, sad memorial service. Then all the friends and relatives who'd come from far away returned to their homes, and Annie and I began to come back into our bodies. At first we simply assumed our lives were over. It meant little to us, personally, if we lived or died. Then we remembered that we still had two children who were dependent on us, and who had lives that were not over. Brooks and Celia still needed to be hugged, yelled at, played with and driven around. We still had important things to do. We did indeed have something to live for. Therefore our lives were not over.

We began our grieving then, and for three years or more Annie and I gave a good part of our lives over to grief. It was not that we retreated into grief. It was more that grieving is what we did to keep from stopping eating and drinking. We knew that if we did our grief sincerely enough and well enough we'd come out on some other side where we wouldn't constantly need to be doing it.

What energy was left over from grieving, we put into being "normal." Normal life had its own form, its own dictates. In our depleted state, normal life led us and not the other way around. When it said smile, we smiled. When it said talk, we talked. It told us when to sleep and rise and work and eat.

Brooks and Celia were most willing to help in this regard. Their innocent needs kept us engaged in the world. But there was something else that went along with the grieving and the being normal. The four of us may have talked about it a few times, but mostly it was unspoken and mutually understood. We were determined not to let the evil thing that had gotten Galen get us. Whatever it was, it would go into the ground with him. It would not be given the satisfaction of destroying our lives, as it had destroyed his.

So, Annie and I had an extra incentive, beyond our natural love, to watch after Celia and Brooks, to care for them, to do everything we could to insure that they survived this horrible experience intact. As for ourselves, we had confidence in the strength of our marriage. It would be our greatest asset in facing this situation. Annie would go about her business, and I would go about mine, but we'd always be in there, cross-checking, tinkering, making whatever adjustments were necessary to insure that the wonderfully strange machinery of our relationship thumped along in good order. We'd get through this, somehow.

Meanwhile, in the face of the horror of Galen's death, there was this other matter, the business of how-could-it-have-happened. Judging by the photos of the sullen, shaved-headed shooter that had appeared in the initial news accounts, and from the reports of what he'd said and done, he seemed to have been a monster. How could the college not have known there was something wrong with him? How could he have gotten the gun and ammunition onto the campus? How could he have gone around with a rifle, shooting people, and why?

As the days after Galen's death commenced their excruciating passage, we kept expecting some word from the college; a detailed explanation of events and an apology. I had the naive and still-dazed fantasy that, after what had happened, the college would be anxious to take care of us. However, when more information finally did arrive, it was from a very different source.

First a sympathetic member of the police investigating squad called and told me that the murder weapon had been a Chinese SKS semi-automatic rifle. Wayne Lo had purchased it used for about $130. This officer told me that all the victims appeared to have been targets of opportunity; they had no particular connection with Wayne. The shooter had simply been shooting, and the victims had been unlucky enough to get in his way.

Then, ten days after the shootings, on Christmas eve, the news media revealed that Wayne Lo had ordered his ammunition via UPS from a company down south called Classic Arms. The package had arrived on campus on Monday, December 14, the morning of the shootings. Dean Bernard Rodgers, the man who had first called us with the news of Galen's murder, had presided over a staff meeting that morning and the package had been brought into the meeting. It was clearly labeled "Classic Arms" but, after some discussion, Dean Rodgers had sent it back to the mail room unopened. Wayne Lo picked it up and took it to his dorm, unsupervised and unimpeded.

Learning these unpleasant facts by reading them in the newspapers and hearing them on TV made them even more disturbing. After his initial call, I'd had two more brief telephone conversations with Dean Rodgers. Both times I had asked him to keep us informed of every detail of the case as soon as it became known. Not only had he failed to do that, it now seemed that he had failed to tell us things he already knew.

Using the information available to us, Annie and I began trying to reconstruct the sequence of events leading to Galen's murder. This exercise led us to believe that the college had mishandled the situation from the start. Dean Rodgers and others had known for the entire day preceding the murders that Wayne Lo had gotten a package from an ammunition company. They had failed either to ascertain the true contents of that package or to prevent Wayne from taking possession of it, yet they were claiming that they had done everything that could have been done. That didn't sound right to us.

We talked these things over during our ghastly Christmas holiday that year … Annie and I, and Annie's mother and sisters and my brother-in-law and even the kids. We believed that the college was wrong in not keeping us informed. We wondered how much more information they were not sharing with us.

By January of 1993 Simon's Rock College had still not given us a detailed explanation of the events leading to the murder of our son. We started thinking about taking legal action. We wanted to learn exactly how college officials had let such a thing happen, and we wanted a jury of our peers to decide how well they'd handled the situation.

We began to search for lawyers, and with this act, we took our final departure from the comforting luminescence of that source-place, and returned to the evils of the world.

The cruelest irony of the situation was that Galen and Simon's Rock College had seemed a perfect match.

In his sophomore year at our local high school, Galen had gotten a brochure in the mail. It was a head-hunting flyer of the sort that was mailed to students in certain zip codes who scored above a certain number on their standardized tests, but this one was particularly well thought out. On the front of this brochure in big block letters were the words, BORED WITH HIGH SCHOOL? Inside, the brochure explained that Simon's Rock College was a small, innovative liberal arts college that took students directly from high school and set them to work on a college curriculum. Students could graduate in two years with an Associate's degree, or in four years with a Bachelor's degree. The brochure warned that Simon's Rock was not for everyone. Students had to be self-motivated, intelligent, and mature enough to function in the less structured environment of a college setting.

Galen was hooked.

We filled out all the applications and then went, that spring, to parent's visiting day, when Galen was to have his interview. This was our first child-at-college experience, and Annie and I were terrified. But for Galen, it was as if he had finally landed on the planet of his origin. The boys at this school had green hair. The girls had no hair at all. While the Dean of Admissions was interviewing Galen, we were taken on a tour of the campus by a heavily pierced and very bright and funny young lady whose name I could neither pronounce nor remember. We also spent some time at an indoctrination session with parents of other prospective students. Here, once again, we were told of the academic rigors of the college, and of the high degree of maturity that would be expected of future students. It was also explained to us how closely monitored these students would be, because, after all, they were only high school kids, and a lot was being expected of them.

This was all meant to be reassuring, but Annie and I were exquisitely uncomfortable. The other parents were a notch or two above us in social standing and income. They had arrived in Volvos and their clothes fit well. Their children seemed ferociously smart and impeccably mannered. Admission to Simon's Rock could possibly be the greatest opportunity of Galen's life. How could he find a place among these superior beings?

Galen seemed not at all concerned. He was happy. As we walked across the campus after our indoctrination, he nodded politely to professors and said hello to the kids who'd been through the sample class session with him. In answer to our nervous questioning, he told us his interview had gone well. He was sure things would work out fine.

He was shocked and hurt, therefore, when the rejection notice came that summer. It was a conditional rejection, but it stung. What it said was that based on Galen's high school transcript (filled with marginal grades ... of course they were marginal. He was BORED WITH HIGH SCHOOL) college officials weren't sure that he could do the work required of him. He was obviously intelligent, as proved by his high SAT scores, but they wondered if he had the maturity to apply himself to his studies and do college level work. So, they were rejecting him. But if he really wanted to attend he could submit an essay about why he thought he should go to Simon's Rock and work hard for the first marking period of his junior year in high school. If his grades showed sufficient improvement, they would reconsider his application.

This was a watershed event for Galen. He was a smart boy, but he was even more headstrong. At every critical point in the past, if the world had failed to conform to his expectations he had simply let the world go on its own misguided way. He had never, ever, deigned to play the world's game. Now, for once, the world was offering something he really wanted, and he knew that he would have to do the world's bidding to get it. He brooded for only a short while and then he wrote to the college. His essay was short and to the point. He said he didn't like the game they were playing with him, but he was convinced he belonged at Simon's Rock. To prove it, he would do what they asked. He would bring his grades up to the level they required. He didn't like it, but he would do it.

I was as proud and happy as if he'd already graduated with high honors. He'd had his first real battle with the world and he'd emerged, I thought, with his head held high. Of course, his grades for that first quarter of his junior year at Gloucester High went right up. He was summoned back to Simon's Rock.

Galen and I went out there alone late in the fall of his junior year. This time we were both nervous. This time he had his meeting with the college Provost, a Burmese man named Ba Win. Ba Win was small and gentle, and seemed an affable man, but on this occasion, ushering Galen into his office, he was stern. One of those interminable waits ensued, then Galen and Ba Win came out of the office, full of the magnitude of what had just passed between them. Ba Win called me in to speak with him. My palms were sweating as I took my seat. He looked at me with that serious, round face and those dark pools of eyes, and then the face creased in the middle. It was a grin. As if he'd been talking about the Thanksgiving turkey we were soon to eat, Ba Win said, "He's ready."

Galen entered Simon's Rock College in the winter term of 1991. The Boston Celtics were on their way to a successful 56–26 season. McHale and Durand were looking forward to another good year.

In the middle of our lawyer search, on Martin Luther King Day in 1993, we drove out to Simon's Rock College to collect Galen's belongings. It was probably too soon to attempt such a thing, but time had stopped for us. In our grief chronology it had already been an eternity since Galen had died. We wanted the last of his things away from that place and back with us.

As soon as we arrived at the college we went to Dean Rodgers' office for a meeting. The Dean was alone up there, somber and waiting. We'd seen him a few times before, on campus visits, and if appearances meant anything, he'd seemed like the right man for his job. Today he was wearing tan hush puppies, wide-wale corduroys, a button-down white oxford shirt under V-neck lamb's wool sweater, and big horn-rimmed glasses; every inch the owlish academician, smoking nervous cigarettes, one after the other. His opening sentence astounded me.

"I'm a man of words." he said, "And for once I can't find anything to say."

A man of words? It seemed a strange identity for Dean Rodgers to assume. If anything, I had thought the head of a college would be a man of truth or a man of knowledge. Didn't men of words go into politics or advertising? The second part of his declaration made me nervous. Did it mean that we would not be given any substantive new information about Galen's death?

Despite his disclaimer, this Man of Words had no trouble finding things to say. Mostly what he said was, "Everything looks different in hindsight" and, "We did everything that could reasonably have been expected of us, given the circumstances."

He gave us his account of what had happened the day of the shootings, and though it mostly recapitulated the media reports, we did learn a couple of new things. Dean Rodgers told us that he'd sent the Classic Arms package back to the mail room after the morning meeting because he believed it was against the law to open another person's mail. It was also his understanding that guns could not be sent through the mail. He knew better now. UPS, not the U.S. Postal Service, had delivered the package and it had contained ammunition, not a gun. But at the time he was making the best decision he could, based on the knowledge available to him. He also told us that he had met with Wayne Lo on the day of the shootings. Still concerned about that package, the Dean had spoken to Wayne in his office sometime around noon. Wayne had seemed calm and polite. He showed the Dean several empty ammunition cans and some gun parts, which he said were the entire contents of the package, and which he claimed were Christmas presents for his father, and accessories for his own gun at home. The Dean had accepted this. There was no way, he told us, that he could have known what Wayne was about to do. No one on earth could have known.

Annie and Brooks and Celia and I, sitting in the office watching him smoke, absorbing his condolences and regrets, as stunned by what he was saying, as if we'd each been whacked on the head. We had so many questions! But at that moment we found ourselves so dazed by the genteel horror of it all that we could hardly focus on the facts of the matter. It was all I could do to inquire if it had been his intention to ascertain the contents of that package from Classic Arms before Wayne got back to his room and opened it in private. The Dean nodded, looking at me sadly over the tops of those glasses.

"Yes. It was my intention. Things just didn't work out that way."

This interview was going awry but we were too confused to set matters right. We had come expecting hard, detailed facts about the entire sequence of events leading to our son's murder. Furthermore, we expected that Dean Rodgers, on the college's behalf, would accept some responsibility for what had happened and make some kind of apology. What we were getting instead sounded like a rehearsed public relations statement. The Dean was trying to absolve himself and the college of their roles in the shootings. Not only was he not going to inform us, he wasn't going to accept any responsibility, either. He wasn't even going to apologize for having mishandled the situation. He was going to try to make us believe there was no reason to apologize.

So, at that crucial moment, I found myself too surprised and upset to ask him why he hadn't made Wayne open that Classic Arms package in his presence, or how it was that no college official was present when Wayne did open it. I could not remember to ask him why he didn't hold the package till Wayne left campus for Christmas vacation. I did not ask him why he hadn't called Mr. Lo to check out Wayne's story that the ammunition containers were a Christmas present for his father. (We learned later that neither Wayne nor his father owned a gun at home.) What should have been my initial incisive examination of Dean Rodgers was a failure.

That interview was a failure for the college too. We were still unresolved. We needed to forgive them if we could. Our meeting was their single best chance to say, "We've made a mess of this. We're sorry. How can we make it better for you?" It would have taken us back to that initial place of compassion. This didn't happen. All we saw on that visit was a man trying to put the best face on things.

After our talk with the Dean, one of the college staff showed us the library entrance where Galen died, and where the kids had set their memorials to him. Our son had an innovative sense of humor, long on the absurd. The chicken was an important totem animal for him, and "chicken fajita" was a phrase of great utility, appearing unpredictably as a non sequitur in almost any utterance, or even as a thought complete and perfect in itself. ("Galen, have you finished your homework yet?"—"Chicken fajita.") Both the bird and the comestible were amply represented in the memorial offerings, giving the whole thing a perfectly Galen-ish wackiness. The student union was plastered with hundreds of last messages to Galen, outpourings of love and grief from his friends. He had so many friends!

We backed our van up to Galen's dorm and emptied his room of its contents. He had spent most of his free time with his girlfriend and his bed had become a midden heap of the stuff of his life. We took away box after box, and then the unused blankets and the sheets. Then the room was empty and the bed was bare, and Brooks laid himself down on it and cried. His sobs rocked the building and picked us up and down with them as we made the last trips back and forth from the van.

It's odd about life. Driving home through the Berkshires it started to snow. The car ahead of us suddenly lost control, wiggled, fishtailed in sweeps of increasing amplitude, and then did a donut, a 360. I pumped my brakes as gently as I could, trying to slow us without losing control, but the road was icy and there was no stopping. We careened toward the vehicle ahead of us, Annie in the front seat next to me, Celia and Brooksie in the back seat, all of us just sitting there without a word watching disaster approach.

Then, as we came upon it, the car ahead slid into another lane, another part of its donut, and we went past, unharmed. In the rearview mirror the car chugged into a snow bank and other vehicles stopped to give assistance. We just noted the incident and kept on going. At that moment I don't think it mattered to any of us whether we went up in flames or not.

The owner of the restaurant where we stopped for dinner that night was very upset. He took one look at us, after dinner, and thought we'd found something wrong with the food or the service. What could we tell him?

What could we tell anyone? We were lost in a vast mystery. One minute Galen had been with us, tall, smart and strong, his beautiful, wisecracking self; off on adventures with his brother, telling sweet stories to his baby sis. The next minute he was utterly and irrevocably gone. It was at once a terrible blow and the greatest Teaching the world had to offer. It was God's Will, but it had happened in the world and so it had causes, and those causes skittered away into webs of anterior causes.

17

As those first weeks wore on, I figured out that if I concentrated on the worldly chain of causes I might finally work my way up to the God's Will part. Perhaps the lengthy process of sorting through all those events and their relationships would help me digest the huge lump of misery that God's Will had left on my plate. Thus I determined the pattern that was to serve me well over the next several years, as I attempted to recover from the death of my son. I would concentrate on the details, the facts, and trust that their greater meaning would emerge of its own accord in the end. It never occurred to me to doubt that there was a greater meaning.

$3
THE TIME MACHINE

Galen's grave sat unmarked for most of that first year after his death. We were just too maimed to do anything about it. But in the fall of 1993, Annie began poking around the local granite quarries. Gloucester is situated on a big hump of granite that sticks ten miles out into the Atlantic Ocean. Where we live, at the northern end of this cape, there are dozens of abandoned granite quarries or "pits" as the locals call them. She had an idea of what she was looking for and she spent several weeks touring the rock heaps surrounding those pits, waiting for the perfect piece of granite to appear. Finally up in Johnson's Quarry she found one she knew would be right. Brooksie and Celia and I went up there with her and inspected it on site, laying on its side in a field of stone rubble. We all agreed it would be just the thing.

She purchased it from the keeper of the quarry and got the local monument company to send it up to Vermont to have two smooth faces and a base cut in it. The local monument guy poured the cement slab for the stone to sit on, but then the winter closed in and the weather was so severe they couldn't get their truck into the graveyard until April.

There was some uncertainty during that long winter's wait, but at least we had something other than bad weather to occupy our thoughts. We'd never designed a grave marker and the monument people had never faced, lettered and installed a hunk of raw granite. We were all curious to see how Annie's idea would work out. Then one April day the big foreign truck appeared and there was our gravestone.

It looks like a strange stone banana, or an ancient boat or a bird or a psychiatrist's couch. It's shaggy lovely granite, and one end of it reaches up. It's not square and polished like all the other headstones. It's tasteful, it fits, but there's no other stone like it in the entire graveyard. Annie did a good job picking it out. It's like Galen. It's like us.

There is a Time Machine in that cemetery, about half a mile away from our grave site, in an older part closer to the road. Galen, Brooks and I discovered it the first year we started playing there. Galen would have been about eight, Brooks six years old. It was late in the fall and on into the winter, when most of the other greenery was gone, making that little area even more anomalous.

The Time Machine was a nineteenth-century family plot about fifteen feet wide and thirty feet deep. It was different from the other plots because on each corner there was a thick cedar tree, and there was a row of evergreen bushes at the back, like the curtain for a stage. The ground within was very serious, very leveled, very discrete. At the front of the plot was an ornate monument bordered by a granite curb setting the plot off from the ground surrounding it.

If you entered it in a certain way, in a certain frame of mind, that plot of ground became the Time Machine. The three of us would run around the monument setting certain vital controls that were carved into the rock or that appeared to our imaginations—setting the Time Machine— and then one of us, usually Galen but sometimes Brooks, pressed the button, a really egregious knob on the front of the monument, and the countdown started ... TEN ... NINE ... EIGHT ... All that buildup of eating breakfast, getting dressed, leaving the house, walking to the cemetery, finding the Time Machine, imagining where we wanted to go, setting the controls correctly, and then we had a ten-count to run like hell as the Machine blasted us to wherever we'd set it for, which was always far in the future. The graveyard then became our ice planet or sand world, and we'd have adventures there, based loosely on the first two Star Wars movies, until we got tired and went home.

These days I can barely recognize that Time Machine when I pass it. Things have changed a lot, or my imperfect memory had made it something it never was, but there have been many occasions since Galen's death when I've wished I could reactivate it.

What would I do if I got it operational? I'd go back just a few years, not ahead thousands. I'd have the pleasure of seeing Galen again, for sure. Rescue him, or change things if I could. Mostly, I would use that machine to try to understand the puzzle of how Galen could have been here in this world and now no longer is. How could there have been a time in my life with no Galen, and then with all that Galen, and then again with no Galen? How can he be so much here, with me always, and so much not here?

This is a tremendous mystery to me. It is even a greater mystery than how a boy could get murdered at the door of a college library. It is the essential mystery and I yearn to get at that essence almost as badly as I yearn to have my boy back with me. It has to do with the past, and with time and place, but it is an unreasonable intuitive yearning. It begins where reason ends.

I have had some experience with reason ending, since I spent most of Galen's first fourteen years at my wit's end. He was difficult. He was smart. He was strong-willed. I'd never had a child before, let alone a smart, strong-willed, boy-child. I remember those first few months with him in our tiny third floor apartment down along the edge of Gloucester harbor. He'd make a noise and I'd wonder, "What is that?" and be astounded, over and over again, that there was no place to go and find out. Automobiles, even washing machines came with instruction manuals; yet they let you take this incredibly complex creation home without so much as a label on it.

My earliest concept of fathering involved a series of unsuccessful strategies for getting the Child to do what the Father wanted as quickly as possible. I thought parents existed for the purpose of teaching children to behave like grownups. I still see parents making that mistake, and sometimes their children even buy into it. Galen certainly didn't. As hard as I tried to teach him I was the parent, he was right back in my face teaching me he was the child, damn it. Our relationship was in part a contest, but it was not a bad relationship. There was plenty of love, lots of fun, and always the gentle mediating presence of Annie, stepping in and defusing each jaw-to-jaw, red-faced confrontation between thirty-one-year-old man and two-year-old boy.

Just because Annie continually saved his hide didn't mean he was obliged to her. Although baby Galen was by nature sensitive and compassionate, he regarded his mother as his slave. He'd boss her around without mercy and start in with the verbal abuse (he was an early talker) when she didn't jump fast enough. Eventually I suggested she wasn't doing Galen any good by putting up with these antics. By tolerating his rotten behavior she was helping to create a monster, or a monstrous side to our beautiful boy. Why, I wanted to know, didn't she stiffen up and say "No." once in a while?

She thought this over, and then in that quiet way of hers replied, "He'll grow out of this. If I'm hard on him now it'll make a part in me hard. Then later when he needs to come to me for softness, it won't be there."

I shut up after that. If there was any hardening to be done, I guessed I'd better be the one to do it, and accept my lot with whatever dignity a red-faced bellowing father could muster.

Then there was his brother. At least for his first two years Galen had Annie and me to himself. Suddenly one day there was this other creature, this *baby* to be reckoned with. Where Galen was big, strong, slow and straight-ahead, his brother Brooks was quick, small and wily. The two would torment one another until Galen's reserve ran out (not a long time) and he clubbed Brooks. Brooks would then go whining or wailing to his parents seeking justice against aggressor Galen ... maybe four times an hour for most of the waking day, from 1977 to 1987. In those years Galen was fond of referring to the day Brooks was born as "the worst day of my life."

Somehow this combat became a part of their play. In its most benign aspect their fighting was like the fighting of bear cubs in their den. Annie was always afraid they'd do one another physical harm. I guessed there was some biological governor to their activities. Brothers had been fighting like this for eons. With one biblical exception it had never amounted to much. If Galen and Brooks were as able to give each other concussions and broken backs as it seemed from their howling and wailing, the race would have died out long ago. I was more concerned that their relationship would never progress beyond combat. As it turned out, I needn't have worried.

There were a lot of things I should have worried about that I didn't. When Anne Marie got pregnant with Galen there were two major problems. We didn't have any money to begin our married life, but then, we weren't married either. I didn't see any reason to be. Anne Marie and I were in love. Wasn't that enough?

Apparently it was not. The political situation with Annie's parents grew tense and heated. I kept suggesting compromises like, let's get married when the baby can walk. These were dashed by the implacable, adamantine will of her mother, and the bland, innocent assumption of her father. He opined that Anne Marie *must* already have been married, since she'd already gotten pregnant. He was shocked to be informed otherwise. The upshot was that we got bundled off into what was as close to a shotgun wedding as ever a middle class couple endured. Which is to say, the only thing missing was the shotgun, and Jane, Annie's mom, supplied that to abundance metaphorically. She was all hard stares and hours of pacing alone along the edge of Gloucester harbor, weeping into the sea. Her daughter was pregnant, and she wasn't marrying a Catholic. She was marrying the heathen son of a traveling salesman, and her poor innocent grandchild would be consigned to Limbo. She was marrying an irreligious bum, not a doctor or a lawyer or any kind of professional. Her daughter was pregnant and she was marrying a wild, conceited, rude young man with no religion and no job. I, in my own way, shared her concerns, at least about the job. I had to figure something out.

During Galen's first two years, when we lived in that apartment on the edge of the harbor, I managed to scrounge up a number of unsatisfactory jobs. The first place I landed was in a local machine shop, in the early fall just before Galen was born. Annie would drag herself out of bed and pack me a lunch. I'd hop on my bike and commute. The work was hard and boring and no one talked. I hated it. For Thanksgiving they gave us each a basket of canned goods. Was that what machine shop workers ate? Then shortly after Christmas Big Fred called me into his office. He looked distraught.

"Kid," he said, "I know you've just had a baby but these are tough times. Our orders are way down and we've got to cut back somewheres. You were the last hired, and you've got to be the first to go. We've gotta ... lay you off."

What a moment! Big Fred was a good man and it was hurting him to tell me this. I knew it would be disrespectful to him to jump up and kiss him, but that's what I wanted to do. I tried to look torn up. He shook my hand and gave me a soulful look.

"You're a smart kid. You'll catch on somewheres else."

I scuttled out of there and caught on at the unemployment office for many happy weeks of food stamps and the dole.

That got us to mud-time in the spring. I went to work for a genius who rebuilt wharves in Gloucester harbor. His name was Francis Burnham and he understood everything about the internal combustion engine, radio waves and electricity. He was a Leonardo of the lever, a complete master of everything inorganic. Like many geniuses, however, his preternatural intelligence was limited in scope. Organic life forms baffled him. He couldn't relate to his helpers, he couldn't remember which tools to bring, he couldn't even order lunch. Some mornings, when I needed to know where we'd be working, I'd telephone the Terminal Garage, the gas station where Francis hung out. His brother Mose would answer the phone.

I'd ask Mose, "Is Francis there?"

"Just a minute," Mose would reply, "I'll ask him."

Mose meant it. Some days Francis just was not there mentally. He'd be walking around the Terminal Garage, humming show tunes, probably thinking three jobs ahead. I'd show up for work and he'd stare at me fixedly ... he recognized me from somewhere. So my job, when I wasn't placing fulcrums under levers or hanging chainfalls, was ordering lunch for Francis, and running around making sure he didn't forget things. I'd like to say I learned something from that brilliant eccentric, but I didn't. The early mornings on the harbor, in secret places under the docks, were unforgettably radiant and beautiful. The rest of the day was long and hard. I'd come home filthy, take a bath, bounce Galen on my knee and go off and drink a six pack and try to write poetry. I was happy with Annie and Galen, but I was not happy.

Then my friend Jean opened an art gallery and found me a profession.

"You've always liked books," she said. "Why don't you start a little shop and sell old books in my gallery?"

That was all I needed. I'd gotten out of the Navy as the Vietnam War was winding down, and had spent the years before my marriage producing an unpublishable novel and several bales of incomprehensible poetry. The demands of married life had forced me into gainful employment, but chainsaws and crowbars were driving me crazy. Here was a chance to work with words, at least.

I quit my job with Francis, built some shelves, and ran off to the library to read everything I could find about old books. It was fascinating. I gathered up old books wherever I could find them. Jean fronted me something like a hundred dollars for this endeavor, and it seemed like a hundred dollars could buy a lot of old books. In fact, people were giving them away. Then it was time to price my wares. I remember it being a big decision whether to price a book thirty-five cents or eighty-five cents (which appeared to be the upper limit of what the market would bear). Jean opened her gallery and people came through and bought a few books. Just like that I was a bookseller. There was an epiphany. Even now I can see the flash of light that accompanied it. I was reading one of the trade magazines when I realized that, with diligence, I could make as much as fifty dollars a week at this. Fifty dollars seemed like plenty.

Soon I was making that fifty dollars a week, but it was not plenty. We'd moved out of the apartment on Gloucester harbor to a little house all our own. The house was situated at the edge of the downtown area, close to the harbor and the wharves. We got a good deal on the rent because the place didn't have any heat. It didn't have any heat because it happened to be on low ground next to a marsh, and in the winter and spring when the frozen ground couldn't absorb the runoff, the basement flooded. The oil burner had been destroyed by high waters years before. We installed a used gas-log stove in the kitchen that only worked if you kept a weight on the safety button that was supposed to turn off the gas if anything went wrong. We put an old wood stove in the front room, too. I ran a stove pipe up through the living room ceiling and into the conked-out oil burner's chimney, thereby providing us with a rudimentary heating system. We quickly learned that green wood did not produce much heat. They were demolishing a building down the street and we spent the rest of that first winter burning all the wooden studs, sills and headers that I could snitch from the site.

For a while we were on welfare. Every week our case worker would squeeze her giant Cadillac into our driveway and her giant frame into our kitchen. She'd glance about, as she went through her preliminary litany, looking for signs of drug use and child abuse, then she'd fix me in her piggy gaze and ask, "Have you gotten a job yet?"

"Yes."

"Good. What is it?"

"Old book seller."

"That's not a job."

"Yes it is."

"Look. I'll give you one more week. But you've got to get a job."

She wasn't a patient woman. Soon we were on our own.

Antiquarian bookselling is a profession notorious for low pay. Famous book collectors are fond of writing memoirs in which they brag about the fabulous rare books they've purchased cheap, at the expense of already starving booksellers. These booksellers are usually portrayed as skinny and ragged bemused souls, in squalid shops, often with a sniveling brat or two on the floor. That's the way I felt for years, trying to establish a business with no cash to invest, needing every nickel to pay the rent and buy food. I supplemented my meager income by painting houses and driving a taxi—miserable, exhausting jobs which took even more time away from developing the book business.

Our situation often seemed impossible, but never futile. I loved bookselling and Annie loved being a mom. We had a car that someone had given us; our health insurance was no-one-get-sick. For vacations Annie took the boys and went to visit her mother. We were heedless and brave. We had no idea how hard all this was. We had love and energy and senses of humor, and we guessed that would have to do.

It did, but I think it made for a unique environment during Galen's and Brooks's formative years. Everything was seat-of-the-pants. We didn't have any money so we did things that didn't cost money. We were very social. We visited a lot and went to a lot of parties. We couldn't afford baby sitters so Galen, and later his brother, always came with us. Being intelligent and early talkers, the boys grew up being more our peers in social situations than "the babies." Galen easily held his own in this milieu. Our adult friends found him amusing and more interesting, I'm sure, than some of their contemporaries. Galen grew up thinking like a grownup in many situations, if not always acting like one.

But then, Galen always was an "old soul"—conservative, set in his ways, domineering—right from birth. Annie and I noticed it immediately, and were always running afoul of Galen's stodgy side. It was rather funny that a baby should be such an old man, and we usually reacted with humor. When Brooks, a natural comedian, came along this behavior was defined in our family unit. Galen was the boss-man, the alpha male. He was also our perpetual straight man. Some of the humor was for revenge or relief, but most of it was aimed at getting him to lighten up a little. Even as late as Galen's last summer at home we were all working on him, trying to get that sense of humor more supple.

To his credit Galen eventually came to understand that most of our efforts were well-intended. The bursting into tears and running from the room happened less and less. It was replaced by grave acknowledgment, sometimes even by a smile. Much as someone with two left feet might learn to dance, Galen learned to take, and give, a joke. With a mind such as his, this ability took its own path. By the time he was of high school age Galen had developed a truly wry and irreverent sense of humor. His freshman year, for example, Galen's girlfriend invited us to her parent's house to celebrate Thanksgiving. We all went over there with our offerings of creamed onions and apple pie, and had a grand time, not learning until later that Galen and Pam had broken up shortly before the holiday. Galen informed us, deadpan, that they'd kept the relationship together "for the sake of the parents."

And then Celia, who was immediately everyone's baby, and a girl besides. Galen and Brooks, therefore, became The Boys and grudgingly began their ascent to real brotherhood. I gave up trying to control everyone (I didn't have the energy.) My mother-in-law and I quit being adversaries and became allies, and under Annie's tutelage our family unit began to solidify.

Our circumstances changed too. My sister had died and left us a little insurance money, which we promptly spent on the down payment for a pretty Queen Anne-style house out on the north edge of Gloucester, just a couple of blocks from that cemetery. The book business began to support us. I quit my taxi driving job and eventually housepainting.

For Galen these were difficult years. He was the first one, the snow-plow. In many ways he got the best we had to give, but he got the worst of it as well; all our inexperience as parents and our inability to direct him. He realized at a very young age he was different. Because he was young he didn't have power enough to articulate that difference, or to alter his surroundings to accommodate it. He just mostly witnessed, and suffered. (And learned, as it later turned out.) He was miserable most of the time. For years he had no friends. He was not a fit companion for the children of firemen and carpenters who inhabited the neighborhood, though it is hard to imagine who he would have been comfortable with. He lived in science fiction and fantasy books and on TV. He read incessantly and did little else, it seemed.

Once when he was in fifth grade I noticed, walking past his room, that he was unable to sleep. I went in and asked him what the matter was. He told me. It took about an hour and a half and the torrent of alienation and despair left me reeling. The poor kid was only eleven and everything seemed so ... so ... black. He was alone. No one liked him. No one would play with him, and everyone made fun of him. A lot of times he said things they were too stupid to understand. But they

29

were too stupid to understand they didn't understand and so they thought *he* was stupid. They laughed at him. He was alone ...

His misery seemed so deep I began to worry about his mental health. My sister had been a schizophrenic, and I was afraid Galen might have inherited this illness. There was his despair and depression, but also his mind had quirks that were difficult for me to understand. He was encyclopedic in an almost eidetic way. He'd go to a movie and when he came home I'd ask him what happened. Instead of saying "The good guy rescued the girl." he'd say, in just that same tone of voice, "Well, there was this guy who lived in a little house at the edge of this town in the northwest, right near Washington, I think. The house had brown clapboards and the window trim was green." and go on and recite the movie scene by scene. To him that was what had happened. I'd beg him to summarize. He'd try for a sentence, then be drawn right back into the texture of the movie, event by event, still alive in his brain.

This made for real trouble at school. Because of his method of consuming information it was impossible for him to process knowledge in the way that his teachers wanted him to. At the same time his native intelligence made their homework instantly do-able and therefore instantly boring and therefore he refused to do any. Consequently the profile emerged of a bright, eager, funny classroom participant who steadfastly refused to do any homework and was therefore continually on the verge of flunking his subjects. He was disillusioned with his teachers and unhappy with his classmates. Annie and I suffered with Galen and worried about him a lot. We took him to the school psychologist.

This guy, much wiser and more experienced than we, assured us that Galen wasn't crazy, that he'd grow through all of this, and that we needed patience in seeing him through these difficult years. He gave us a book to read. The book said that being a parent was often a frightening job and that we should try to be brave and go about our work with courage. This seemed like good advice, and we tried to heed it. If the black obstacle surfaced we'd plow right through it.

For his part, Galen maintained courage at all times. Despite his misery in school he got up each morning and dragged himself off for another day of boredom and abuse. His report card was riddled with Ds and incompletes and the occasional F, but his attendance was always perfect. We asked him why he never missed a day of school. He replied, "I'm always afraid that the one day I'd miss would be the one day they'd have something to teach me."

It took a while, but form slowly found its way into this adolescent mess. It was probably in the summer of his seventh-grade year that a skateboard appeared, and with it friends, similarly alienated and goober-ish, and their whole skateboard culture. For them it was a way of life, an identity in the midst of confusion and turmoil. For us it was aural mostly, the distinctive THUNK and then diminishing roll of the board being thrown down, jumped upon and skated away. It was a relief. At least the boys were outside getting some exercise. One could deal with broken limbs.

I had built an addition onto our house. The bottom floor contained the overflow from my growing book business. The top floor was partly Celia's bedroom, but mostly what became known as the playroom. The playroom had a thick carpet, some beat up furniture, the kids' library and a big TV. There was a candy store down the street run by an ill-tempered neanderthal named Black Arthur (we never could figure out why we all loved him). The boys would go down there and get terror-ized by Arthur. They'd come back with candy by the bagful and lay around on the floor and play Dungeons and Dragons. Then we got our first VCR, and Arthur started renting videos, and the kids would watch movies by the hours. When the door opened the weird reek of hormones and candy chemicals would drift out.

So the boys oozed around in there, in that revolting pupal state for a few years, and when they emerged they were teenagers. Or so it seems at my memory's first glance. Actually the process was prolonged and not without difficulties. Fortunately, throughout these years there was the socializing presence of the Unitarian Universalist Church.

Annie was a lapsed Catholic and I was a lapsed Congregationalist. We both began our lapses as soon as we got out on our own, and we were both perfectly happy not to have taken up with any form of organized religion. God was fine with us; churches were not. As a result, though we were well grounded spiritually, we were not versed in the finer points of religious doctrine. On his own, and inspired initially by questions about philosophical matters that we were unable to answer satisfactorily, Galen discovered the Unitarians, and started attending youth services with a friend of his who lived down the street. It was a happy meeting. The UUs taught comparative religion, and I think Galen got enough information to begin working toward the answers he needed.

The friend down the street had a father, a sweet man with a gift for this sort of thing, who organized a Unitarian youth group, and soon this became the focus of the boys' social development. There were meetings every Sunday night. Galen would make chocolate chip cookies and under the patient eye of this wonderful adult, they all got together and … who knows what they did? Somehow it answered. That agonizing isolation began to break down. There were other kids as sensitive, intelligent and confused as Galen.

The world opened up even more when the boys discovered that the Unitarians sponsored Conferences. These were weekend co-ed sleepovers held at Unitarian Universalist Churches throughout New England. And then there were UU summer conferences for kids from as far away as New York and Maryland. Galen, and Brooks after him, made a whole network of friends, male and female, along the eastern seaboard, who became so many nieces and nephews to us.

Many of them wound up spending time, prolonged time, with us, and the playroom became a sort of salon for this group. They appeared to follow their own UU Conference rules (no violence, no drugs, no overt sex) and transferred their conference activities to our house. Countless times, as we hauled up to bed, Annie and I would look in through that glass door and the floor would be a solid mass of young teenaged boys and girls, in rapt attention, faces illuminated by the flicker of whatever movie they'd rented at Black Arthur's, and later, discussions downstairs and the smell of late-night coffee brewing.

The wonderful thing was, they were good kids—intelligent, sensitive, physically attractive. They were much more interesting than adults, because for them everything was fresh and new and *very* important. They could be witty and were always unintentionally funny. This was the kind of "Youth" Annie and I "worked with"—kids with no major defects who were attractive, intelligent, funny and self-motivated. This was our flock.

Galen was an important figure to this gang. He was a good listener, and he tended to be very sensitive and supportive. His earlier troubles had provided him with a wealth of understanding, and his solutions to the problems of his peers tended to be original, imaginative and whimsical, when solutions were possible at all. I think he was the village explainer, the sage.

One of his favorite techniques was a sort of relief-by-expansion. Galen was a devotee of Richard Feynman, the Nobel-Prize-winning physicist and author. Some friend would be in the playroom near tears, laying out whatever insoluble dilemma he or she was facing, and Galen would be all grave nods. The next time I'd pass, he'd be taking a Feynmanesque riff on the metaphorical similarities between the problem at hand and the actions of certain curious sub-atomic particles. By my third trip up the stairs, they'd be rhapsodizing about cosmology or the startling fact of existence itself. The problem would not have been solved or removed;

it would have been put in perspective. That breadth of thought was one of Galen's gifts.

But I'd like to let him give you an example of this in his own words. A while after he died, I had sense enough to rescue everything he wrote on our several computers from off their various hard drives and floppy discs and put it all in hard copy form. There are maybe thirty pages of poems, stories, journal entries and miscellaneous writings. This particular one is from the spring of Galen's sixteenth year. He's writing an essay applying for the position of Registrar at the Unitarian Universalist Star Island Conference, and is answering question #4. (I don't have the question but it was probably something like "Why do you want to be on the staff?")

> So I want to be part of the staff... for a number of reasons, and, as may be expected these are in a complex reticulum spanning my subconscious, Freudian drives and unfulfilled self-actualization needs, but knowing my application is late going out and our beloved chair is a busy man, I'll try a different approach.
>
> My story starts in the basement of a UU church on Cleaves Street, Rockport, Massachusetts. It was here where a young man, feeling persecuted by his peers, found shelter among a group that was accepting by nature. Through this group I discovered several things including love, being in love, extroversion, and my natural existentialism. Also, I discovered YRUU. This new group showed me more of the same but more importantly it showed me that what I experienced in my homey basement of a picturesque Rockport church was applicable to hundreds of others. About halfway into my second year (I'll be entering my sixth in September) I discovered a new angle on YRUU. That was the parts of the weekend in which certain diligent individuals prepared meals and attempted to restore the church to its original state. I had some

experience in these fields having worked a couple of summers in restaurants, and wanting to give back to the conference something more than love (since I felt I had been given so much more), I set to the work which none but a masochistic few seemed to enjoy. I discovered ... that those who enjoyed it were generally the charismatic leaders of the conference and were easy to bond with while drying dishes or sweeping floors ... I realized that the extra-little-bit-besides-love that they gave to conferences was life. I in turn felt the urge to give as much as I could, which included life.

Star Island has given me a lesson in sublime and beautiful conference experience, and in the same spirit which I felt to clean up as a twelve-year-old I'd like to feel for staffing as a sixteen-year-old ...

What I feel I can offer the staff is some experience and some insight into the wrongness of sushi.

Isn't that impressive? Clearly, the boy had done some maturing in those last few years, but I think what really happened was that he got his internal wiring hooked up. All those vast heaps of knowledge and feeling finally got interconnected and the effect was synergic, dazzling. I tell you, in all honesty, the working of that mind and heart was one of my favorite things on this earth to behold. As badly as I have missed my son, as bitterly as I have grieved, I have taken occasion to thank God for the blessing of that experience.

He was a lovely dude; and I finally got to know him, as anything other than a sweet, complicated handful of a son, on the squash court.

Galen had always been big, but, except for a few years' fascination with karate, had loathed organized sports. In a mental contest he could hold his own with anybody, or find a way to make it seem, in his mind, that he'd won or at least tied. With physical sports the result was too clear-cut. There was a winner and a loser. Galen wasn't comfortable with that and didn't want to risk it. We'd had some spectacular fights in his eighth and ninth years when I'd tried to teach him soccer. I managed to ruin baseball for him forever, by trying to get him to play. The kid had the body of a tight end and refused to get off the couch; yet here was his pipsqueak of a brother playing guard on the PeeWee football team. Go figure.

All through their growing up years I'd been a happy hacker at squash, playing the game with great gusto and attention, but never getting very good. I'd started too late, in my thirties, and had taught myself, and had just too many bad habits and not enough correctly grooved neural pathways. Suddenly one day toward the far side of puberty Galen wanted to go down to the Y and learn how to play squash. I couldn't imagine what had gotten into him. He and Brooksie both understood how much I enjoyed the game, but because it was so difficult and so specialized, it was the one sport I'd never attempted to force on either of them. There's probably a deep teaching in there somewhere.

So we began, every Sunday afternoon and whatever weekday evenings we could snatch, in the winter of Galen's fourteenth year, to learn the difficult game, and this time I was a patient teacher and he an attentive student. Naturally Brooks was there too and it was fun to watch the contrast in styles. Galen was studied, hesitant and analytical. He actually tried to remember things I told him and make his body do them. Brooks threw himself onto the court with abandon, letting his body teach him, and after a while, something his body learned would coincide with something I'd said, and he'd make it a habit.

After a winter they were good enough to stand there and play each other. It became one of my great joys over the next few years to sneak up onto the balcony and watch my two teenaged boys go at it on the court. All those years of scrabbling, punching and hair-pulling, and it had come to,

"Was that out?"

"Yeah, I think so."

"OK."

Or even, "Good shot, Brooks!"

"Thanks, Galen."

The other great pleasure was the opportunity our lessons afforded Galen and me, finally, to learn to talk. There'd always been chatter aplenty, and no little communication, but this experience gave it a form.

It began as a simple thing, as a need for me to express the game to him in terms he could relate to. What worked best was when the squash game was a metaphor for life, when things that happened on the court stood for things that happened in life. For example, he'd say, "This is too hard. I'll never learn how to do it."

I'd say, "It's very hard. But you'll learn how to do it. Anyone can learn if they know the Secret."

"Secret? What Secret?"

"One hundred thousand."

"One hundred thousand?"

"The Secret is that there is no secret. It's just repetition. All you have to do is hit that ball a hundred thousand times and you'll be a good player. There! See? Even while we've been talking you just hit it five more times. But people don't understand that. They think they can get good if they only hit it a thousand times. Then they get discouraged. They see a good player and they wonder 'What's his secret?' Well, his secret is that he hit the ball a hundred thousand times."

He'd nod and continue hitting the ball. Instead of protesting or coming back with a smart remark, he was chewing on it, picturing hitting the ball one hundred thousand times, and how repetition could be a "secret." I could see he liked that sort of idea.

These were good moments for us. He would actually try to listen to something I'd said, to add it to his own store of knowledge. From there on we had a very different relationship.

My book business was evolving. I was spending less time in the shop, more time on the road, buying from other dealers, doing book shows and selling rare books by mail. In those years there was a book I used to see a lot. It was a coffee table book about the Plains Indians, and it had been remaindered, so it was everywhere. It was called *Mystic Warriors of the Plains,* or some such. Taking off from that, I used to see myself, in only a half-kidding light, as a sort of modern analog to the Indian hunter. My van was my pony, I was hunting books instead of buffalo, my range was Boston to Washington instead of the Great Plains. It was quite a stretch, but just exactly the sort of stretch I had always been capable of making, particularly as far as my own endeavors were concerned.

Galen came with me on some of my book trips, so he had some idea of what was going on. Slowly, building on our squash experience, we began to have some heady conversations while driving, especially when it was too dark for him to read and too early for him to sleep. We'd talk about people or we'd talk about life, or both, since one always tended to lead to the other. Our talk had that mildly crazy metaphorical quality where the way you got ready for a squash game had something to do with the way you lived your life. I used to tell Galen I was a Mystical Warrior of the Eastern Macro-Metro Corridor. He dug it.

Some times, instead of two marginal middle-class white people schlugging books around, we'd be the mystical warrior and his apprentice. That was the feeling, though it was never stated explicitly; just the boy and me, talking our way down the road. We were on a path fathers and sons had been traversing since time began, but it felt new to us, and we were glad to be there.

4
THE TRIAL

Our search for a lawyer continued. Late in January of 1993 we talked to a big guy with a balding pate, bright, intense eyes and big hands. He told us things had gone very badly for us, and that we could not expect him, or anyone, to make them better. All he could do would be to try his hardest to see that things went right from here on. We liked him. We liked the hands. Annie and I went home and talked it over. We decided that since we had no idea what to look for in a lawyer, we might as well pick someone we liked. So we had a lawyer, simple as that. His name was Neil Rossman. His firm was Rossman, Rossman & Eschelbacher. We never did meet Eschelbacher.

As news reports continued to appear, we learned more, and none of what we learned spoke well for the college. The people in charge had known for the entire day that Wayne Lo had received a large package from a firearms company. The newspapers also reported that college officials had gotten an anonymous phone call, not long before the shooting started, warning them that Wayne had a gun.

In our opinion they had made some very poor decisions and bore at least some of the responsibility for Galen's death. In March of 1993, the estate of Galen Gibson sued Bernard Rodgers, Ba Win, and several other people employed by Simon's Rock College. We thought we were beginning to make progress.

As eager as we were to press forward with our civil suit, the criminal issues had to be resolved first.

After two false starts in 1993, Wayne Lo's murder trial finally got underway in January of 1994. The proceedings had been transferred from the locale of the crimes in Berkshire County, to the Hampden County courthouse in Springfield, Massachusetts, about two and a half hours west of our home in Gloucester. There was no question whether we'd attend.

Annie and I had a deep-seated need to learn all the facts surrounding Galen's murder. Although we were very different people in many ways, we shared the same basic values. One of these was a belief in the redemptive power of truth. If the truth didn't always set us free, at least it kept us clean, and made our lives less complicated.

Part of our anger at Simon's Rock College, and one of the main reasons for the lawsuit, was our belief that they had failed to respect our need for the truth. Of course, with the initiation of the lawsuit, the already remote possibility of us learning anything new from them ceased entirely. So, we were eager for this criminal trial to begin because we were certain that it would provide some of the factual information we needed.

We needed it, but we dreaded it, too. Only fourteen months had elapsed since Galen's death, and our wounds were still open. Each day these criminal proceedings would present new ways to remind us of this. Seeing Galen's friends and schoolmates, seeing Bernie Rodgers, seeing cops, seeing the murder weapon, seeing Wayne Lo, silent and dark at the defense table, hearing a detailed recapitulation of events leading up to the shootings, hearing about the shootings themselves ... all these things would be tremendously painful, and at first we were unsure of our ability to endure the discomfort.

As the trial drew nearer, however, our belief in the necessity of learning the truth about what happened overcame our fear of the pain. We weren't sure exactly why we had to do it, we just knew we had to do it, and do it as well as we could, out of respect for Galen, and out of respect for our own lives.

Annie and I set about our preparations with all the long-faced diligence of people planning a difficult trip to an unpleasant place. We bought a reliable, low-mileage used car specifically for the Gloucester-Springfield commute. Some friends in the book world helped us find an apartment in Springfield just a few miles from the courthouse. Brooks and Galen's friend Lulu was taking a year off school, and she volunteered to live at our house while we were gone, and cook for the kids, and drive Celia to her activities. Brooks got his grandmother's old car, so he could ferry himself around and help Lulu with the Celia duties. Annie wrote out schedules and shopping lists and I lay in a good store of firewood and groceries. We assembled our courtroom wardrobes, packed our bags, and loaded them in the car.

We'd leave Gloucester early each Monday morning, and arrive in Springfield in time for the beginning of the week's proceedings. Friday afternoon at the end of the court session, we'd hop in our trusty new used car and get back to the Boston area just in time for rush hour. To the best of my recollection, it snowed each Monday morning and each Friday afternoon for the duration of the trial. We hardly noticed.

During the week, our lives centered around the courthouse. Annie and I would rise each morning, and glance about the strange apartment, wondering where we were. We'd have coffee and a snack, and drive down to the courthouse, where we'd be received by our friendly parking lot attendant, the court officers, the DA's people, and the cops. We'd take our place at the front of the visitor's gallery, and the day would begin. We'd break for lunch and eat at Tilly's, the local courthouse joint, with whatever friends or family were keeping us company in court that day, then we'd return for the afternoon session. At the end of the day there would be drinks at our apartment and a review of the most recent proceedings, then dinner at a restaurant (cooking seemed to require more concentration than we could muster) and long phone calls from restaurant lobbies to Celia, Brooks and Lulu.

In the fourth week, Celia began her midwinter school vacation and joined us in Springfield. Brooks played hooky or took long weekends and spent as much time with us as he could. It was a difficult situation. I don't know where we got the grit and endurance to meet the ordeal, but we did, individually and as a family unit. In fact, we were splendid.

Some of this was due to our shared determination not to be destroyed by the thing that had destroyed Galen. We each worked hard to develop strategies for dealing with this painful disruption. Brooks and Celia, I think, turned it into something of a lark. Lulu was cool and funny and fun, somewhere between Peter Pan and Auntie Mame. Our babies faced those long weekday spans with courage and humor, (talk about shared basic values!) and Annie and I would finish each nightly phone call bursting with pride in them, and concern, and boundless sadness that any of this had to be happening at all.

For me, it helped to concentrate on the aspects of my situation that allowed for a workmanlike approach. Even before the trial began, I resolved to take notes of the proceedings. I wanted to record the series of witnesses and the thread of each examination, cross- and recross-, while they were taking place. I thought such a running commentary might prove useful to our lawyer in preparing for our civil case. Also, I wanted to memorialize this momentous event somehow, to fix it in time, and I could think of no better way to do this than to try to keep a journal.

I brought a notepad to court each morning, and scribbled away, recording as much as I could of what was going on. Then, next morning over coffee at the apartment, I transcribed my handwritten notes into the computer. Almost immediately, however, the process took an unforeseen course. It felt surprisingly good to work up those courtroom notes, to get some sense of the form of the proceedings, to actually be *doing* something with what was going on. By the third morning I was getting up at six o'clock and spending a couple of hours enthusiastically, almost gleefully, writing my report of the past day's events. In fact, the activity transformed me. Instead of being a victim of the trial, instead of being the passive recipient of all this painful and difficult information, I could take an active role. I was reporting the trial.

This not to say that the situation ever became easy. I was hanging on by my fingernails, so pummeled by the relentless revelation of facts regarding the murder of my son that I didn't really understand the full meaning or actual significance of the things I was writing down. It was simply the exercise of writing that was helping me; I just kept my head down and concentrated on doing the job.

On the third morning of the trial I looked over next to me and there was Annie, finishing a pastel drawing of the Clerk of Courts. She had a sketching pad in her lap, and it was already full of portraits.

But it was different for her. I approached my new "job" with the intensity of a drowning man struggling to stay afloat. Annie had already gone under. Her "job," the sketching, was more of a pastime than a life preserver. So, as I thrashed about in my efforts to process this terrible information, to palliate its effects on me, she sat there and took it all in. Straight. Stubbornly, quietly, beautifully certain that there was more of her than there was of it, and if not, too bad.

The criminal trial lasted from January 10th to February 3rd, 1994. The first two weeks of testimony were concerned with establishing that Wayne Lo was the shooter and that he had murdered two people and wounded four more. Dozens of witnesses testified, including two of the boys who had been wounded, and Theresa Beavers, the security guard who had been shot repeatedly at close range and was still recovering physically and emotionally.

We learned many important things during this first part of the trial; chief among them was the exact sequence of events leading to Galen's murder. Sometime around 10:15 P.M. on December 14, Wayne took his loaded gun and extra ammunition clips and walked from his dormitory to the front guard shack. After shooting Theresa Beavers, and while still in the vicinity of the guard shack, he shot and killed a teacher, Ñacuñán Sáez. Ñacuñán was returning to campus, apparently having forgotten something. He must have slowed or stopped his car as he approached the guard shack, and Wayne stepped out and shot him through the driver's side window. The car rolled into a snow bank a few yards from the guard shack and Wayne began walking toward the library. Very soon after this, three students drove onto campus. They saw Ñacuñán's body in the car, and, thinking there'd been an accident, they rushed to the library to get help, passing Wayne on their way. Galen was the first one to offer his assistance. Wayne shot him from the sidewalk while he was coming out the library door.

Physical evidence from the crime scene indicated that Wayne had difficulty getting his gun to operate properly. Unspent cartridges were recovered from some of the stops along his deadly walk. Apparently, he'd had to recycle the gun manually, ejecting jammed shells and inserting new ones. He had purchased about 200 rounds of ammunition, but he'd fired less than two dozen. He may have been fiddling with his gun when the three students passed him on their way to the library. He may have surrendered because his gun didn't work. We'll never know for sure. Wayne Lo had nothing to say on the subject.

We learned in excruciating detail the nature of the deaths of Ñacuñán Sáez and of Galen Gibson. We learned that Galen had been shot twice, in the chest and in the side. The side bullet also grazed his elbow, consistent with his arm being at his side, putting on his coat to run outdoors. The chest shot was fatal. The side shot was not. No succession was established. No distance was given. The chest shot shattered his sternum, passed into the chest cavity, severed blood vessels, passed through a lung, severed the trachea, passed through the seventh rib and exited the back. Galen bled approximately two and a half liters into the chest cavity. Death was caused by blood loss and accompanying shock and ensued in several minutes, ten or twenty at most. At one point, the prosecution produced a toothbrush that Galen had been carrying in his pocket (one of Galen's charming eccentricities was that he frequently carried a toothbrush around with him, as if he never knew where he'd find himself waking up). This toothbrush had been damaged, presumably by one of the bullets that had passed through Galen's body, and the prosecution wanted the expert witness to verify that the damage to the toothbrush had been caused by a bullet. To her credit, the criminalist, one Mary-Kate Lumley, testified that she could not say to a certainty that the toothbrush had suffered bullet-damage, because she had never before examined a bullet-damaged toothbrush. That was the sort of thing we endured on a daily basis.

Such testimony and documentary evidence fixed, as matters of irrefutable fact, things we'd only inferred from news reports or rumors. Thus, we were able once and for all to visualize the delivery of the ammunition package, the administrative meeting at which the package was discussed and then released, Wayne's taking possession of it, his hiding the bullets, his taxi ride to the gun shop, the purchase of the rifle, and his return to campus with the rife hidden in a guitar case.

Then, after this material had been presented, the prosecution produced a witness whose testimony had a profound effect on our understanding of what had happened that night. One of Wayne's friends, a boy named Jeremy Roberts, had realized at dinner that something was wrong, that Wayne really might have a gun and might use it. After dinner, between 7:00 and 8:00 o'clock, he made several attempts to reach campus security. It was the first we'd heard of this.

According to Jeremy Roberts' testimony, there was no one at the campus security number, just an answering machine. He was afraid to leave an incriminating message in case he was wrong about Wayne. He then called the Residence Director of the dorm in which Wayne lived. This

neys, occasionally writing something on the legal-sized pad in front of him. How I wished I could compare his notes with my own!

The prosecution and the defense hammered away at each other throughout those snowy weeks in the winter of 1994. Then, when they could hammer no more, the matter was turned over to the jury to decide. While they deliberated, all of us on the prosecution side spent an uncomfortable two days talking among ourselves, playing cards, trying to read, waiting for the verdict. Finally, on the afternoon of February 3rd, we were called back into the courtroom. We took our accustomed seats, a sinking-elevator feeling in our bellies, and watched the jury file in.

As soon as the first juror came into the room, I saw it in her eyes, and then in the eyes of most of the others. I knew they had decided he was guilty. They were relieved when they looked at us, and it was their relief that I saw. Sure enough, guilty. Guilty of Murder in the First Degree, twice. Guilty, of all the other lesser counts. Wayne Lo would spend the rest of his life in prison with no chance of parole.

We cried and hugged our fellow victims, cried and thanked our friends the cops, (how close we'd grown in four weeks!) told the reporters we were glad it was done, and went home.

We'd gotten through it, somehow, and I had it all written down. However, I was too numbed, too desperately battered by the process, to make immediate use of the information I had recorded. I had all the words on paper, but it would be years before I had sufficient clarity to understand what they meant.

✸§5
THE ROAD

Here's how I saw the situation:

We finish the criminal trial, put Wayne Lo away for life, then go after the people at the college. The Commonwealth of Massachusetts needed only to show that Wayne was guilty of murder, not that college officials were guilty of stupidity and cowardice. So we'd have our civil trial and all the events leading up to the shootings would be investigated in detail, from the point of view of what the college did or did not do. This investigation would take place in a public forum, and college officials would have to stand up, under oath, and give a public accounting of how that package from Classic Arms got into Wayne Lo's hands, and why they did not stop him on the night of December 14, 1992, and why they did not call the police. Then the jury would render their verdict. Preferably, we'd win a big judgment. Then I'd say something like, "We don't want the money. We want the college to make a public apology. And they have to name a building after Galen. And Bernie Rodgers has to KISS MY ASS."

This was a measure of how far I had drifted from the realities of the situation.

I waited, with increasing discomfort, while our lawyers prepared their case against the people at the college. My discomfort arose from the surprising fact that, despite the passage of time, I was not getting over Galen's death. I was not finding acceptance. I was not finding forgiveness. I was not finding peace.

I had survived the criminal trial, but it had only inflamed me. I was more certain than ever that Bernie Rodgers and Ba Win had mishandled events. The fact that they were denying this enraged me. I wanted them punished. I fantasized throttling Bernie Rodgers, or meeting him in a bar and punching him in the nose, but I wasn't going to do any of this. I had turned it all over to the judicial system, and I was counting on them to do it for me. The problem was, they were taking their sweet time about it, and I was suffering.

Annie was suffering too, but in a very different way. Where mine was all writhing on the surface, busy with matters of vengeance and rage, hers was quiet and deep. The surface was placid, and sad, and just a little loopy.

I'd get up every morning with Brooks and make his breakfast and a bag lunch. Then Annie would get up with Celia, and help her get ready while I sat and drank my coffee. When the kids were off to school, Annie and I would have a cup of coffee together. Then she'd start reading a book and I'd go into my study and begin my day's work cataloging books. When I came out for lunch, Annie would still be sitting there at the kitchen table in her bathrobe, reading.

She began keeping in close contact with the Publisher's Clearing House, that magazine subscription outfit with the Prize Truck and the oversized $25 million checks. Two or three times a week we'd get another packet of junk mail promising untold riches, and very assiduously, Annie would fill out each form, rip out each ticket, check each box, complete each card, paste the little colored stamps in their proper squares, and mail the whole thing back. The family joke was, "It's Mom's new job." She'd look at us deadpan and intone, "My name is Anne Marie Crotty. I never leave the house."

Annie interacted with her friends, and with the other mothers in Celia's ice skating and school and social worlds. She was a good wife and companion to me, and a good mom to Brooks and Celia, and to all the kids who hung around our house. She wasn't morose, she didn't brood, but if you saw her every day as I did, you would have noticed a change.

Inside, she seemed to stop. There was something important to be done, and nothing else could go forward for her until it had been accomplished. So she stayed home and read her books and sat with her grief. And while she was doing her grieving, she did the Publisher's Clearing House. She knew it was nuts, but it occupied her. Or it contained the nuttiness. Instead of going genuinely crazy and ruining us all, she isolated the craziness into one obsession. We all took it as just that; Mom was crazy. But it was kind of funny, and we got all those magazines, and what if one day the Prize Truck really did pull up in front of our house?

In the summer of 1994, Simon's Rock and their insurance company, wonderfully named Great American, offered to settle out of court for $250,000. We, of course, refused. The whole purpose of the trial was public accountability, not affixing a dollar amount to our dead son. There was a mediation session at which nothing was mediated, more delay, and then stasis. No trial was held. No date had even been set. Our lawyers continued to talk to their lawyers, to gather information, to file requests of the court. It was a curious condition, probably quite normal for situations of this kind, but otherwise beyond the pale of human experience. Everybody knew nothing was happening and everybody bustled around, not admitting it. It was maddening.

I use the word "maddening" in a literal sense, because I was actually getting a little crazy by then. It was beginning to look as if there would be no civil trial. There would be no public disclosure from college officials, no wronged father seeking justice against great odds, just some insurance adjuster talking with our lawyers and their lawyers. There would be five guys in suits between me and college officials at all times. Bernie Rodgers could go the rest of his life denying everything, claiming he'd acted well in a difficult situation, and I could go on fantasizing my revenge forever and it wouldn't mean a thing. Nothing would happen, nothing would change.

In the midst of this anguish I did something that seemed crazy at the time, but it only seemed crazy because I was crazy. I went to Pittsfield, Massachusetts and talked to the man who ran the shop where Wayne Lo had bought the gun. I knew I had better get out of my own head, if I was going to survive, and confront the sources of my grief. Then I began to get caught up in the idea. It seemed like a bold thing to do. I would go out there and get the facts for myself. I would learn the whole story. The gun shop seemed like the obvious place to start.

I would assemble an airtight case against the college and send it to my lawyers or get it published in the *New York Times*. The point was that I would get out of my own condition and into the facts of this matter. Just as I had found during the criminal trial, the facts would be a relief to me. I started thinking of the situation as if it were a detective job, as if I were investigating a case.

Then that generalized detective image mixed with another more particular one. I remembered a movie I'd seen back in the 1960s. It was called *Point Blank*. In this movie Lee Marvin played a very tough character named Walker. Walker gets double crossed by his girlfriend. She and her bad partners shoot him and take all the money and leave him for dead on Alcatraz Island, but he's so tough that he swims back to San Francisco with a slug in him. Then, very methodically, the Lee Marvin character begins tracking down the people behind the double cross. There's a whole hierarchy of bad guys for him to move through, and from each one he learns the identity of the next higher up. He isn't going to stop until he finds the one guy who is ultimately responsible for what happened to him. Finally, he gets to the guy at the very top, but this guy is not the big boss, not the mastermind, he's just an accountant. Walker discovers that the double cross had been nothing more than a business decision. He'd been seeking personal vengeance against an ultimately impersonal corporate structure. It was a perfect sixties message, delivered by Lee Marvin at his cold, ruthless best, but I was inspired by the messenger, not the message.

This image of Lee Marvin as the methodical and brutal Walker actually got me out to the gun shop. I would continue to be reminded of painful things, I would talk to people about painful subjects, but now that I was the Lee Marvin character, there was no pain, there were only facts. The memories of Galen were there, and I had memories of feelings too, but they were from a different lifetime. I was a Lee Marvin story-getting machine. The pain belonged to someone else.

❧§6
DAVE

The day began with a dream.

The dream had to do with a theorem regarding Galen's death. In my dream there were two branching lines of events and even a single change on any point of either of the lines would change everything on both lines. Over and over in my dream I formulated this concept, sometimes as pure geometry, sometimes as speech or action. This change concept had somehow to do with Galen's salvation or my solution to or prevention of his murder. It was one of those obsessive repetitive dreams that usually caused me to wake in an uncomfortable sweat. This time the dream turned narrative and representational before I woke.

I was bringing an old book into a big office for a Bernie Rodgers-like figure to examine. He did so and at the point in the book where the French "word" *educationaire* occurred, a folded piece of blank soft white paper had been inserted. "You see!" he exclaimed excitedly, showing me the paper. "This proves Galen had thought of (the murder) ahead of time! It changes everything." I picked up his excitement. One point on the line had changed! Then I realized that I had put that paper in there myself, when I was working with the book before I showed it to him.

I told him so and then I was awake.

As I lay there, staring at the wall, the irrational power of the dream was already asserting itself. "I moved that paper, moved the point. Maybe I can follow that bullet back." I got up and went to visit the man who sold the gun that took my son's life.

Western Massachusetts was hot and crowded. The Berkshires were gearing up for the beginning of the Tanglewood Music Festival and the thermometer on every savings bank was pushing 95. Traffic light waits were interminable and consequently Pittsfield, once I got off the Massachusetts Pike, seemed a lot farther away than I remembered it.

Eventually I got into town and spotted Pittsfield Sporting Goods, a big storefront right on the main drag. I followed the signs around to the parking lot in back, parked the van and entered, noting a sign on the door with the satisfaction that comes from having one's expectations met. It was printed on a home computer in cheap dot-matrix fashion and it said that they also bought and sold coins, baseball cards, comics and precious metals. That sounded about right, precious metals and semi-automatic weapons.

I had plenty of expectations. I'd been spinning out scenarios all morning. What would the gun guy (Dave was his name) and his gun shop be like? What would I say to him? I tried to imagine two or three basic ways our interview might go, and to formulate an approach for each of them. Maybe he'd be aggressive. Maybe defensive and silent. Maybe friendly and devious. I wanted to have a plan to meet each possibility. The closer I came to the actual meeting, however, the more I saw that it was just going to be a matter of being ready for anything. My plan was to be very aware, to improvise, to be quick on my feet. I could do that.

Inside the store my expectations were not met. The place was full of running shoes and basketballs, tents, tennis racquets and golf clubs. It was a ... a Sporting Goods store. A pimply-faced kid came up to help and I said, "This isn't Dave's Sporting Goods, is it." He smiled and shook his head, and gave me to understand that Dave's was down the road about two miles. I got back in the van and drove.

This time there was no mistaking it: a rambling building which had probably been a ranch-style dwelling before going commercial and getting its windows walled over. It had a gently sloped roof with a lot of overhang and its ridge line roughly paralleled the road. The gable end facing me was white with "Dave's Sporting Goods" painted right onto the wall in big dark block letters. In bigger letters under that was the word GUNS. I figured I had the right place.

At Wayne Lo's criminal trial I had kept what I thought were careful notes regarding the proceedings, but my memories of Dave's appearance were few and dim. I remembered a gray-haired caveman sort of a guy giving the District Attorney's people a hard time about having to wait around the courtroom. His testimony about the sale of the gun was straightforward but had seemed surly and grudging. I was surprised to realize that he was one of the few witnesses whose full name I had either forgotten or failed to record. Gray haired, surly and burly. That was all I had to go in with. Talk about prepared.

I took a deep breath and climbed sweating from the van. In the parking lot a gray-haired burly guy had just escorted a customer to his truck, with all the backslapping and friendly chatter that might accompany a successful sale. I followed him in on back into the store. As soon as we were inside he turned.

"You Dave?"

"Sure am ..." he replied, but there was something about that pause.

"*The* Dave? The Dave in Dave's Sporting Goods?"

He grinned. "One of the Daves. There's five Daves work at this place. Dave senior, the owner, he isn't here right now, but that's his son, Dave Junior, over there if you want to talk to him." This was obviously not the surly Dave.

The store area was configured like a dwelling with its interior walls knocked out and big carrying beams spanning the ceilings holding up the roof and attic. One wing, maybe what had been living room and dining room, was all fishing gear. A bait cooler and storeroom were back where the kitchen and pantry had probably been. Hunting and target bows and archery supplies were hung all over the central carrying beam and guns were on racks at the other end of the store, with long counters along three of the outside walls. It was cool from the air conditioning and a little under-lit. There were no windows.

Dave junior was a burly young man in his late twenties with black hair and mustache. He was selling a bass rig to a middle-aged couple, and he'd spent enough time bass fishing to do a good job with the sale. The couple had already decided on the reel and was working on the rod, so I wandered over to the gun section.

Despite the emotional insulation my new identity provided, I began to tremble surrounded by all those weapons. I'd done some hunting as a kid, and had gotten the standard small-arms training in the navy, but it had been twenty-five years since I'd picked up a firearm of any kind, and Galen's murder had created unpleasant associations in my mind. For people who are not involved with guns as a matter of course, the firearm is a potent symbol. We have none of the recreational and pleasurable associations to attach to it. For us, guns do one thing—they kill—and it's initially weird and scary being surrounded by them. It was hard to focus. It was hard to breathe. There was a heavy set guy at the end of the aisle (Christ, were all these guys burly?) inspecting the wares. He'd pick up a rifle, snap the bolt, heft it, shoulder it, look down the sight, and squeeze off an imaginary round at the wall. I watched him for a while and began to calm down. If he could pick those guns up and throw them around like that, at least I could stand next to them.

The guns were contained in four racks on the floor and one on the wall behind the glass counter. They seemed mostly to be hunting rifles and shotguns, new and used in about equal proportion, some very space-age looking survival sorts of guns that came apart and could be carried around, and then a number of home-owner models like the "Defender" which appeared to be a shotgun with a pistol grip instead of a shoulder piece. It retailed for $395.

The middle-aged couple had moved to the front counter near the guns now. Dave Junior had the reel on the rod and was spooling l ne onto the reel while he and the couple talked about Lake George, the "Queen of Lakes" as the middle aged man called it. Dave told a story of how clear the water was. He'd lost a reel just like this one on a shoal in about ten feet of water, and had come back the following week with a mask to recover it.

Another clerk, one of the Daves no doubt, was waiting on the burly gun customer. Two women had come in and were inspecting camping gear. A young boy in front of me said he was going fishing in Maine and wanted to know what kind of fish he might catch and what kind of lures to use. Dave finished with the middle aged couple and was about to go looking for salmon and small mouthed bass gear for the kid. I asked him when Dave Senior would be back.

"After one-thirty." he said, "He's got a meeting with the accountant." We exchanged knowing smiles and I left, trying to picture burly surly Dave in earnest conversation with his accountant.

I had over an hour and a half so, in a masterstroke of improvisation, I drove down to Simon's Rock College via Routes 7 and 20, through Stockbridge to Great Barrington. This was the same way the cabbie had driven Wayne Lo from the college to the gun shop and back on December 14, 1992. However, on this day, in July of 1994, it was hard to think of winter. On this day, it was so hot the landscape throbbed. Green had exploded everywhere and summer was still young enough that the vegetation hadn't started turning brown. It just sat there throbbing, giving off moist oxygen. The countryside was like a tropical rainforest.

Downtown Great Barrington, the road to Simon's Rock, the drive to the campus and still no ghosts. I thought of the movie *Robocop*, in which high-tech scientists rebuild the hero and remove his personal memories so that he can be a perfect crime fighting machine. The hook to the plot is that little shreds of his memory remain and bits of his past life keep flashing back to him while he's doing his crime busting. It was an inane and gratuitously violent movie actually, but now that I was on the case, that plot device had resonance. As I drove through the familiar terrain, fragments of my old life with Galen came back to me, but there was no pain. I had been rebuilt.

If Galen's murder had changed security policies at Simon's Rock, you wouldn't have known it from the reception I got at the guard shack. I had to stop in front of the window and yell to get the guard's attention. She was a cheery, grandmotherly lady and she told me, when I asked, that the Galen Gibson memorial was down the road on the right; I'd recognize it when I saw the bench.

I drove a few hundred yards and then I saw the wooden bench. It was across a little creek from the administration building, at one end of an open field below the student union and dorms. The memorial behind it was a hexagonal pole about seven feet tall. It was a little wider in the middle, maybe eight inches, and it tapered to about six inches at each end. The top was cut at a bias and capped with copper. On one of the faces the word P E A C E was spelled vertically in roman capitals. That was it. Nothing about Galen. Just a wannabe tree, standing alone in a field, non-referential, sentimental and not at all Galen. To make the setting even stranger the bench, which logically should have been facing the monument or looking down the field, was turned to face the stream, so that its back was to the six-sided pole. If you came to view the memorial and sat on the bench, you wouldn't see it. This was symbolic I thought, taking a rest on the bench, of how the administration had turned their backs on what had happened to my son. Their desire to put it all behind them and move on was natural, but it was self-serving too.

It was a little cooler here at least. I thought back to the sequence of events as I remembered them from the criminal trial. Across the road and a few hundred feet to the right was the small stand of pines where Wayne Lo had waited that night. He'd already shot the security guard,

Theresa Beavers, and then murdered the teacher, Ñacuñán Sáez, who had paused at the guard shack while driving back onto campus. The three kids who'd driven onto campus just after this noticed Wayne standing in the pines next to the library, probably fiddling with his gun. He'd shouted something like, "Get the fuck out of here." They ignored him and went into the library. By the time Galen had come out to help, Wayne had gotten his gun operational.

I followed all this in my imagination. Then I got off the bench, walked to the library, and moved my body over the same course that had been Galen's last walk on this earth, back through the big doors, through the atrium, against the wooden inner doors, where, according to trial testimony, the chest-shot victim had exhaled a bloody mist onto the wood, and into the library where he'd collapsed and died. The distance was somewhat longer than I had pictured it. I saw too that the front walkway sloped down from the library. That would explain how some of the bullets had entered high in the walls near the ceiling or had exited through the roof, Galen's lovely spirit after them.

The library was deserted in the midday heat, giving me ample room for these thoughts and investigations. There's not much else to say about revisiting this scene. Galen was dead. I had tried with all my might to bring him back, but he was not coming. I had suffered much more, in other places, than I did in that library. It was an analytical exercise for me. If I had any emotion it was, predictably, a resurgence of my anger. Not at Wayne Lo, or that Galen was dead, but that there was no display in a glass case, no sign, nothing to tell the story of what had happened. That Galen had lived and been happy here, that he'd loved this library, that he'd died running out of it to help someone; none of these facts, which were of such importance to me, were deemed worthy of note by the college.

I decided to skip the rest of my campus tour and proceed back up Route 7 to meet burly surly Dave. I was curious about the route of Wayne

Lo's deadly walk, but it seemed that the vegetation was too dense in this season for easy passage. Streams and ponds that he might have walked over in December would have to be waded in July.

At the gun shop Dave Junior went downstairs and got Senior. The man came up the stairs and looked me in the eye a little quizzically. I shook his hand and introduced myself. He asked what he could do for me. I said I needed to talk with him for a few minutes but it would be a little embarrassing to do that right in the store. "Well," he said easily, "let's go outside where it's a hundred five." He motioned me through the door to the front porch and we stood in the heat on the edge of the parking lot.

He was a stocky man, with an open face. I said, "I'm the guy whose son got killed by Wayne Lo."

It was like I'd punched him. He sagged a little and hurt filled his eyes. He stammered an apology and then kept repeating, "What can I do for you? What do you need? What can I tell you?" Not like he was trying to get rid of me, but as if he were trying to soothe a hurt friend or fill a hole that existed in both of us. We talked.

I learned a few things in our half hour in the sun. Dave had been in business for thirty years and had sold about thirty thousand firearms in that time. (He consistently called them firearms. I kept saying "weapons" just out of habit from my navy days, I guess. He made no effort to correct me.) There had been six deaths from those 30,000 firearms: the two at Simon's Rock, two other murders and two suicides. The SKS was a firearm he didn't handle much. It had come in used from a man named Hernandez who lived right up the street. Why did people buy SKS-type firearms? He shrugged his shoulders and shook his head. "People collect all kinds of crazy things." he said, "I don't know why they do, I've never thought much about it and to be honest I don't care. But I'll tell you one thing for sure. If you want people to buy more assault rifles all you gotta do is tell them that pretty soon you're not going to let them buy any at all. Right? All you gotta do is tell people they can't have something and that makes them want it more." He stood there sweating, head shaking at the irony of the situation, at the foolishness of his fellow beings. We savored that for a moment and plowed on.

No, his store had not advertised the used SKS in the paper. Dave suspected that Wayne Lo had been calling for months to see if such a model had come in. There were half a dozen gun shops Lo might have bought an SKS from, but Dave's Sporting Goods was the only one with an 800 number. He thought that Lo had used the 800 number repeatedly until he learned that an SKS was in stock. It would have been a toll free call, important for a college kid of limited means, and he could have made it from the privacy of his room. How he wished he hadn't sold that gun to that kid!

Then he told me that the cops hadn't come around at all until about a week before Wayne Lo's murder trial. They'd called him once to verify the story, but had never come out and talked with him until just before the trial began. Even then it was perfunctory. This seemed important to me. It had been my assumption, based on the testimony of one of the psychiatrists at the criminal trial, that Wayne Lo had read about the used SKS in a newspaper ad immediately before the killings.

The story developed a little differently if Wayne Lo had in fact been calling Dave's 800 number "for months." It would lend credence to the District Attorney's contention that Lo's plan had been formed and the type of weapon (something cheap and easily available, with a lot of firepower) had been selected since the fall. It would add weight to the creepy notion that Simon's Rock College had been feeding, housing and educating a killer-in-waiting for months.

Dave had made a point of talking to Lo before the sale, just to try to see if he was OK. They'd joked about the Yankees. Dave was a big Red Sox fan and Wayne Lo had been wearing a Yankees cap. "Anyone who walks into my store in a Yankees cap is going to get a hard time from me," he said, "And I gave it to him." Apparently the reaction had not been noticeably abnormal. Dave didn't remember exactly what Lo had said, but it hadn't seemed inappropriate. He told me he'd also made a joke with Lo about the pronunciation of Helena, just to see if Lo would pronounce that city's name the way Montana people did. Satisfied that the kid was stable and on the level, Dave let the other clerk, Dave, complete the transaction. The item purchased was a little out of the ordinary, but the kid seemed to check out.

As we talked and sweated people kept passing in and out of the shop. It was clear Dave had a healthy business going, and it was clear why. Each person who passed us greeted Dave by name, and Dave responded by name. One old geezer with dog hair all over his T-shirt wanted to give Dave a blow-by-blow description, right then and there, of his prostate operation. Dave gently shooed him inside. Dave Benham appeared to be a straightforward man. He went about his business honestly and earnestly. He cared about people.

This was not what I'd expected at all. In the course of the morning I'd played out my fantasy scenarios involving me and a defensive Dave, certainly surly, maybe confrontational, hostile, but I had never even considered a situation where two people simply talk.

This guy was not unintelligent, not insensitive. He wasn't a philosophical or introspective sort, but he had a heart. He was showing me that it hurt. It hurt for me and my boy. It hurt that bad things happened in the world. It hurt for himself and his family; that many townspeople and college kids had accused him of being responsible for Galen's death. Sure, he'd sold the gun. And he'd had many a staff meeting and many a sleepless night after that sale wondering if there was any way he could've kept that gun out of Wayne Lo's hands. It was done now. It was a tragedy, but it could not be undone.

I realized that whatever I thought I was going to find here, I'd found something else. It never occurred to Dave that the way to have kept the gun out of Wayne Lo's hands was to not sell guns. Dave was who he was, and who he was sold firearms of all kinds, had been for thirty years. This guy was just a piece of the big fate-machine that put Galen and that bullet together. He was as feckless and uncomplicated as the piece of metal that tore through my son's chest. Was it the bullet's fault? Sure, as much as it was Dave's. If there was blame to be assigned, there ought to be responsibility, and the possibility at least, that the responsible party had had a choice of actions and chose the wrong one. Dave and the bullet, it seemed to me then, did not fall into that category. They simply were what they were; minor elements at the end of a long chain.

He wasn't going to tell me all he knew or thought about the legal requirements for gun ownership. He wasn't going to tell me all he knew or thought about foreign importation of assault-style weapons, or about Classic Arms. He said he never bought that stuff wholesale new (meaning cheap imported SKS-type guns), and that he didn't trust some of the mail order concerns (meaning outfits like Classic Arms), but that was all he said. Maybe he was holding something back from me; maybe this was just a kind of speculation he did not indulge in. Either way, I wasn't going to get any more information by continuing to ask.

Instead we talked for a bit about him. His business hadn't been particularly affected by the shootings, but he personally had. The local paper had undertaken a campaign to vilify him, and the local congressman had accused him to his face of being responsible for Galen's death. That hurt him. It hurt his family. He seemed to understand about politics and selling newspapers. But understanding did not make it easier. There was plenty of blame to go around, he said. He was not ready to bear it all.

Then our talk was over. I was to call him anytime, if there was ever anything he could do to help me. It was that simply said and that genuinely offered.

7

GREAT AMERICAN

I should have been more attentive. My Bernie Rodgers dream was showing me a path through my suffering, a path I followed briefly on my trip to the gun shop. As I had done at the criminal trial, I recorded my visit with Dave Benham. I wrote it up in a straightforward manner, like case notes, and stored it in my computer in a file reserved for information about Galen's murder. As before, this exercise had a beneficial effect. It felt good to have done something. It felt good to have that file to refer to for matters of fact.

I had taken the first, tentative steps out of my predicament, but the way was not yet clear to me, and I wandered.

As the second anniversary of Galen's death approached, my obsession with our civil action against the college began to reassert itself. Our lawyer was going to file a motion to have the trial moved to a faster track. He was nearly finished with his preparations. Perhaps we'd have our day in court soon. I was back in my revenge mode, and, not coincidentally, deeper in misery than ever.

Time was not healing my wounds. If anything, it was having the opposite effect. Annie and I had been in shock that first year, and then we'd been numbed and distracted by the criminal trial. Now, it was like coming back from a difficult session with the dentist, and having the novocaine wear off. We were getting our feelings back and we were both acutely aware of how much we hurt. The jagged mystery tumbled over and over inside us. How could it have been *him*, of all the hundreds of students? Of all the thousands of things that could have happened, how could it have been Galen at that library door? How could he be gone forever? All around us, it seemed, people were expecting us to be getting better, to be getting over it. We were getting worse! The magazines from Publisher's Clearing House piled up. My rage increased.

The winter passed with no relief. Then, in May of 1995, I got a call from our lawyer telling me there had been a new development.

The lawyers representing Simon's Rock College and the lawyers representing Great American Insurance Company did not seem eager to begin a civil trial. They knew how bad the college might look if the matter were presented in an unsympathetic way, and they knew that the more time they put between the murders and our trial, the more they would gain. Memories would dim, the horror of Wayne Lo's actions would be covered over by newer horrors. Responsible individuals might move or even die, and the college could divorce itself from its role in the tragedy. They 'd been stalling for two years and now they had come up with a legal maneuver that blasted our distant civil trial into an even more remote orbit.

They decided to depose Wayne Lo. They wanted to question him, under oath, and record his answers for possible use in our civil case.

The odds were very long against their ever using his testimony in their own defense. He was a sociopath and a murderer. The truth of his statements could not be trusted. He could easily do the college more harm than good, and it was likely that he would want to. None of this mattered. It only mattered that the college said they needed his testimony to prepare their defense.

In Massachusetts every person who is sentenced to first degree murder is entitled by law to an automatic appeal. There are many murderers, and many appeals to be heard. There was really no telling when Wayne Lo's appeal would be heard. That meant there was no telling when the college would be able to depose him because, theoretically, deposing him prior to his appeal might deprive him of his Fifth Amendment rights.

There was no telling when we'd have our civil trial because the trial could not go forward until the college had been able to complete the preparation of its defense, and the college could not complete its preparation until it had deposed Wayne Lo, and it could not depose Wayne Lo until Wayne Lo's appeal had been heard, and there was no telling when Wayne Lo's appeal would be heard.

This was bad news indeed, and it got worse. As our lawyer explained matters, the true origin of the delay was not Simon's Rock College. The case was out of their hands by this time. The real problem was an insurance problem.

Great American was only the primary insurer for the college. When large damages were possible, a secondary insurer backed up the primary insurer. If the college's liability went beyond the limits of the primary insurer's policy, the secondary insurer would pay the difference. In our case the problem concerned a matter of definition. Great American and the secondary insurer were arguing over how to define the Wayne Lo incident. Great American said Wayne Lo's entire rampage represented a single incident. It would pay up to its limit on all the damages won by all the victims, then the secondary insurer would pay the balance. The secondary insurer disagreed. They said each individual represented a separate incident. Therefore Great American would pay up to its maximum for damages that might be won by Theresa Beavers, Ñacuñán Sáez, Galen Gibson, the other wounded students, and all other potential claimants, after which the secondary insurer would pay the balance.

Of course nothing had been decided yet. No civil suits against the college had begun, no judgments had been rendered. But the potential difference between the two interpretations could be millions of dollars. Great American and the secondary insurer could not agree on how to settle their problem, so they were suing each other! Until the two insurance companies had ironed out their lawsuit they would do everything they could to prevent our lawsuit from taking place.

It would be a long time before we got our day in court.

One morning, shortly after learning this, I woke up and lay in bed with a strange and wonderful image in my head. The birds were making a racket outside. Sweet smelling spring air drifted in the window. I lay there next to my lovely Annie and beheld the thing that filled my mind almost as if it were a vision.

It wasn't a vision, though. It was another movie, but not a real movie. It was an amalgam of movies, and I played it over and over.

It starred Clint Eastwood, and he was a homesteader, a retired gunslinger. In this movie the bad guys come and kill the Young Man. Clint is out in the yard feeding his chickens, and somebody tells him what happened. He goes in his house and gets his gun down from over the fireplace and then he climbs on his horse and starts down the road after those bad guys … not racing around, but relentless. One by one he catches up with them. Some grovel, some fight back. Some die on the road, some in whorehouses, some in high places. But they all get what's coming to them. Finally after he's found the last bad guy he rides home and hangs up his gun and goes back out in the yard and feeds his chickens.

I must've lain there watching it for an hour. By the time I got up, the sun was bright.

I was ready to go out and buy a gun.

⚘§8
CLINT, LEE & ME

It was frightening and funny at the same time. I was so distraught by the murder of my son that I was ready to get a gun and murder someone. I suppose that was the point at which I bottomed out. The jolt of my landing shocked me into thinking about what was happening to me.

I was suffering because I hadn't seen deeply enough into the process that had caught me up. I knew I wanted revenge for what had happened to Galen, and I knew this revenge would not come through any of my florid and violent fantasies, but only through knowledge. I thought the civil trial would reveal the truth and that public opinion would serve as a just punishment for Bernie Rodgers and Simon's Rock College. But I hadn't thought the whole thing through.

My pursuit of vengeance had at its core those seemingly endless chains of causes that I had recognized immediately after Galen's death. I should have understood that by initiating legal action against the college I was setting in motion yet another series of causes which would have their effects on my life. I should have understood that by investing myself so completely in the judicial system to further my vengeful aims, I had made myself a prisoner of that system.

What if we never had a trial? What if I or one of the principals died before a trial? What if they lied and the jury believed them? What if they told the truth and the jury decided they'd done the best they could? What if everything came to pass just as I hoped and I still found myself on the other side of it, a suffering mess? I needed to get out of that loop.

As I considered the compelling vividness of the Lee Marvin and Clint Eastwood fantasies, it occurred to me that they were my own productions, and that I was producing them for a reason. Talking to Dave Benham had been a good thing. I could sense that it represented the beginning of a solution to my problem. If pretending that I was a movie tough-guy helped accomplish this, so be it. Perhaps I could use these crazy fantasies to keep me from going crazy. Perhaps they were no more than tools for gaining knowledge. Certainly knowledge could be used for revenge, but it might also bring understanding. Understanding might lead to acceptance or even forgiveness.

Once I realized this, the rage began to release its hold on me.

My first breakthrough came at the end of a very hot day in July, 1995, just about a year after my visit with Dave Benham. For some months I'd been thinking about the ingrown, cancerous futility of my anger, and about possible ways to get beyond it. I hadn't come up with much more than the concept of using those Clint and Lee icons as tools, but I was still working on it. This particular evening, after a fruitless day of book scouting, I found myself in central Massachusetts, at the intersections of Routes I-91, I-90 and 5, too tired and cranky to drive any farther.

Route 5 had been an old wagon road that ran along the Connecticut River. It had always been a commercial route, and in the 1970s and 1980s malls and shopping centers sprang up along much of its length. Here at the fertile junction of two interstate highways, commerce had gone a little wild. It was one giant strip mall, miles of businesses, punctuated by ganglia of more densely developed shopping areas. The right-of-way for Route 5 had been developed back in the Model-T era, and was hopelessly inadequate for the volume of traffic it was now required to carry. The road was a mess, the worst of modern auto-America, impersonal and dysfunctional on a human level, piled up around the ideas of the automobile and the consumer. Traffic would start up, move about fifty feet and stop again. I had plenty of time to enjoy the scenery. Wal-Mart, McDonald's, Pizza Hut, Sears.

The first motel I saw that looked like it might be relatively roach-free was a Super Ramada City. From the name and sprawl of the place I figured it was one of those motels with rooms, conference spaces, exhibition halls and a restaurant organized around an indoor tropical rainforest. In the rainforest would be a bamboo cabana containing a bar, next to which would be a swimming pool. I pictured that bar and I pictured that pool, and the soft green of the indoor plants. I pulled in.

It was cool in the lobby, but there was an indefinable sense of wrongness, of something out of place. However they did have a single room and the rate was reduced from the usual ninety-five dollars to sixty-five dollars tonight. I got my key, drove my van around to the appropriate wing of Super Ramada City and took my bag up to my room, feeling all the while that something was slightly amiss.

In my room, the digital clock on the TV was broken. It was all amped up and the big red numbers flashed a new minute every five seconds or so and would not stop. I threw a towel over it, but I couldn't arrange the towel so that it concealed the clock without covering the TV too. I gave up and went to the tropical rainforest.

Sure enough, that bamboo cabana was there, right by the pool. I slid onto a stool and ordered a beer. The rainforest was just what I'd imagined, but I'd forgotten about the smell of chlorine from the pool. I didn't like chlorine in my rainforests. I didn't even like rainforests. They were wet and sticky.

I went back to the parking lot to get my computer out of the van, and discovered what was wrong. There were half a dozen other vehicles out there and they were all vans like mine or pickup trucks with caps on the back. In each of these vans or trucks was a wire animal cage. I stopped on the hot pavement and listened. From the direction of Super Ramada City came a faint but distinct yapping. The place sounded like a kennel. I walked back in and went through the lobby. The guy at the desk smiled when he saw me coming.

"There's a dog show here, right?"

"Yes Sir!" he piped, "Not one dog show, actually. There are four different breed shows here. Starting today and running through the weekend." Big smile.

Now that I looked around the lobby I saw two short brown dogs. That was what had been wrong. Dogs do not belong in motel lobbies. Out in the rainforest there had been a big tan dog. That would be two breeds right there, if I knew my dogs, short brown and big tan. That's what had seemed wrong. That's why the rates were reduced. The place was a dog pound for the weekend and I was stuck in the middle of it.

Back in the room I poured a bourbon and lay on the bed. The clock on the TV roared away in those large red wrong numbers, 1:02, 1:03 ... I closed my eyes. Here I was, in the middle of a fucking kennel with a dead son, no lawsuit, and a world of misery, and what did I have to work with? The brains God gave me, such as they were, and two tools, or maybe one. Or maybe three.

For the past couple of weeks I'd been having a recurring idea. It felt like another one of my fantasies but it wasn't a movie. It was a story about a journey. A guy is on a journey, sort of like Clint, but with no revenge motive. The journey is through a strange land, and what the story is all about is that the guy just wants to get home. The wily Odysseus? A little too grand. Maybe something like Nathaniel Bishop's excellent *Voyage of the Paper Canoe* wherein the author takes a trip down the Mississippi from Quebec to the Gulf of Mexico. *The Paper Canoe.* A perfect title for me, though in that book the narrator didn't want to get home badly enough. Maybe Joshua Slocum's *Sailing Alone Around the World.* That guy knew he never *was* going to get back home because there was no more home to get to.

My mind wandered off. I took a glug of bourbon. If you have a tool, you use it to do a job. In my case the tool, my fantasies, was just a way of enabling myself to go out and get the story. That's what I was really thinking about, wasn't it? Finding out as much as I could about what happened to Galen, and why it happened and who was involved?

I could imagine a story out there in the great wide world, all spread out and misshapen like Mercator's projection. The story was dispersed in time and space, but it was not lost. It seemed to me, in this imagining, that all the pieces of the story were preserved out there and were waiting for me to discover them. If I could find them and put them all together, the story of what had happened would exist in something close to its original form. Every role would be known and the heroes and villains would be there for all to see. Any one of us could look back on that story and take from it what we needed. It might not be what we wanted, but it would be as close to what happened as a story could provide, and that would finish the line of events that had started with Galen, and taken a horrible turn with his murder, and changed all our lives forever.

Wayne Lo was locked up. There was nothing more I could do about him. But I was furious at Bernie Rodgers for the way he'd handled things on the day of the shootings, and for the way he'd tried to avoid responsibility for what I considered to be his bad decisions. I was furious at the college for trying to slither out of the lawsuit.

Now I thought I could see a solution. I'd write a book. If I couldn't make it into a book, if it didn't fit, or organize, or turn out that way, at least I'd be the world's expert on the case, and I'd have all the notes written up, and I could say, "There. I've given it my best. Now I'm done."

What made it seem possible was that the story was out there on the road; right where I'd be all the time anyway. Finding those fugitive pieces of the story would be like discovering and snagging rare books. It would take long road hours, time spent in strange places with strange people, close attention to detail and a good memory for odd bits of information. I could do that! I was the Mystical Warrior of the Eastern Macro-Metro Corridor, wasn't I?

I could feel time sweeping me along, just like that stupid digital clock on the TV. I could feel my life changing in the years since Galen had died. I could feel myself forgetting things. I knew I'd have to start on the story soon.

November would be the perfect time. It would take about four months to get the loose ends of my business tied down. I'd get out one last catalog with a lot of rare books in it, and get enough money in the bank to coast for a while. The last big book show of the season was in the middle of November. That would be a little more income. Then I could start trying to do this Galen thing. Just like Clint and Lee, and Joshua Slocum and Nathaniel Bishop and, what the hell, Odysseus too. I finished my drink and washed up and went out to dinner.

I didn't want to get back in the van so I began to walk. I felt a little giddy and—what was that nineties word—empowered. I'd been thinking about this in parts and pieces for two years or more. One time I'd think, "I need to get the whole story down." Another time I'd think, "I really should take some time off and look into this Galen business." Now I had it all together. The story would redeem the experience, if I could get it all. And if I could get it, I'd write it all down. I really was going to do this thing.

I got to the end of the long drive leading out of Super Ramada City and realized that walking was a very weird thing to be doing in this landscape. It was just getting dark. All around me electric signs flashed dinner messages, but getting to them on foot was going to be tricky. The traffic had let up a little but cars still zoomed down Route 5 in the dusk and they were not looking for pedestrians. There was no sidewalk.

Here my journey had just begun and already I was walking where no man dared to walk.

I cut across the lot of a Family Restaurant and through some hedges to a muffler shop, then past a Dunkin Donuts to a small sub-mall, a collection of a dozen or so businesses in unconnected one or two story frame buildings. In this little mall was a security company, a take-out Chinese restaurant, a beauty parlor, a shoe store, a karate studio, a meat wholesaler and, charmingly, a training center for the trowel arts, with pillars, gates, walls and porticoes, all student projects, constructed in front of it. These cheesy little enterprises were remarkable in their own way, as much a force of nature as the weed shoots that pushed though cracks in the pavement under my feet. Finally, just beyond the mini-mall, I found what looked like it might be an acceptable eatery.

It was cool and dark inside, not particularly crowded. The decor was dark country wood and the menu was heavy American. The bar looked well stocked. More liquor than I could drink that night, at least. I ordered a bourbon and soda and drank half of it, thinking about actually beginning to write a story. I thought about the places such an adventure might take me. I thought about the places I'd been already.

Then for an astounding two minutes, I could not remember where I was. I remembered what I was doing, and I remembered who I was, but as I looked intently around the restaurant I had no idea whether I was in Burlington, Vermont or Albany, New York or Portland, Maine or Evanston, Illinois or Whippany, New Jersey—or where? The fact was that it could've been any of those places, and many more. This was a remarkable feature of the country in which my journey took place; much of it could be anywhere else. And if that was true, where did it leave me?

✢9
GOD'S WILL

By November of 1995 I was ready.

Annie and I were sitting at the kitchen table, surrounded by our after-dinner mess. I'd just given her the front section of the newspaper, which I always read first, and had taken, in exchange, the sports section, which I preferred and saved for last. I opened the paper and told her, "I'm going to investigate Galen's murder and write a book about it."

"What?"

"I'm going to go out there and find out about this thing for myself."

She put her paper down. "Why would you want to do that?"

"It'll make me feel better." I said.

"It will? Talking to all those people? Digging up all that awful stuff?"

"This lawsuit bullshit is making me crazy. I've got to do something."

"You already *are* crazy."

"Then it couldn't hurt, could it?"

"No, I don't suppose. I don't have to help you, do I?"

"Just with the dishes."

She was stuck, and she knew it. I had a terrible memory for dates, and I'd be dragging her back with me every time I had a question about the order of events. I'd be sharing my latest revelations with her when I came off the road, because we always talked about what happened out there. Perhaps worst of all, she'd be forced to bear witness to my obsessive hashing and rehashing of motives. It would be unpleasant for her, especially since she didn't have the emotional cover that my Clint and Lee persona provided me. But she would bear it bravely because she thought it might do me some good. Also, we both knew that if I ever did get the story assembled, it would be a way to air our grievance against Simon's Rock College. We were beginning to lose faith in the possibility of our civil suit ever taking place.

If Annie considered my plan marginal, Brooks thought it was down-right dumb. Who would want to go back there and dig up all that stuff he was working so hard to move past? His old man. That was who. Celia didn't have a strong opinion about it either way, but if there was going to be a book, she wanted to be damned certain that she was in it. And could I put her friends in a chapter too?

In fact, as I had guessed when this idea first came to me, the Galen project wasn't going to cause any major disruptions. I did not go to work like other fathers. I made noises in my study. Then I went away for a few days. Then I came back and slept. Then I went back in my study. It had been like this for a while, and it was not about to change. There may have been a little strain because now I was working at two jobs, but for the most part, my investigations fit well into the somewhat wrinkled fabric of our family life.

First I went back over all the newspaper articles I'd saved, and then the notes and letters pertaining to the shooting, and the notes I'd written about things that occurred to me after Galen died. I even read copies of letters I'd sent to people in the past three years, looking for things there that I might have forgotten since. Then I went back to my notes on the criminal trial.

It was not until this review, in the fall of 1995, nearly three years after Galen's death, that I began to understand the limits of these notes and of the trial itself. Recording the proceedings had been a therapeutic exercise, but I saw now that part of my frustration in the intervening months must have arisen from the limits of the information I had recorded. Far from telling the whole story of what happened the night

Galen was killed, the proceedings only provided information of a certain kind.

Although the witnesses were helpful in recreating the general sequence of events, their testimony was less effective at establishing who was where when, and surprisingly, almost useless at establishing motivation. I realized that Wayne Lo didn't have to tell us anything if he didn't want to. And he didn't want to. He was never called to the witness stand. Nor was the reasoning of any of the other characters in the drama important to the prosecution. The question was always "What happened next?" never, "Why did you do what you did?"

I had been in the curious position of sitting in the courtroom, just a few feet from the people who knew what had happened, and who were bound by oath to give answers truthfully, and I could not ask them the questions I needed answered. The district attorney didn't care how or why Bernie Rodgers had failed to prevent Wayne Lo from getting the ammo package; he just needed to establish that the package had arrived on campus. He didn't care that no one had stopped Wayne; he just needed to prove that Wayne had done the shooting. I had a story with characters and events, but nothing connecting them.

Despite this difficulty, my review of the trial got me oriented. At a year's remove from the ebb and flow of the courtroom battle, certain patterns emerged.

The most obvious of these had to do with Wayne Lo. On looking over the evidence, it seemed to me that Wayne's anger had a history, and that it was directed, at least in part, against the college. According to testimony given by students and teachers, Wayne Lo had espoused far right-wing views and had made derogatory remarks against Jews, gays, blacks and the handicapped. Aside from his few friends who held similar views, most of the college kids avoided him. Earlier that fall he'd written a paper advocating that all people with AIDS be herded into concentration camps. His classmates had derided him. His teacher had censured him.

Just before Thanksgiving vacation, Wayne had come down with the chicken pox, and was prohibited by the airline from flying home. During vacations the few students who remained on campus were required to live in one monitored area. Wayne had returned to his own dorm room too early, and had been caught and punished by his Residence Director, Floyd Robinson. In the course of an argument with Robinson, Wayne stated that he had "the power to bring the college to its knees."

Students testified that, earlier that fall, he had expressed interest in obtaining a gun. A Residence Advisor testified that Wayne had talked about shooting up the dining hall. Apparently, this kind of gallows humor was not unusual among the students; one of Galen's friends told me that the warning, "I'm in a bad mood. Don't go to the dining hall today." was a standard joke on campus. Certainly there was stress in the students' lives, and increasing violence in the world around them. Joking about it helped to put it in perspective, made it easier to deal with. But Wayne Lo didn't get the joke. He got a gun.

His anger against the college had been growing at least since the fall, and the District Attorney prosecuting the case demonstrated that Wayne had acted on it in a methodical way. He pointed out that Wayne purchased the parts to modify the gun (the package from Classic Arms) several days *before* purchasing the gun. This implied that he knew ahead of time what kind of gun he was going to buy; that he had a plan already in place.

The same could not be said for the college, or its chief administrator. Despite Wayne's increasingly hostile behavior, and despite the Classic arms package and Jeremy Roberts' warning telephone call, Dean Rodgers had no clear and forceful plan for dealing with the threat posed by Wayne Lo; he seemed reluctant to recognize there was a threat at all.

This typified the college's reaction to Wayne Lo. As I continued to review the trial notes, I came to believe that there were a few defining points on the line of events leading to the shootings. Each of these was characterized by bad communications and false assumptions.

The first of these decisive points was the arrival of the ammo package on campus. Because it was labeled "Classic Arms" it was noticed by the mail room lady and brought to the attention of college staff members. The package was then taken to a morning meeting of school officials and discussed, but was returned unopened to the mail room. Sometime before noon Wayne picked the package up and took it back to his dorm.

Several people at that meeting had reservations about the contents of the package, but Dean Rodgers, apparently thinking it illegal to interfere with anyone's mail, refused to open it and returned it to the mail room. Did the Dean have a specific plan for ascertaining its contents? Was his plan attempted but improperly carried out? The trial testimony was unclear on these important questions.

This led to the second point. When Trinka Robinson learned that Wayne had been allowed to pick up the package she followed him back to his room, and almost saved the day by arriving just as he was opening it. Wayne refused to let her watch him, citing a rule in the college handbook that said that two college officials had to be present during a room search. Baffled, Trinka went off to phone Bernie Rodgers. When she came back, Wayne had already hidden the bullets.

Finally, there was a critical interval during the time Trinka and her children were being evacuated. While everyone was bustling around her apartment, a weekly dorm meeting was taking place right in the building. Both Wayne Lo and Floyd Robinson were present. It broke up some time around 9:30 P.M. Floyd returned to his apartment and Wayne returned to his room. According to Theresa Beavers's testimony, and to telephone records, it was about 10:15 when Wayne began shooting. For some part of the forty-five minutes during which college officials knew about the package from Classic Arms and about the threat Wayne posed, they knew where Wayne was.

After I'd finished going over the trial notes, I turned my attention to the depositions that our lawyer had taken for our civil case. When I read through these, I realized the complexity of events leading up to the shootings, and from how many viewpoints that day had been seen. A dozen students, teachers and staff at the college had been interviewed. Some of the depositions were unproductive from my point of view. Others provided information that shed light on questions the criminal trial had raised.

Trinka Robinson, who had not testified at the criminal trial, stated that she left that morning staff meeting thinking Bernie had arranged to have Wayne open the package in his presence. She was surprised to learn that Wayne had picked up the package at the mail room and that he was on his way to the dorm. When she called Bernie for guidance in dealing with the situation, Bernie said she should search the package *but not the room.* She returned to the room and the contents of the package (minus the bullets) were spread out on the bed. She reported back to Bernie that it had taken Wayne some time to open the door, and that she couldn't be certain that Wayne wasn't hiding something.

In his deposition, Bernie Rodgers had some interesting things to say about the morning meeting. He knew the school had policies about the students' privacy, and he did not think the school had the right to interfere with another person's mail. He stated that he had directed Trinka to find out what was in the package, but that he did not specifically tell her to be there when the package was opened.

According to the story the depositions told, Bernie and Trinka each left that morning meeting thinking the other would determine the contents of the package. Residence director Andrew Jillings stated in his deposition that he thought a note would be attached to the package, directing Wayne to open it in the presence of a college official. Susan Austin, another staff person present that morning, said that as she recalled it, the consensus of the meeting was that Trinka should be present when Wayne opened the package.

Bad communication and weak administration.

However, there was still a chance to retrieve the situation. Wayne had wanted to transfer to another school, and had previously scheduled a meeting for that morning to discuss his request with the Dean. When Trinka called Bernie for advice about entering Wayne's room, Bernie told her to tell Wayne to bring the package to their meeting. Dean Rodgers had a new plan now. He was going to find out what had been in that package by asking Wayne. In his deposition, the Dean said that Wayne was very calm and straightforward, and that he did not appear to be defensive or upset. This satisfied Bernie that Wayne was telling the truth, that there had been no infraction of college rules, and that Wayne did not have a gun.

Jeremy Roberts' warning telephone call was the third critical point. Bernie stated that he thought it was probably a crank call, but that it should be investigated. This investigation would determine whether or not the police should be summoned. However, Bernie was unclear as to who would conduct this investigation and when, exactly, it would be accomplished.

In his deposition, Ba Win stated that, after he had finished moving Trinka and her children to his house, he called Dean Rodgers and told him that he was going to go back and search the room and look for Wayne. He was expecting the Residence Director Andrew Jillings to arrive and accompany him on his search. Jillings was off campus, but was due back momentarily. Ba Win had left messages for Jillings to call him immediately on his return.

So, Bernie Rodgers had a plan to investigate the situation. Ba Win had a plan to apprehend Wayne Lo. But Wayne had his own plan and his own timetable. The college's plan was based on the false assumption that they had plenty of time. The anonymous caller had said the shooting would occur "tomorrow." Bernie Rodgers was so uncertain about the reliability of this call that he did not summon the police; yet the timing of the actions the college took was based on the fact that the caller had said the shooting would not take place until the next day.

While Ba Win was on the phone with Bernie, he heard the first shots. Theresa Beavers. Ñacuñán Sáez.

Then there was the deposition of Irvinia Scott, a residence director at Crosby House, one of the other dorms on campus. The story she told was unrelated to any of the key moments I had identified, but it shed some light on the issue of communication among college officials. She stated that, a month or more after the shootings, a cleaning lady discovered a number of bullets in the weight room in Crosby House. Knowing that Wayne had lifted weights there on the evening of the shootings, Irvinia took the bullets to Bernie Rodgers and asked him what she should do with them. According to her deposition he told her to throw them away. She took them to the police.

Bernie stated in his deposition that he did not remember telling her to throw them away, but that he may well have said it "as a joke."

There was more, much more. In one way, these depositions portrayed the people who gave them simply as fallible human beings who responded in a variety of ways to a complex and extraordinary situation. In another way, it seemed to me that the depositions enhanced the troubling testimony given at the criminal trial. Where was campus security when Jeremy Roberts made his first phone calls? How had Bernie Rodgers, a trained and capable administrator, let that package get away? He said he wasn't sure if the warning call was genuine, but he already knew Wayne had received a package from an ammunition company. Shouldn't this have been sufficient evidence to warrant a call to the police? If he wasn't going to call the police, shouldn't he have gotten campus security after Wayne, even while he knew Ba Win was going to evacuate Trinka? What about all the other people in the dorm with Wayne? These were the sorts of questions my studies raised. As much as they increased my understanding, they also fueled my anger.

However, the most chilling thing I learned in reviewing all these records didn't have to do with any of the people involved; it had to do with the weapon. Wayne had purchased a cheap Chinese version of the SKS semi-automatic rifle. It was sold with a ten round magazine. From the mail order people he'd ordered a folding plastic stock and several thirty-round magazines.

We learned during the trial that the rifle had jammed repeatedly during Wayne's spree. He shot Theresa Beavers and the gun jammed. He shot Ñacuñán Sáez and the gun jammed. He shot Galen and the gun jammed. He shot two other boys and the gun jammed and he gave up.

Scrape marks on the top of some of the cartridges made it apparent that the bolt was riding over the top of the cartridge rather than feeding it into the firing chamber. We never learned at the trial whether the misfit occurred because of a physical defect in the magazines or because Wayne was simply not inserting them with enough force.

Imagine him, then, on that same evening, with a fully functional weapon. Imagine him taking his murderous walk with two hundred rounds of ammunition, loaded in clips of thirty shots each that fired as fast as he could pull the trigger. Imagine that, instead of having to stop, frustrated, every few shots, and fiddle with his jammed weapon, Wayne had been able to *simply keep shooting.* Imagine Wayne's excitement. Imagine the effect of those two hundred rounds of ammunition as opposed to twenty. It was only the malfunction of the weapon that saved dozens of lives, and perhaps, an entire college.

This, too, was God's Will, as much as it was a mundane event with causes of its own.

was a woman named Trinka Robinson. Wayne had argued with her in the past and Jeremy knew that Wayne held a grudge against her and her husband Floyd. According to Jeremy's testimony, he told Trinka that he thought Wayne "has a gun and will hurt someone or himself" and that this would happen "tomorrow." He hung up the phone without identifying himself.

Trinka called Dean Rodgers, and then the Provost, Ba Win. By 9:30 P.M. at the latest, the Provost and the Dean of Simon's Rock College had both been informed that Wayne had a gun. This was approximately forty-five minutes before the shooting started. The Dean testified that he did not call the police because he thought the matter needed more investigation. Despite his knowledge of the Classic Arms package, he thought this was probably a crank call. He offered to drive in and help Trinka if she wanted him to, but she thought it better to contact Ba Win, who lived closer to campus. The Provost came to the dormitory and directed the evacuation of Trinka Robinson and her two children. While Trinka was being moved, she and Ba Win learned that Wayne Lo was present in the dorm. Ba Win testified that he had planned to bring Trinka to his home, and then wait for Andrew Jillings before returning to campus. Together, they would question Wayne.

The shooting started before Jillings reached Ba Win.

The second half of the trial was devoted to biographical and psychological testimony about Wayne Lo. There had been little the defense could do to contest that Wayne had done the shooting, but there was more room for them to maneuver when it came to the question of why the shooting had taken place. They wanted to show that their client was not guilty by reason of insanity. The prosecution countered that Wayne Lo might have been a sick member of society, but he was not innocent by reason of insanity. Through it all the young killer sat stone-faced, in fresh-pressed suits and shirts from home, rarely speaking to his attor-

PART
TWO

❧10
THE WALKABOUT

After a while I got tired of looking at pieces of paper.

Early in December of 1995 I drove to Brooklyn and stayed the evening with my old friend Brown at his place in Greenpoint. The road was dark and I felt alone. Heading through the rain down I-95 and the Brooklyn Queens Expressway, I listened to the music of Thelonius Monk, and cried some. Some for Galen and my family, and some for myself. After a while Monk brought me back ... that piano solo on the version of "Straight No Chaser" he recorded with Charlie Rouse, and its wealth of courage and humor... Not for the first time, I listened to Thelonius Sphere Monk and thought, "If he can do that, I can do this."

Brown was my oldest friend on the planet. In the early 1960s, after seven moves and a near-divorce, my peripatetic and troubled family found itself in a classic split-level ranch on Lagoon Boulevard in Massapequa, Long Island, New York. Brown and I were in several high school classes together, and, being two of the brighter, less motivated students, we soon became friends. As my parents' increasingly venomous battles poisoned the air around our house, I was drawn more and more to Brown's ramshackle old duplex, right on the edge of one of the canals that led out to the Great South Bay. His family seemed everything mine was not. They were Texans, originally, and they still talked with a twang. All four children had odd nicknames (Taffy, Bo, Bossie and Tub), but the cat was called Puss. Mrs. Brown was an artist and a teacher, and Mr. Brown was writing a book about Hemingway, with whom he had corresponded. They ate their summer dinners together on a screened-in porch at the edge of the canal, and after dinner, instead of fighting, they talked. Mr. Brown was likely to hold forth on Russian history or the Civil War or existentialism and the Church, or the New York Giants, and interruptions were welcomed. Through the end of high school, and into our college years, Brown and I hunted and fished on the Great South Bay. We chased girls and drank beers and read books and had ideas together, and as we grew up and became initiated to sex and finance and birth and death we kept in close touch and conferred on these matters. My relationship with Brown had more spirit value than even Monk's music. His family was a model for the one I hoped to have, and he was a model for me. In those first days after Galen died he was there to prop me up and walk me around until I could stand on my own again.

His employees had given him some fancy Scotch for his birthday, and we sipped and talked while he made dinner and then we talked and ate. Brown's widowed mother was failing, and he was taking it hard. The problem of caring for her was looming large. The other thing that consumed him was his quest for a mate. He'd been divorced years before, and though he'd moved through a succession of women and relationships, he had finally come to realize that he wasn't likely to find a wife in the hard-drinking bar scene he frequented. So he began answering personal ads, then placing his own ads. Eventually he hired a consultant, a matchmaker. His claim was that all he wanted was a wife and kids, and I had no reason to doubt him. But there was something else going on. It seemed to me the quest had assumed a form of its own and that going out on these prearranged blind dates had become an end in itself. There must have been a recreational element in it for him. It was certainly a better way to spend his time than drinking whiskey and snorting cocaine—more interesting than the movies, less physically demanding than mountain climbing. He estimated he'd been on a hundred of these dates, ranging from very good to very bad indeed. The worst was meeting the other person and realizing from the first instant that the two of you are going to intensely dislike one another. It was a curious experience, he said, spending time in the company of someone who does not like the way you look, sound, smell or think. It was a curious exercise to learn that you could have such an effect on people.

Brown had always had that ability to see things as they actually were, to look at reality dispassionately and without sentimentality. He was the most fearless person I'd ever known. Part of it was a moral quality, part of it was his wiring. He also had a rare ability to think things through, to see through to the consequences of actions. Perhaps fearlessness was a necessary requisite for someone who could see things as they were and see their consequences too.

Next morning over breakfast I told him what I intended to do and he listened, assented. It was a good plan, he said. It was a necessary thing to do. Brown and I both tended to be orderly people about our interior lives. We didn't like loose ends or messy deals. We'd both go to great lengths to keep the books clean, and I think Brown best understood my endeavor in that light; at least he helped me see it that way. Whether or not I succeeded in this project, or whatever I was trying to do about Galen, at least I wouldn't wake up in twenty years and wish I had tried, and realize it was too late. Was such a rationale understandable to the world at large? Brown understood it, and that was good enough for me.

I left my van in Brooklyn and took the subway into Manhattan to meet Eva and Howard Thomas. After Wayne Lo had finished shooting up the library he moved across the lower campus and shot two more kids, one of whom was their son Richard. The Thomases had decided to sue the college in the summer of 1995 and had called us to ask if they could use our lawyer. We told them yes, and wished them well, but we'd all been preoccupied and we didn't talk about much more than the lawyer issue. Now I wanted to hear their story in detail. Obviously they'd realized something, or had gotten angry about something. I assumed they knew what we knew. I wanted to find out if they knew anything else, anything about the behavior of the college officials that had pushed them into action. I had called Eva the week before and as it turned out they were going to be in the city on this particular Saturday. We arranged a meeting at her husband's office.

The address was on Park Ave, a big new glass and gray metal skyscraper. Her husband's firm had the thirty-ninth floor to themselves. I got off the elevator and wandered past the reception desk into a room full of filing cabinets. The place was deserted. I gave a few tentative shouts and a kid with an armful of folders came out of another room and showed me where to go.

I found Howard Thomas back in a corner office with a spectacular view of the Triborough Bridge and northeastern Manhattan. It was a large room but it was cluttered with bookshelves and desks and with at least three computers and related hardware. Howard himself was on a speakerphone with someone and they were talking about computers. They were trying to do something with Norton Navigator and Windows 95. Whatever they were trying wasn't working and Howard was becoming frustrated. Finally he hung up and said hello and shook my hand. He was round and furry, wearing jeans with rolled-up cuffs. He'd taken off his shoes and one of his socks had a hole in the toe. A computer geek for a big law firm? I couldn't quite get a make on him. When I'd met his wife at the trial she'd looked like she had money. I was confused.

We'd just started talking when a woman came in and said, "You're gonna love this . . ." She proceeded to relay some bad news to Howard, something about someone demanding something. "He can't get away with that," said Howard. There was more back and forth about this guy's demands and how far Howard had already extended himself, then the lady asked, "What should I tell him?" Howard Thomas replied,

"Tell him to go fuck himself." and I relaxed. This guy was no computer jock, he was a lawyer. A litigator. A kick-ass, big-city lawyer with a corner office.

Eva joined us just after this. At the trial she'd been confident and bubbly, our frequent luncheon companion. Her son had survived the shootings, and in a way she had been trying to energize or support us. Now she was quiet and pale. As I was to learn, some things had changed for her. Howard, with help from her on specifics, began his narrative.

The semester after the shooting, Richard had done pretty well. In fact he did quite well, primarily because he was getting a lot of attention and support. People were solicitous and concerned about him. They wanted to hear his story and were willing to make concessions for him on account of what he'd been through. Eva and Howard made it clear that Ricky had some psychological problems prior to the shooting. He'd been seeing therapists and struggling to some extent with depression. To their surprise he seemed to make progress as he recovered from his wounds.

Howard said that the next year, his senior year, Richard "crashed and burned." People were no longer lavishing attention on him. In fact, as time went on, Richard came to feel that students and faculty subtly avoided him. He felt he was a visible reminder of an unpleasant incident, an incident that the rest of the community wanted to put behind them. They were uncomfortable with the memories that Richard Thomas represented.

The college provided what would have been reasonable measures for a troubled student, but Howard did not feel that those measures, such as counseling, were necessarily sufficient for a traumatized shooting victim. He did not feel they provided any extra support that might have been occasioned by Ricky's extraordinary circumstances. Whatever they provided, it did not seem to help. Ricky was unable to concentrate on his schoolwork. The college responded by allowing him to carry a reduced course-load (Howard Thomas called it a "case load," laughed, and corrected himself). This continued through the year until finally, by the end of the second semester, Richard Thomas was enrolled in a single course, and failing that one. Simon's Rock did not graduate him that spring.

Howard said that at that point he wrote a letter to the college. In the letter he said that although Richard had suffered through a difficult and unsatisfactory year, he did not consider the college entirely responsible for Richard's difficulties. He wrote that he did not intend to pursue the college regarding its responsibilities toward his son, and that he was willing to simply let matters rest, and move on. Apparently, Howard did not intend to finish paying Richard's tuition either. The details on this point were sketchy and I thought it would be indelicate to pursue them. However, the gist of the matter, as I got it, was that this was a sort of "no fault" proposition, made to the college by Howard Thomas. The college had failed his son to a certain degree; there was a certain amount of unpaid tuition. Howard was suggesting that both parties leave it at that.

He got no response to this letter. It was not until a year and a half later that the college acknowledged receiving it.

Meanwhile Richard had come home for the summer and continued his slide. He continued to get professional help, and these professionals became alarmed for his well-being. Things got so bad that Howard and Eva committed Richard to some kind of emergency psychiatric facility for thirty days. He had a violent episode while he was at this facility.

When he came home the Thomases sent him to a longer term custodial care facility in Vermont. This place cost seven thousand dollars a month and the stay was not covered by insurance. The boy remained there for a time, the expenses piled up, and the parents realized they were spending a hell of a lot of money for their son not to get any better. They brought him home.

Richard tried to pull himself together and enroll in a few courses at a local college. To do this he needed proof that he had sufficient credits in high school English. (Because students go directly from high school into Simon's Rock College, they do not have high school degrees. All their necessary high school work is accomplished as the student works toward his college Associate or Bachelor's degree.) The Thomases requested Richard's transcript from Simon's Rock. To their surprise school officials refused to release the transcript because the Thomases had an unpaid tuition bill.

Howard Thomas said he got quite a runaround trying to find someone at the college who was responsible for this decision. Finally he reached someone who told him, regarding his year-and-a-half-old letter, "Oh, I was just going to call you about that."

This person told Howard that it was simply not college policy to release any transcripts while there was tuition due. Howard reminded him of the substance of his letter, and of the unusual nature of this particular case, and suggested that perhaps it fell outside the boundaries of their "policy." No, said the official, he would make no exceptions. Perhaps, said Howard, he should discuss this matter with the college officials who were responsible for determining this policy before making a final decision. No, said the official, *he* was responsible for determining policy, and the policy would stand. Howard suggested that sometime in the future they would meet again, and no matter who "won" regarding this policy issue, the fight would have wound up costing Simon's Rock many, many times the amount of the unpaid tuition. The college official was unmoved.

Annoyed, Howard Thomas contacted our lawyer. It was at this time that he claimed to have learned things about the shooting that he had not been aware of before. He seemed particularly disturbed by the fact that Ba Win evacuated the Residence Directors (Floyd and Trinka Robinson) from the dorm and did not evacuate or even warn the students.

We began to talk about other aspects of the shooting but Howard Thomas did not seem interested in the particulars of chronology or the persons involved. He had already made up his mind that the institution was guilty of negligence, and guilty of insensitivity. He said he was interested simply in punishing them.

Nor was he interested in finding the highest powered lawyer who might extract the highest damages from the college. Our lawyers had done their work, and had prepared their case. He was satisfied with them on a professional level, and was convinced that they would serve his purposes well enough.

Regarding the timetable of the trial, he saw things as I did. I asked him if he thought the insurance companies were delaying matters in hopes that the issue would be less inflammatory, or that people would have forgotten testimony, or simply because they could hold onto their money longer. Howard Thomas, the New York litigator with the corner office, said no. The reason the trial was being delayed was because of the fight between the two insurance companies themselves.

From Howard Thomas' perspective on the thirty-ninth floor, it was clear that neither insurer wanted our trial to go forward until they had decided this matter between themselves. The decision by Simon's Rock lawyers to depose Wayne Lo, and the matter of his Fifth Amendment rights, were in Howard's words "window dressing." Just a trumped-up reason to delay our trial until they got their own business sorted out.

The Thomases did not share my impatience for the civil trial to begin. Partly, I supposed, it was because they were lawyers, and had no illusions about the way matters proceeded. But there was more. Richard Thomas was at home now and he had not improved a bit. Their son's plight, day to day, took up whatever energy they had. For these people, severe depression and the constant threat of Richard's suicide were the aftermath of Wayne Lo's rampage. "He's stuck in that shooting." Eva Thomas told me, "And he can't get out."

If Ricky Thomas was stuck in the shooting, Rob Horowitz was stuck in himself. Rob was one of Galen's friends from the college. He had graduated the semester Galen died and was now living in New York. After I finished with Eva and Howard Thomas, I walked down to the Chelsea district to visit him.

Galen had told me about Rob. Most of us know people like him, pains in the neck who are somehow, at the same time, so lovable that we can't help but have affection for them. Rob's negative qualities were apparent enough. He was insecure and self-absorbed. On the positive side, seeing him through Galen's eyes, he had a good cynical sense of humor, and an almost childish forthrightness. He was smart and sensitive too, although I got the idea that the boundary between "sensitive," "hypersensitive," and "neurotic" was constantly being drawn and redrawn. Whatever his mix was, it had appealed to Galen. He and Rob were buddies for both of Galen's years at Simon's Rock. They had girlfriends who lived in the same dorm and they were involved in the theater program together.

Theater had been one of Galen's main preoccupations all through his adolescent years. It was, I think, one of the ways he finally socialized himself. He had always been a fixer of things. He had a lot of native mechanical smarts, and endless patience with physical objects. In junior high he began to get involved in the technical end of school productions, set design and construction, sound and lighting. In high school he pretty much *was* the technical staff. There was a professional theater company in our town and Galen soon had a job there. It was a great fit. Galen provided capable, willing and cheap labor, and this equity theater company provided him with the kind of professional education rich kids pay thousands of dollars for at camps in the Berkshires. Better still, it was the real world. Galen had to learn to deal with other people, had to learn the glories of making his personal agenda secondary to the group effort. It was a good education for him, and he carried his knowledge and enthusiasm to the theater program at Simon's Rock.

In his senior year Rob cajoled Galen into designing the sets and lighting for his production of a play about the Holocaust. Galen was not particularly interested in the Holocaust; certainly he did not view it with Rob's intensity, but he agreed to do the job. His friendship with Rob made him commit to the task and his professional standards made him want to do it well. During his last summer at home, I remember Galen complaining about the play, as he forced himself to read it over and over, thinking about lighting and sets. The last time I saw Galen alive was in the fall of 1992. I'd stopped by the college on one of my road trips, and he took me down to the theater building and proudly showed me some of the sets he had constructed. Just the two of us, after dinner, walking through that big dark theater, Galen telling me stories from his professional life. It was a good moment. From talking to Rob it was clear that he and Galen had some good moments, too.

After graduation Rob moved to Manhattan only to discover that theater wasn't really for him. He was living in a room at the Chelsea hotel, and while it was fun finally going into that famous old Manhattan landmark, it was a little disappointing to see that it was just an old hotel. No underground media stars stumbling around in drug-hazes, no flamboyant queens crowding the lobby. A lot of younger people. A very friendly maid who struck up a conversation on the elevator. It reminded me more of a college dorm than of Andy Warhol.

Rob's room had a bed, a desk and a closet. The bathroom was down the hall. The place was, in fact, just like a dorm, save for the handsome large windows that opened onto a small balcony on the street side, mellow afternoon light pouring through the dusty glass.

We sat for a moment, then Rob announced he was hungry and led me to a restaurant around the corner. There was a wait, and as we stood at the restaurant door a group of four Asian people, two mothers and two small children, made their way around us and stood near the only empty table, the one that was being cleaned off for us. "Hey!" shouted Rob to the restaurant and its staff. "Those people just pushed past us and they're trying to take our table. Did you see that? They can't do that!" The lady who was cleaning the table looked at him, looked at them, finished cleaning, and left. They just stood there, filled with uncertainty. Our waitress came back and led us to the table. Then Rob told his story.

He said he'd been in the library with Galen that night. They'd heard the shots, or noises, but had not connected them with anything threatening. Tom McElderry, one of the three kids who'd driven past Ñacuñán Sáez' car, burst into the room saying there'd been an accident. Rose Gowen, the girl at the circulation desk, tried to get help on the library phone. Galen went out to the front door to offer assistance. There were more noises and Galen walked in, holding his chest. He said, "I've been shot. Get help." Rob said, "Are you kidding?" Galen just took his hands away from his chest. They were covered with blood. There was a bloody hole in him.

Then the room exploded with gunfire. Everyone, including Galen, went down. Glass was flying, the gun banging, bullets zinging around. Tom McElderry was shot in the leg. Rose was on the floor with the phone, still trying to call for help. Kids were screaming. Rob ran out the back door of the library, and through the woods to get help at the guard shack.

This sounded like a smart thing to me. It sounded like a survival move, one of those actions that are quicker than thought. You just do it and it's appropriate. As Rob chewed through his lunch and his story I imagined again the scenario in which Wayne Lo has a fully functional weapon and a backpack full of thirty-round ammo clips. He stands at that door and shoots until everyone in the room is hit. Maybe he moves through the library, firing. Getting out the back and going for help seemed like just exactly the thing to have done.

Yet it was Rob's condition, or maybe a condition common to survivors of such catastrophes, that he was burdened with guilt about leaving the library, about not having suffered all of what his comrades suffered, about leaving his friend Galen to die without him. Rob Horowitz, producer and director of the famous holocaust play, was carrying some of the same lousy baggage a concentration camp survivor might have carried. He tried to put the best face on it, presenting the issue of his flight to me in a non-committal way, but the question burned in his eyes. The question was not, "Am I guilty?" The question was, "*Why* am I guilty?" I had no answer for that.

We went back to his apartment and talked a little more. He wanted me to read the screenplay he'd written about the shooting. I flipped through it as we talked. It seemed to be about the trauma. There were visions of blood and flashbacks to that terrible moment in the library.

Our talk in his room yielded a remembered detail or two. He told me that Karen Beaumont, one of the theater people, was convinced that another student named Kevin Wolak had helped Wayne with the gun. Rob also confirmed the Thomases' contention about their son becoming a pariah. After a while the students began to avoid everyone connected with Galen or the shootings. They were a reminder of something bad.

Then we lapsed into desultory chat, which included a brief narration of Rob's recent sexual encounters. This was another of Rob's character traits that would probably have to go in the "obnoxious" category. In fact his screenplay had two explicit sex scenes in it, which I thought a little unusual for the story of a tragic shooting. On the other hand, in the "endearing" column, Rob would catch himself bragging and say, "I can't help it. I'm a *very* sexual person." These opposites were continually at war in the kid. Obnoxiously, he tended to have trouble with women. I don't think he really liked them very much. Yet, endearingly, after Galen died he stayed around the college for an extra semester taking care of Danica, Galen's distraught and nearly destroyed girlfriend. He rented an apartment off campus and let her stay with him. As some of Galen's other friends had confirmed, he wasn't hitting on her. He was genuinely "there" for her. He told me how each of them would wake in the middle of those long nights to discover the other walking around the apartment, unable to sleep, and they'd sit and talk. They got each other through those first few rough months.

Out of the blue a thought occurred to me. I asked Rob if he thought Wayne Lo was a virgin. He pondered for a moment, then answered with the ease of a man on familiar ground, "Almost certainly."

Eventually the time got heavy. I'd planned to take Rob down to Tribeca to have dinner with my son Brooks and Brown and some friends, but I'd allocated too much time for our talk. We'd finished in two hours and still had two hours left. We weren't going to make it. Rob said he'd show up at the Tribeca restaurant later, but that first he wanted to see if he had a date that night. "A girl I met at the William Morris Agency... I really can't stand her. I don't know why I'm going out with her..." Nervously dialing the numbers of her several answering machines, one after the other, "I don't know... I almost love her. But I don't think it's a relationship that's going to last..." I left before we got around to their sex life. Rob promised to meet me in Tribeca. I was certain he wouldn't.

I was right, and I was sorry that he didn't make it. Dinner was wonderful. By then, Brooks was going to college at NYU. I met him and Brown and Brown's friends Susan Dumois and Bobby Ross downtown and we drank and ate and laughed. We then went to the bar where Susan worked and drank more; drank too much, but only a little too much. Then Brooks and Brown and I went back to Brown's and had a nightcap, talking by this time very much like men who had drunk only a little too much.

Later, I wondered that, of all things, *this* should be what I did with my Brooks. On the other hand, there was little help for it. Brown and I were drunks. This had nothing to do with Galen's death. It was, as the insurance people say, "a pre-existing condition." Drinking was a vice I had cultivated throughout my adult life, for the most part with energy and enjoyment. I would like to be clear about it here, because of the warning flags mention of the topic raises for people in this day and age, and because this account aspires to deal with facts. The fact is, I was practiced, modulated, and functional, but I was a drunk nonetheless. Brooks, or Galen before him, would have told you the same thing, and I'd be ashamed of them if they didn't. The other fact is, I'd never had a drink with Galen. So I drank, that first night drinking with Brooks, for both of us.

It was in the course of our dinner that Brown and Bobby Ross and Susan and I were talking about those stupefying staggering states of intoxication that drunks sometimes find themselves in. Brown referred to the discourse that occurs on such occasions as "speaking in tongues." Bobby Ross, a large black man who favored cowboy hats and turquoise rings, said that when he sees someone in that state, he considers that person as being on his "walkabout."

The image and its aboriginal connotation charmed me. I decided at that moment that my finding-out-about Galen exercise was as close to a walkabout as I'd ever do. It would be no drunken wiggle if I could help it, but it was sure to be as far removed from the normal course of my activities as either the aforesaid bender or the aboriginal Australian rite. A Crusade Against Injustice was pompous. A Father's Struggle to Learn the Truth sounded just a little boring. But a Walkabout ... I could do that!

Several mornings later I was on my way to the town of Housatonic in western Massachusetts. I was going to have breakfast with a girl named Margaret Ladner and lunch with a man named Derek Gentile. Even on a walkabout regular meals were important.

There'd been a sprinkling of snow and the Berkshires backcountry looked beautiful. Margaret lived in an apartment in a white house on the edge of a woods, and she looked beautiful too. She was petite, with angular features and deep, luminous eyes. Over the years I had observed that her looks and quiet manner sometimes made her seem more pensive than she actually felt. This morning, however, she was radiant. Rob had told me she had a new boyfriend, a real boyfriend, and maybe that's what having a boyfriend will do for a girl. We drove in to the town of Great Barrington and while we talked, had breakfast at a place called Martin's.

The talk with her was a little different, since she hadn't been present at the shooting. She'd been in a dorm when it happened. Her father came and picked her up next day and she stayed off campus for a few weeks, only returning when normal school activities resumed.

Margaret was an old friend of Galen's from the Unitarian Universalist kids network, which was complex and tightly interwoven. In those teenage years, bonds got forged with startling speed. What always surprised and pleased Annie and me was Galen's ability to maintain these friendships over time. So, in distinction to Lulu, who was from the Boston group of UUs, Margaret was from the Maryland group. The Maryland group also included Jeanna, who was Margaret's and Galen's close friend, and who later became Brooks' girlfriend. The UU group overlapped with friends from Simon's Rock, like Rob and Danica. In fact, Galen had gotten Margaret to apply to Simon's Rock, and she was just finishing her first semester there when he'd been killed. She hadn't really known Danica or Rob until she returned to Simon's Rock after the shooting. Then they'd banded together, a tight little knot of Galen's closest friends.

According to Margaret, the college had done a pretty good job in the months after the shooting, getting the student body in general through this terrible experience. There was counseling, understanding, sympathy and openness to grief and its byproducts. A memorial committee was formed. The memorial bench and pole that I had seen were eventually set in place, some trees were planted, and a plaque was placed in the atrium where Galen had been shot.

From her account, I got a sense of the institution directing warm and sensitive care inward to its own and not much at all to the outside world. I guessed that, almost immediately, a decision had been made not to yield the slightest bit on any matter that the outside world might perceive as an admission of guilt. In retrospect it was probably a stupid policy. But the survival of the institution was at stake, and once they embarked on it, they were stuck with it. Thus Richard Thomas' transcript was withheld pending payment of his back tuition. Thus we heard not a word from the administration after our first conversations with Bernie Rodgers. Thus Simon's Rock College wound up getting sued.

I didn't get any hard information from her, really, just an image of her and Danica and Rob hanging on to each other, trying to deal with something that no one should have to deal with, trying to grow up, trying to get homework done. We talked about how distraught Danica had been, and how Rob had been supportive of her. She too said that the incident had tended, over time, to isolate those most closely associated with it. It was so painful and so awful, many of the students didn't want to dwell on it. I asked her what she thought the effect of the shooting had been on her. She looked at me with those big green eyes of hers, unblinking.

"I used to think everything would work out in the end; that there was nothing that couldn't get fixed up eventually. The night Galen died I called up Jeanna and tried to tell her what had happened. But I couldn't. I kept crying and crying and I couldn't get the words out. Jeanna kept trying to calm me down. She kept saying, 'Everything's all right. It's going to be OK,' and I told her, 'No. It's not going to be OK.' And she said, 'Yes it is.' And then I told her what had happened and she said, 'You were right. It's not going to be OK.'"

Derek Gentile wasn't at the Great Barrington office of the *Berkshire Eagle* when I arrived for our luncheon date. The only people at work were a reporter with her feet on the desk and a receptionist. They were cute and I was feeling cute. I told the reporter to put her feet down and get to work. She told me she was thinking. I said, "O.K. Which one of you is Derek Gentile?"

After that burst of wit, things were friendly at the *Berkshire Eagle*. Derek had forgotten our appointment, which apparently was not unusual. I shouldn't worry, however, since he lived just down the street. The reporter called him. "Yes," she said patiently into the receiver, "Today is Tuesday ... It *is* noon."

Gentile was one of the local reporters who'd covered the shootings. He showed up smelling of toothpaste, a big guy in a sweatshirt with no pretension about him. He wandered around the office looking for a notebook, then we went to lunch. He asked me where I wanted to eat. I told him it was his call. He said he knew this nice little place and of course we wound up back at Martin's. On the way, Gentile said hello to about half a dozen passers-by. At the restaurant he knew the waitress by name, but I one-upped him when she recognized me from breakfast.

I explained my walkabout to him, and as he began to understand what I was up to, he took his notebook out. I stopped. I told him this was not a story right now, it was something else, and that it wouldn't be fair to me or to my family if there were an article in the local paper announcing that I was snooping around.

He nodded, sighed, and started to put the notebook away. I told him to wait a minute, that there might be another interesting angle to this. I had spent a lot of time thinking about the shootings, and had picked up a few loose ends. For example, I told him, I'd heard a rumor during the criminal trial that Wayne Lo had tried to buy a gun the week before December 14, from another gun dealer in the area. When this unnamed gun dealer saw that Wayne Lo was a college student he refused the sale and threw Wayne out. If true, this would place the actions of Dave's Sporting Goods in a rather different light. We knew from the criminal trial that there were state and federal laws against having firearms on a college campus. The first gun dealer, if he existed, would have connected Wayne's Montana driver's license and the student ID and inferred that the weapon was going back to a college campus. It could be argued that Dave, if he were truly a *responsible* dealer, should have made the same inference.

Gentile's eyes were opening. His last piece of French toast was getting cold. I told him more. We knew that Wayne Lo had to hang around the college campus all through the Thanksgiving break. We knew that Thanksgiving was when merchants started heavy advertising. We knew that hunting season was underway. It was reasonable to guess that, especially in this area, sporting goods dealers would start advertising hunting and fishing equipment. During the criminal trial one of the psychiatrists had testified that Wayne had learned about his gun from a newspaper advertisement. Although Dave said he did not advertise the SKS in the local newspapers, perhaps this other gun dealer had. Perhaps this other dealer's identity might be discovered by searching back issues of the *Berkshire Eagle*. The reporter smiled. "That's good." he said, "I like that." I liked it, too. We were beginning to see the possibility of a mutually beneficial relationship.

Then I asked him about the Beavers' Workmen's Compensation hearing. This was the real reason I'd wanted to talk with Gentile, and now that the channels were open between us, he proved to be an enthusiastic informant.

Theresa Beavers had gone from the Robinson's dorm apartment to her post at the guard shack on December 14, and a few minutes later had been the first one shot by Wayne. He had fired through the half-opened door of the shack, then shot again and again, bullets tearing through her, nearly destroying her insides. She'd had the presence of mind to fall against the door to keep him from entering, and to play dead until he moved on, but she had been badly wounded and was still recovering from her injuries. Some of them, she now realized, would be permanent. Theresa's husband, Bruce, had been disabled from a prior injury. That was why she'd taken the Simon's Rock security job in the first place. When she became disabled herself, Bruce was well enough to provide her with the full-time care she needed, but neither of them could work at a paying job. Clearly, Theresa and Bruce Beavers were in a bad way, but, in a manner that reminded me of the policy they'd displayed toward the Thomases and toward our family, the college had failed to offer Theresa any additional help with her medical bills. According to Theresa, Simon's Rock picked up the balance of payments between what Workman's Compensation was providing and the salary she would have received from the college, but that was all. These payments amounted to about $90 a week, and they stopped when the Beavers pressed their claim against the college.

Gradually Bruce and Theresa learned more about what had happened prior to the shootings, and they got angry. Like Howard Thomas they were angry that the college had information about Wayne Lo that it kept to itself before the shootings. By Theresa's own account, no one had told her that Wayne had a gun. If she had known ahead of time that he was armed and planning to shoot people, things might have gone very differently for her when Wayne approached the guard shack.

Under state laws, a worker cannot sue his or her employer for a work-related injury or disability. However, Theresa Beavers could recover triple her medical costs if she could prove extreme negligence on the part of Simon's Rock. There is precise legal terminology for all of this, but essentially a great degree of negligence has to be proved. The Beavers found a lawyer to represent them in a hearing before the Workmen's Compensation Board regarding this negligence matter.

The hearing had been held some months before and had gone badly for the college; so badly, in fact, that the college and their insurance company settled with the Beavers. Bruce and Theresa had come to our house and told us about it just as I was beginning my walkabout. Their story had sounded so incredible I wanted to verify it from another source.

Gentile had been at their Workmen's Compensation hearing, covering it for the *Berkshire Eagle*. He told me that, as the Beavers' lawyer developed the chronology, a key moment had come on Monday night, just before the shootings. Ba Win was at Floyd and Trinka's apartment in the Kendrick House dorm. Trinka and her two small children were there. Two Residence Advisors, Susan Austin and Irvinia Scott, (the woman who later brought the bullets to Bernie Rodgers) were there. There was much running around, everyone trying to get Trinka and the kids and their necessary belongings out of the dorm. Then Floyd came back to the rooms. He had just finished overseeing a dorm meeting in the basement of the building, the meeting at which Wayne had been present.

The Beavers' lawyer led Ba Win through all this testimony, then asked him two questions, to which Ba Win responded with a series of answers. Both Derek Gentile and Theresa Beavers remembered the questions, and they recalled the essence of the answers. They both agreed in their report of Ba Win's final answer, but neither of my informants could recall the exact sequence of the answers.

The first question was why no one went to Wayne's room right at that moment. They knew from Floyd that Wayne was there. They knew Wayne had a package from Classic Arms. They knew from the anonymous phone call that he had a gun. If they weren't going to call the police, why didn't they just get Wayne and stop him before he caused any harm?

Ba Win said he suggested to Floyd that they go to Wayne's room, but that Floyd had refused, saying he'd been there earlier. (This was supported by Ba Win's deposition.)

The lawyer then asked Ba Win, "Why didn't you go to Wayne's room yourself?"

Apparently, Ba Win gave several answers. According to Theresa Beavers, he pointed out that college rules required two staff members to be present at a room search. He said that Wayne was Asian, and that he would never do anything to bring shame to his family. He said that Trinka was hysterical and had to be tended to.

After each of these answers, according to Derek Gentile and Theresa Beavers, the lawyer bore in again, asking, "Why didn't you go after Wayne yourself?" Finally, according to Theresa's report, Ba Win became emotional. His eyes welled up, his face reddened, and he told the lawyer that he knew he would be the first one shot. Gentile's account substantiated Theresa's story. He too reported Ba Win becoming emotional and finally saying, "I knew I would be the first one shot."

This was astounding, and initially it filled me with fury, because on its face it sounded to me like an admission of cowardice. However, there may have been other explanations. In his deposition, Ba Win said that he'd suggested going to Wayne's room with Floyd, but that when Floyd refused, he planned to get Andrew Jillings and go after Wayne. In other words, he had a plan. At this time he was still thinking he had until the next day before the shooting started. He was never asked in the deposition why he didn't go after Wayne alone, but common sense suggests that, if Wayne were armed and unstable, two men might have a chance at subduing him, whereas one man alone would simply be shot. Perhaps that was what Ba Win meant when he said he'd be the first one shot. Perhaps he was expressing the futility of going in there alone, not cowardice in refusing to do so.

We talked about this a bit, in terms of the different ways Bernie and Ba Win had reacted in the aftermath of the shootings. To Gentile, who'd been on the story since its beginning, it seemed as if Bernie had decided immediately that he'd done the best he could. He was so entrenched in this position, it was as if he were in denial. Ba Win, on the other hand, seemed troubled by events. This might be a guilty conscience, or it might be a reaction to the inescapable tragedy in which he found himself; that, by the time it got to where he could to anything, the only thing to do was walk into Wayne's room and get shot. Perhaps he, like Rob Horowitz, was suffering from a kind of survivor guilt. Perhaps he also felt badly that the college's legal difficulties were preventing him from having contact with the victims. The summer after Galen died, Ba Win had sent us a small gift and a terse but moving note of sympathy. Perhaps he would have liked to say more.

We'll never know precisely what he said at that hearing, because immediately after his last answer to the lawyer's insistent question, the college's attorneys requested a recess, during which they settled their case with the Beavers. Because it was settled in this fashion, it was never, in the eyes of the court, an official event. The transcript of the testimony was never written out and preserved as part of an official record. I called and wrote lawyers and judges all the way up the line, but there was nothing that could be done. There was no written record of Ba Win's testimony. All I had was Theresa's version, seconded by the reporter.

I didn't know what to make of it. But whatever Ba Win had said, the college settled that Workman's Compensation case right after he said it.

It was about an hour's drive from Pittsfield back to Northampton, and I had a pleasant trip of it, thinking about everything I'd learned. There was a book auction scheduled that evening at a hotel; a large collection of works printed by the Anthoensen Press was up for sale. These included a number of well-produced books on local and maritime history, and there was money to be made for me. I'd reserved a room in the hotel and planned to attend the auction. During the preview I met a couple of old-time booksellers from Philadelphia. We had a drink and made arrangements to split a few lots and not get in one another's way.

The auction went pretty much as we expected, and we got most of what we wanted. Then we went out to dinner and had a grand time complaining and telling lies. This difficult and sad Galen business was having a wonderful effect on my professional life. Work was a refuge from the pain, and in the years following Galen's death I worked hard. My business prospered. Dealing with my son's murder was so difficult that the challenging intricacies of running my own business seemed easy by comparison. And in the spiritual devastation that followed the catastrophe, the greatest risks became easy. Nothing mattered anymore. Galen was dead. Whether or not I wound up in the poorhouse was of small moment. Therefore I could look at every opportunity not from a standpoint of anxiety but with a cold and calculating eye, and leap from one precipice to the next without a thought. Ten thousand dollars, a hundred thousand dollars? What did it matter? Such a bad thing had happened to me that for the first time in my life I was no longer afraid of bad things happening. Furthermore, what had formerly seemed like hard work was now nothing but a pleasant interlude, a break from the Galen business. I returned to my room that evening satisfied and at peace. For the moment, Life was good.

Life was cold, with another inch of snow, the next morning. I'd thought of possibly going back out west to Pittsfield first thing, talking to the clerk at Dave's Sporting Goods or doing research at the main office of the *Berkshire Eagle*, but I was too full of peace and satisfaction, and bourbon and lamb chops. I lounged around the hotel till mid-morning, then drove out to see Bruce and Theresa Beavers.

They lived in a little log cabin way out in the sticks in western Massachusetts, and I remembered that this choice of a location had something to do with Theresa's post-traumatic stress. She'd been afraid, in more congested areas, of people coming in through windows. Being isolated out in the woods somehow made her feel safer.

Bruce and Theresa were large people; not fat, but big. When they had visited us at our house I'd learned that they were Mormons and now as I thought of them they seemed to me to carry that peculiar aura Mormons sometimes will. It was definitely white-bread but ... how could I describe it? One time my Uncle Frank was telling me about meeting a young Mormon couple. He was a devout Irish Catholic, and was prepared to be revolted by these heathens, but instead, he couldn't help but like them, "because they were so *clean*." The Beavers had that, whatever it was.

Annie and I had met them first at the criminal trial a year after the shootings. Poor Theresa, in a wheelchair at the time, had been terrified that we would think she was responsible for Galen's death. She had seemed very vulnerable and afraid, and she was visibly relieved to discover that we bore her no ill will. We couldn't help but like, and pity, them both; wounded Theresa and big affable Bruce, trying his damnedest to keep it all together.

We didn't really talk with them much at the trial. Looking back on it now, it seemed strange how little we talked to anybody; how little communication there was between the parties involved in the shootings. Certainly the event itself was so monstrous that it was painful to discuss it with anyone except our most intimate family and friends. Then too, there was our civil suit. We felt uncomfortable about that. We were not litigious people. We were the kind of folks who really did think there were too many lawyers. Yet here we were, with a serious beef, and the only means our society provided for us to settle it was through the courts. The courts were a great mystery. Court procedure was all mystery, and the lawyers were like priests and they never talked to us, except on ceremonial occasions. I assumed that I shouldn't talk to anybody either. I felt extremely nervous about exchanging information with people, as if I were somehow going to ruin things for our lawyer, wreck our case because of a simple human need to know. It had taken me three years to get past that nervousness, and even then it was the deeper need that had driven me to it. As I began my walkabout I still thought I was doing something close to wrong talking to people who might be involved in our legal action. I had these funny ideas about spoiling witnesses.

In our limited conversations at the criminal trial I had assumed that Bruce and Theresa Beavers weren't especially smart. When they came to visit us after their Workmen's Compensation hearing, I was disabused of that assumption. They were plenty smart. Furthermore, they didn't waste their time smoking or drinking, their kids were mostly grown, and neither of them could work. There were no distractions in any of those areas. They were totally focused on what had happened to them. What they did with their time was talk and think about the shooting and its aftermath, and who bore responsibility, and how they came to be where they were. Their Workmen's Compensation hearing had been a success, but they weren't finished. Now they were going after Dave's Sporting Goods for selling a firearm that Dave should have known was being taken to a college campus. They were also going after Classic Arms, for shipping ammunition to a college.

Their mastery of the chronology of Wayne Lo's spree was nearly encyclopedic. Because Theresa had worked at the college she had connections and she knew the personalities of all the people involved. Bruce and Theresa knew, chapter and verse, state and federal laws regarding Workmen's Compensation. They could cite, by number, pending legislation that would have bearing on cases like theirs. They knew legal precedents for cases like the Simon's Rock shootings. By the time they left our house after that first visit, I had a very different picture of them. There was a good dose of respect in with the affection and pity.

On my drive through the rolling snow-covered woods along Route 20 I tried to think of specific details to ask them. Dozens of questions had occurred to me since they'd come and told us their story. But my mind kept drifting back to the effect of the shooting. Wayne Lo's crime had changed their lives forever. I wondered if the shooting hadn't in an odd way become their lives. Certainly they now dwelled in the shooting, as surely as they lived in that snug log house half a mile down the road from nowhere, and when they looked out their window all they saw in the yard was the shooting, and as far as they could see or imagine, it was the shooting.

Theresa met me at the door of their house and gave me a hug. I shook hands with Bruce, took off my coat and sat down on the couch. Artificial Christmas tree, bird feeder on the snow-covered deck, wood stove, unlit. It was chilly in there, maybe because the Beavers didn't need much heat. Maybe because they were broke. I congratulated them again on their victory at the Workmen's Compensation hearing. They said the settlement wasn't nearly as much as everyone thought, and that the check hadn't yet arrived. They said they had actually been told it was "in the mail."

We talked about the shooting. As I sat there, asking my questions and answering theirs, my mouth was working, and my brain was processing the conversation, but I was moving away in a strange direction.

I was suffused with affection for these large, earnest people, and I could feel theirs for me. We sat there exchanging difficult, even gruesome information, yet the feeling that informed this exchange was one of cheer and good will. It was intense, a little dotty, like three cheery cheery happy faces pasted over three oceans of misery.

But more. I'll bet that if we had started talking about misery the oceans would not have welled up and drowned us. The misery was not what it was about for us. That was not what was interesting anymore. Those oceans were behind us. We had survived the wreck and were crawling up the beach. We were survivors.

And that was the source of the goofy radiant good will. We had come through something very terrible together. No one else could know what that was like. We were still as messed up in our heads as Theresa's insides were messed up by those bullets, and we'd all sport limps of one kind or another, but by God, we'd gotten through it. The Evil Thing that had gotten Wayne Lo and Galen and Ñacuñán Sáez had *not* gotten us, and there was joy in that. There was a simple magnificent accomplishment about not getting dragged back into that ocean of misery, and as we sat there and yakked, beaming at one another, we celebrated it with conspiratorial glee.

Back home from my visit with Bruce and Theresa, I moped around for a few days, victim of road food and information overload. Babies died on TV, politicians gestured. I slid into depression, then a period of manic effort, trying to catch up on the business that had gone undone since I'd started my walkabout. I researched, priced and wrote up about 300 antiquarian books for my next catalog. I went on long jogs. Not fast, but in great earnest. Slowly, things settled back into that nominal dailiness that is the stuff of life and health. And Annie and I talked, as was our wont, about everything.

Winter was always the worst time for us. Beginning with Galen's birthday on September 27th, through to the anniversary of his murder on December 14, the misery of Christmas and then the recollection of the murder trial in January, it was a deep, long swamp.

One evening during this interlude Annie and I fell to talking about which aspects of the whole mess were still on our minds the most. Celia had finished her dinner and left us for that vastly more interesting family, *The Simpsons*. We were at the kitchen table, as usual, talking about this difficult stuff, laughing and crying. We had both become very adept at crying. Annie could talk right through it. Her eyes would overflow, and the tears would run into the hollows of her cheeks, and she'd keep right on going. It was more of a production for me, but at least I got something out. First I'd lose control of my lips, then my throat would constrict, then I'd snuffle, then cry, then talk. As bad as it felt coming on, it always felt better to have done. At any rate, on this particular evening, Annie confided in me that she was hung up on the "Why," the senselessness of having a beautiful creature like Galen die so prematurely. He had so much to give to the world and was so ready to give it. Why was he not allowed to give what he had? I told her I just believed there was a greater purpose, and that I'd go crazy if I had to wonder about the Why. She asked me what I thought about. I told her I still couldn't let go of Galen's last moments on this earth, of his last day, his last steps, his last words and thoughts and breaths. She told me she'd go crazy if she had to think about that. Then we went upstairs and watched the rest of *The Simpsons*.

But it was his last day that got us back there, finally. Thursday, December 14, 1995, on the third anniversary of Galen's murder, Annie and Celia and I got in the van and drove to Simon's Rock College. There was a supporting structure of reasons, as usual. Margaret Ladner, the girl I'd recently visited, was having her senior art show at the college and it was being hung in the atrium of the library where Galen had been shot. We wanted to see the art show and we thought it would be a good exercise to simply turn up at Simon's Rock College and see what happened.

When we woke that morning, gentle snow had just started falling. The house was quiet and gray, and Annie, Celia and I had a sense of something ceremonial, almost as if we were going to Grandma's for a holiday, but going to a funeral too. Naturally we were all thinking about Galen, and the college, and Brooks, away at school, and our lives when Galen was here, and our lives now. Our heads were very full and we moved in a measured way and spoke softly.

My thoughts ran like this: "It's the morning of the fourteenth. Galen was probably just getting up now. He'd look out the window and see the snow, this snow, just like I'm seeing it ..." All day it went like that, the things he must've seen and touched and smelled, as I saw and touched and smelled them. It was this sensate world he'd departed, that I could almost put him back into with my imagination. Everything I did, I did for him now, too.

As we drove west the soft flakes kept coming down. We talked about other times we'd made this drive. I told Annie and Celia, once again, the story of Galen's Standing Ovation; how, when he and I were unloading stuff at his dorm at the beginning of his last year, someone had called, "Hey Galen!" and then a kid farther up the hill had picked it up, "Hey Galen!" and how then it had simply rolled up the hill from one kid to the next, to the balcony of the Student Union, where a dozen kids were lounging in the autumnal sun, and they'd all gotten up at once and given it a great, goofy, "Hey Galen!"

We talked about the last time we'd taken this drive as a family, that day three years ago when we'd cleaned out Galen's room. It was, we agreed, very different this time. Three years, day by day, was a long while. Some wounds were starting to heal. The last trip had felt horrible. This trip felt right. By the time we got to Margaret's white house in Housatonic there were five or six inches of snow on the ground. It was going to be an interesting day.

Margaret greeted us in the kitchen and Jeanna was there, too. Jeanna was an old member of the Maryland UU gang, and she was the girl Margaret had called after Galen's murder. She'd grown up with Margaret in Maryland and had been a friend of Galen, too. In fact Galen had a crush on her, years before, but she'd jilted him. Then they'd become good buddies. Galen had said to Brooks on occasion, "Brooksie, you ought to get to know Jeanna. I think you and she would get along." When Galen died, the person Brooks asked for was Jeanna. She came to our house and stayed with Brooks through those awful days, and in a sense she never left. We started new lives after Galen died, a new family. Jeanna was part of it.

There had been some trouble between Margaret and her over the past few years. Jeanna, the classic redhead, could be strong-willed and opinionated at times. She was absolutely furious at the college for letting Galen die. She could not understand how Margaret could continue going there. To Margaret, the college was one thing and Galen was another. She grieved for Galen, but her life was still at the college. In the years after Galen's death, Jeanna and Margaret drifted apart. As Margaret expressed it, Jeanna had always been the dominant one and this break gave Margaret a chance to assert herself, to find her own life. It seemed to me she was pretty well along that road already, because the exercise didn't take her long. Jeanna was on her way to see Brooks in New York, and had just stopped at Margaret's last night. She and Margaret had had a great talk, and everything was back to normal now. I knew that a lot of it had to do with the college, and straightening Jeanna's feelings out about that. We weren't the only ones with work to do on this visit.

First, of course, there was lunch. And of course lunch was at Martin's. And of course Gentile the reporter was there, as well as couple of local booksellers of my acquaintance. They offered polite hellos and were kind enough to leave us alone. I made a big deal about being such a well-known guy, and confided to my audience that I was thinking of running for mayor. They tolerated me. I was buying.

Then to the college. Past the empty guard shack, down the road that Wayne Lo paced, pine trees and snow all around. Out of the van and up the sidewalk to the library. Galen would be lounging inside, talking with Rose at the circulation desk. On the walk in front of the building were two candles and a wreath for Galen and Ñacuñán.

Inside, along the walls of the atrium, the space you passed through before you entered the library, were Margaret's photographs and prints. Small images mostly, in small mats, hung up and down, as Annie observed, like musical notes on a staff; people Margaret had seen and lived with on her travels in Africa and Sri Lanka, all people, eyes staring back out at us, people with lives and stories of their own.

At the back of the atrium was the doorway to the library where Galen had lay down and died. Kids went in and out of that door, looking at us, somehow knowing who we were, being quiet. In the center of the atrium was a pool with plants and a little brook running eternally through it. At the front end of this pool was a brass plaque bearing Galen's and Ñacuñán's names, the college's memorial to the two murder victims. The last time I was here, on my way to visit Dave, I hadn't even noticed it.

We sat at the edge of the pool, Annie, Celia, Jeanna, Margaret and I. Time had stopped now. Galen was forever at that desk, deep in chat with Rose. The kindly old janitor came along and told us about Ace, the frog, who'd lived in that pool ever since it had been built four years ago. He capered around a bit trying to find the frog, but Ace was nowhere to be seen. Margaret told us the story of how they'd once gotten a female for Ace, but he'd eaten her.

I looked about me and thought again of Galen's last moments, but here, of all places, I could not concentrate on Galen's death. I walked around the circumference of the atrium, taking in Margaret's work. It was tentative, small, precise. She was still holding herself back, unsure. But the images worked. The stories flowed out of them. Quiet Margaret Ladner had the eyes for other people and their stories.

We sat a while longer, then went out front again. The snow was still coming down in those big fat soft flakes. The pines were bent over with just the perfect burden of white. It was all white and dark green and brown and the flakes diffused the light, brought the sky right down among us. Down the walk, across the road to the brook, across the bridge to the field with that funny looking pole with "Peace" written on it, and the wooden bench. Annie and Celia and Jeanna and Margaret waded over the snowbank and walked the hundred yards to the memorial. I meandered up the path a bit. There was Kendrick dorm on my left, the Student Union just up the hill. On the other side of Kendrick was where I used to back the van up and load and unload Galen and his stuff, where he'd gotten his Standing Ovation, where we'd cleaned out his room for the last time.

It was beautiful here, peaceful. Students passed by. Some said hello. I felt as if I recognized them all and they all knew me. This was the place Galen had loved, and I could feel what he loved about it. I knew that this first part of my walkabout was done.

There had been a shooting. There was a shooter and he was in jail. Everyone else was a victim: Bruce and Theresa, Annie and me and Celia and Brooks, and Margaret with her lost innocence and Rob with his bloody freakouts, and all Galen's friends so hurt, and Ba Win with his guilt and Bernie and the whole institution with their denial, and Dave with a lawsuit slapped on him, and Mr. and Mrs. Lo, whose son turned out to be a monster . . .

I walked up the path to the end of Kendrick. There was a big tree with a rope swing on it. I could feel Galen around me. I felt so strongly that if I just walked around the corner of the dorm, where the snowy path continued up the hill, I'd see him walking toward me; that if I just walked a little more I'd find him.

I stood still for a minute and then I turned back. I'd been down that road before and I knew where it led.

❧11
PICTURES FROM AN INSTITUTION

I kept going back and forth about Andrew Jillings. I'd liked him when I met him at the criminal trial, but he'd seemed more hesitant and unsure in his deposition. Along with Ba Win and Bernie, he was one of the few staff people involved in the shootings who still worked for the college. It would have been very disappointing to discover that he was protecting them in any way.

After the first part of my walkabout was done, I decided he should be the next person to visit. I wanted to sound him out about his possible change of heart, but also I was curious about how, after three years, the faculty people were processing the shootings; about how Ba Win was faring, and if Bernie Rodgers gave any sign that he bore responsibility for what happened to my son. I needed to talk with someone connected to these people, and Jillings seemed like the obvious choice.

After a few tries I managed to contact him at Simon's Rock College, and in the most general terms let him know what I was doing. I told him my visit would be non-threatening to him and the college, and that the questions I had were to satisfy my own curiosity, and were not related in any way to our lawsuit. He agreed to see me. In fact, he said he was looking forward to it. He seemed the same good-natured, open person I'd met at the criminal trial.

So it came to pass that I found myself having breakfast at Martin's in Great Barrington again. This time I didn't see anyone I knew. I debated the Egg McMartin, but I finally settled on the salsa omelet with cheese. I watched the morning frost melt off the big front window and listened to the small town small talk around me. Then I called Andrew from a pay phone to let him know I had arrived, drove out to the college and parked behind Kendrick. Jillings was waiting outside on the walk.

As I climbed out of the van I could feel it was different here yet again. Maybe the change was a result of something I'd resolved on my last visit, or maybe it was just familiarity with the scenery. A lot of the emotional charge was off the place. It felt almost neutral being here. The students were still on winter break and the campus was deserted. Everything was still covered with snow but now the sky was open and bright blue. The landscape rolled up away from me, the Student Union at the top of the hill, and the three dorms around me, Kendrick, Crosby and Dolliver. They were all modern-looking tan brick structures; they'd probably all been built in the 1960s or 1970s, and they weren't so big that they disrupted the setting. I guessed they'd house fifty to seventy-five students each.

Of the three, Kendrick was built lowest to the ground. It had been constructed against the side of the hill, so that its main entrance, the one Jillings and I took, was over a walkway. Inside we were at the top of a hollow cube two stories high. Around the perimeter of this cube, upstairs and down, were living quarters. In the center was an open lounge area with couches and plants. On the top floor was a balcony that looked down onto the lounge area. The layout reminded me of the cellblock in a James Cagney movie. A central stairway led down to the lower level, and just at the bottom of the stairs to the left was Andrew's apartment. He was still a Residence Director, whose job it was to care for all the kids in this dorm, and he shared his suite with a fellow RD. As we were walking into the room and he was apologizing perfunctorily for the mess, I asked him where Floyd and Trinka had lived in 1992. "Right here." he replied, "This was their apartment."

Slam. The door shut and I was right back into it. This was where Ba Win and the others had run around helping Trinka and her kids evacuate on the night of the shootings. This was where they'd done whatever they'd done instead of apprehending Wayne Lo. I climbed into my tough-guy identity with no more thought than getting dressed for work. Just the facts. Right, Clint?

Jillings was most forthcoming with information. I remembered what I'd liked about him. He stood about five feet, ten inches, square build, ruddy features, sandy hair, British accent. He projected the aura of a Regular Guy. Not a remarkable guy, not a genius; simply a man who could stand on his own two feet and look you in the eye—a man you could count on. As we made ourselves comfortable in the squat institutional living room of his apartment I was at ease with him and receptive of what he had to say.

He told me that people actually made their livings being Residence Directors. It was a profession, though it was not his profession. He was probably just thirty years old, maybe late twenties. He hadn't decided what his profession would be, but he was not going to be an RD for the rest of his life, especially not here. Simon's Rock was a dead end job. There was nowhere to go after being RD except Dean of Students and that, he said with evident distaste, was not a job he would take "for any money." At the same time, he cared about the college. It was a safe haven for him, he said, a good stopping place and a comfortable community.

He was dismissive of the so-called professionals in the field, of their inadequate training and "people-factory" approach. He had majored in physical education as an undergraduate and done some grad work at a large mid-western university in the US. There they actually offered a course of study in being a Residence Director. I asked him if he thought that type of professional training might have been useful in the case of someone like Wayne Lo. No, he said, it wasn't the right kind of training. It was all logistics, management of the basic needs of large numbers. In a typical university setting, a career RD could be responsible for three hundred students. "As if one RD were responsible for the entire student body at Simon's Rock. Now what kind of 'care' could a person possibly provide in those circumstances?" He told me he and the other RD were responsible for fifty-five students in Kendrick, and that it "was a full time job, and then some."

He was serious about his work. We talked about the kids a bit; about how when Richard Thomas had begun his final year's collapse, Jillings had taken him under his wing. It had finally gotten to where Jillings would have to bathe him. Ricky had gotten so dysfunctional he wouldn't clean himself. After a while he'd start to smell and Andrew would say, "OK, Ricky, time for a shower..." Josh Faber, the other boy who'd been shot, was also in his dorm. Jillings liked Josh. He was resilient and had recovered well. Of Tom McElderry, the kid who'd been shot in the library, there had been no sign. He'd graduated and left it all behind him.

I asked him what he'd thought of Wayne before the shootings. He told me that Wayne and Kevin Wolak and Eddie Caruso had been a gang of three. There had been no one else, really, except maybe Jeremy Roberts and one or two others on the periphery, but these boys had other interests, could detach themselves. Caruso, Wolak and Lo were the angry ones. They'd sit at a table in the corner in the dining room and glower at everyone. "It was scary." Jillings said. The intimation was not that he was personally frightened, but that they were trying to be intimidating to other students, and succeeding in part. When Caruso had gotten thrown out of school for his threatening behavior toward a female student, Lo and Wolak had a martyr figure, an excuse for their anger. Ultimately, the whole posse boiled down to Wayne Lo and Kevin Wolak. I asked Jillings about the supposition put forth by Karen Beaumont and Rob Horowitz, that Wolak had helped Wayne Lo order and modify the weapon. Jillings had heard nothing about it, but admitted he was curious as to where Wayne had gotten the know-how. He said he was also curious about where Wayne had hidden the gun after he'd brought it on campus.

We talked about the criminal trial; how, much to both our surprises, we'd gotten to respect and like the cops involved in the case. We even talked about Galen a bit. Andrew said he'd gone rock climbing with Galen that last fall, and that it had been an enjoyable afternoon. I could feel his reluctance to go any farther. Galen was the part of all this that still hurt. I could understand. It was a lot easier trying to reconstruct a crime than it was trying to consider the fact that innocent children die terrible deaths before our eyes.

So our talk just wandered along, my agenda be damned. Everything, after all, was important. Somehow we got to the faculty. I asked about Susan Austin, the other Residence Director who had been at the morning meeting and in the dorm room during the Robinson's evacuation. According to the information our lawyer had gathered, she was the only other person (besides Irvinia Scott, the RD who had taken the bullets to Bernie) who'd had serious problems with the Classic Arms package. Yet, unlike Irvinia, she still worked for the college. Jillings explained that she had been undergoing cancer treatments at the time and had needed the security and comfort that the college had provided. In a way, he said, she couldn't leave.

That reinforced my picture of the college being warm and fuzzy inside and a stone wall outside. Jillings talked about how it had felt like "Us and Them" in the weeks just after the shootings; media people all waiting outside the walls like vultures, and the unforgiving outside world they represented. He spoke of the first time he had to go into town after the shootings, to the pharmacy just down the hill to pick up a prescription for a student, and how strange it had felt in public; how, when he'd had to give the information for the prescription and gave the address as Simon's Rock, it felt as if everyone in the place shut up for a moment.

Had there been a stone-wall policy? According to Jillings, there had been a policy decreed "almost immediately" which curtailed certain responses, or required them to act in ways they might not have wanted to act. "I've got to watch it here." he grinned, "Or I'll get myself in trouble." But there were people, he continued, who'd otherwise be acting differently, especially with regard to the Gibsons. I got the distinct impression he was referring to Ba Win.

He said that, in most respects, there'd been a curious lack of information from the highest levels of the administration. For days, he told me, Theresa Beavers was in hospital and people thought that they weren't supposed to visit her. It was upsetting to finally learn that Theresa had been eager to see people, that she needed reassurance that no one thought Wayne Lo's rampage had been her fault.

We spoke of Ba Win and his apparent distress, which Jillings confirmed. We spoke of Bernie Rodgers. Andrew Jillings admitted that Bernie was "harder to read." He'd seen him cry once, but in general Bernie's feelings were not displayed to other members of the administration. "We were not the people he let down his hair for," as Jillings put it. If Bernie did have feelings of responsibility or even remorse, they were shared with people higher up the ladder, with the people at Bard, the parent institution, with Leon Botstein, president of Bard.

That was the only time Andrew got a tad defensive. According to the deposition our lawyer had taken, Andrew had met with Dean Rodgers on the afternoon of the shootings. While we were on the subject of Bernie, I asked him what that afternoon meeting had been about. Jillings said that he'd told Bernie what Trinka had told him about the contents of the Classic Arms package, but that he couldn't remember more than that. Then he told me that it was very difficult to remember a specific conversation from any time in the past, and that he thought it was unreasonable for people to expect him to remember things that had been said in passing three years before. The force and specificity of that declaration surprised me. Perhaps he'd already been challenged about his recollection of these events. Perhaps he felt a little sensitive about it. Perhaps, speaking to me, a man for whom he had some good feeling and sympathy, he wanted it understood that he was not lying. I did understand that, and I felt as if I was beginning to understand Andrew Jillings.

I asked him why everybody was looking for him on December 14. He smiled in a self-deprecating sort of way and told me that because he'd had some experience in the British marines everybody on the campus took him to be the local weapons expert. That was why someone, he couldn't remember who, had stopped him on the way into the Monday morning meeting and showed him the package from Classic Arms. That was why Trinka had called him to report what she'd seen in Wayne's room after he'd taken the package back to his dorm.

Was that why Ba Win had left messages for him on Monday night before the shooting started? Jillings replied that Ba Win had needed someone he could trust in that situation. He said that he and Ba Win had known one another for ten years, that they'd worked together in other circumstances, a summer camp in the area, that they were close personal friends, that Ba Win trusted him, that, "he knew my mind."

"So," I said, "Ba Win was right here in this room with Trinka and her kids, and they're all packing up, and Floyd comes back from the dorm meeting and Ba Win says let's go to Wayne's room and Floyd won't do it."

Jillings nodded and I went on to the next part. "And he didn't want to go himself because, as we learned from the Workmen's Compensation hearing, he thought he would be shot."

Jillings replied, "Ba Win had a terrible decision to make. Now he has to live with the fact that if he had decided on one course of action, we might well be dead."

It was a startling statement, and it seemed enigmatic until I realized that Jillings wasn't answering my leading question about Ba Win's motivation. He was referring to Ba Win's dilemma ... that whatever he did that night, someone would die.

"So Ba Win knew Floyd couldn't help with the problem. He needed you, his old friend, a man he could rely on. That was why he left the message for you to call him. He probably left it all over campus."

"Exactly." said Jillings, "Ba Win was going to wait for me, and then we were going to go to Wayne's room together. That was his plan."

Bright snowy sunlight poured in through the sliding glass door at the end of Jillings' living room. Clint, Lee and I noted these things, our faces impassive. We were looking through the sun to a night three years ago, not fifty yards from this place, where Wayne Lo sat hunched over his gun, getting himself ready to kill. Around him, the air was screaming.

I suggested to Andrew that we walk for a bit, and go over these events as they happened in the places they actually occurred. So we got up, put on our coats, and walked through the evening of December 14, 1992.

We left Trinka and Floyd's apartment, went diagonally across the central open area, and down a flight of stairs to a place aptly named "The Pit." This was the basement, more or less, of the building. It served as a recreation room, meeting space and general purpose common area for the dorm. The walls were unfinished concrete. There was leftover junk from various parties and events piled around the room. A little water had leaked onto the floor from the melting snow.

As I had learned at the criminal trial, this was where they'd had that dorm meeting at nine o'clock Monday night. Wayne Lo had already hidden the ammo, purchased the gun, come back to college, hidden the gun, taken a test, and eaten dinner. Now he was one of the students attending the dorm meeting. Floyd Robinson, fulfilling part of his obligation as RD for the dorm, had conducted the meeting and when it was over he and Wayne had argued. One of the purposes of these meetings,

Jillings told me, was to consider matters of dorm discipline, any infraction less serious than sex, alcohol, or drug violations. At this particular dorm meeting a punishment had been meted out for some abuse of the room policy. Wayne was arguing with Floyd that the penalty was less severe than the one he'd been given for returning to his room too soon over Thanksgiving vacation.

What the outcome of this was, or what Floyd said, we don't know exactly. But Jillings and I talked about it as we walked back up the concrete stairs to the first floor, much as Wayne and Floyd might have done on that Monday night.

We got to the top of the stairwell, turned away from the outside wall, and were looking directly at the door of Floyd and Trinka's apartment, just a few feet to our right. If people had been packing up and moving around in there; if Ba Win and Trinka and her two babies, and Susan Austin and Irvinia Scott were throwing things in duffel bags and taking them out to Ba Win's car, there was no way Wayne wouldn't have noticed. There was no way he couldn't have seen, or at least heard the commotion. He had to know that his plan, whatever it was, had been uncovered. It seemed very possible that Ba Win's effort to evacuate Trinka and Floyd had also alerted Wayne Lo.

At this point, according to Floyd Robinson's deposition, he and his wife and their children and Ba Win got into Ba Win's car and drove to his house. No provisions were made for another Residence Director to stay and monitor the scene. Floyd spoke of the confusion surrounding the event. Trinka, in her deposition, stated that there was no policy that an RD had to be present in their dormitory at all times. Still, it appears that they simply cleared out, leaving Wayne alone.

We walked to Wayne's room. It was on the same floor as Floyd and Trinka's apartment, and it was tiny; just a bed, a closet, a desk and a dresser. There was a window at the foot of the bed that looked across the yard right at the sliding glass door in the living room of Trinka's apartment. If Wayne had hidden the gun in his room, he could've started shooting right there. Either he had something else in mind, or the gun was somewhere else, or both.

Andrew showed me how Trinka had looked in Wayne's room that Monday morning to examine the "contents" of the Classic Arms package, spread out on the bed. From the open doorway, she could have seen all of the room, except for the closet, which was right behind the open entry door.

This was an interesting part of the sequence. Wayne had cited that section in the college handbook about needing two faculty to conduct a room search, and Trinka had gone off to call Bernie. While she was gone, I guessed, Wayne had hidden the bullets in his closet, or in his dresser, or under his bed. In the course of their telephone call, Bernie had given Trinka specific instructions to search the package and not the room, so she would have just come in, probably leaving the door open, and looked at what was on the bed. The open entry door prevented her from seeing into the closet, and without getting on her hands and knees, she wasn't going to be able to see under Wayne's bed. Given her orders and the layout of the room, there was no way she was going to see anything in Wayne's room except what Wayne wanted her to see. It was partly on the basis of this flawed information that the rest of the administration's decisions were made.

We walked outside, and surveyed the route Wayne had taken on the night of the shootings. We talked about Jillings' route that same evening; how when he'd returned to campus and gotten Ba Win's urgent message, he had jogged across the long field to Ba Win's house, hearing the gunshots that had been the wounding of Theresa and the murder of Ñacuñán. No sooner had Andrew set foot in Ba Win's doorway than the third group of shots, Galen, rang out. Ba Win said simply, "Go." and Andrew took off at a dead run for the campus, using the road this time. Andrew said he'd learned later that what Ba Win had meant was, "Go get in my car and we'll drive to the campus." but the distance was slight and Andrew knew there was no time to be lost. His route brought him first to the guard shack. He saw the car stalled a few yards away, and ran to it, where he discovered Ñacuñán. He felt for a pulse, (that was the image he could not shake, the one he woke up with on bad nights, the head-shot bloody corpse of Ñacuñán Sáez) then went back to the guard shack where he discovered and helped Theresa. That was where he was when Rob Horowitz ran up, fresh from the shooting at the library.

We rehearsed, one more time, the incredible story of Simon Bromberg, a student who had returned early from the Christmas concert that had been held on campus that evening. This story had been told first at the criminal trial and had remained, for all of us, a strange anomaly.

Simon, standing at the bottom entry to the deserted Student Union had heard the noises of Wayne's gunshots. He saw Wayne with a gun, some distance away, and went inside and watched through the big glass window there as Wayne walked up the path, still holding the gun. He did not leave. Wayne entered the student union and said to Simon, "Don't move or I'll fucking kill you." Wayne sat on the couch, took off his backpack and withdrew two full clips of ammunition. Bromberg asked, "What are you doing?" Wayne Lo replied, "I'm killing people. I'm fucking shooting people." Lo then told Bromberg to call the cops. Simon dialed 911 and got a busy signal. He told Wayne, "It's busy," and asked if he could leave. Wayne said yes. Simon got to the exit and remembered that he'd left his jacket and chorus music back on the chair in the room with Wayne, so he *went back into that room*, back into the room with the killer, picked up jacket and music, and left Wayne to call the police himself.

It was a koan I'd never get to the heart of. It went like this: Simon Bromberg. Galen Gibson. I looked at Jillings and he looked at me. I could see he was aware of the sequence of my thoughts. This kind of attention must have been one of the things Ba Win valued in him. We walked back to my van without speaking.

I liked Andrew Jillings. I liked the way he'd behaved that night, and I liked the way he'd helped me today. I had no doubt that if he had gotten there in time, he and Ba Win would have gone after Wayne. I told him he should come to visit me and my family some time. He said he'd like that. He said he'd never seen Galen's grave. I said then by all means he must come, it was a remarkable grave. He said he would. I went to shake his hand, but he hugged me, surprising me, for a moment, out of my Clint and Lee persona.

I poked around the western end of Massachusetts and then down the New York Thruway, ostensibly on other business, but mostly musing on Andrew Jillings. Jillings was a company man, probably descended from a long British line of Jillings company men. Adequately bright, probably loyal, possessed of physical courage and little imagination or intuition. Nothing remarkable about him except that he was a good solid guy who valued being active and who placed utmost importance on being of use to the people around him. The world could do worse than be filled with more guys like him. If he'd been on campus when Ba Win had needed him, things might have been very different for all of us. But it was simply not in his makeup to question the sequence of events or the decisions that had been made on the night of December 14. People like Jillings didn't ask those kinds of questions. It was not a moral failing. It was simply who he was.

I had one other stop that day, at the Hudson Mall in Kingston, New York, about halfway between Albany and Manhattan. I arrived an hour early and, never one to waste a minute, did some shopping. At J.C. Penney's I got myself a new pair of blue jeans, the so-called "loose fit" fat old man kind, and a leather belt. From a handcart out front of B. Dalton's Bookstore I picked up an illustrated History of Baseball calendar (based on the award-winning PBS television series) for my office, and an Angels calendar (based on the great art of the western world) for Annie to hang in the kitchen, both at half-price. In B. Dalton's I bought the latest Robert Parker *Spencer* novel and then I walked over to the food court. I found a seat in front of Papa Gino's and read the first few chapters. It was a comfortable interlude. I'd never been to the Hudson Mall, but I felt right at home. It was just like the mall down the road from my house.

At 4:55 I walked through the main arcade to Filenes and sat on a bench in front of the entrance. At a little after 5:00 Irvinia Scott came up to me and asked if I were Mr. Gibson. I was Greg, I told her. We shook hands. I asked if she'd eaten. She said she'd had a late lunch. She asked where I'd like to talk. "How about my office?" I said, motioning toward the bench.

Because of the strident, forceful way she'd spoken against the college in her deposition, I'd been expecting a big strong black woman. Irvinia was slender and fine-boned, pretty, quite dark and real put-together, not a stitch out of place. In a sea of denials, equivocations and lapses of memory, her deposition had been a bright spot for our lawyer. She'd believed right from the start that the college people were making bad decisions, and had not hesitated to say so.

Irvinia had come to work at Simon's Rock in the fall of 1992. She'd completed her undergraduate studies in the Boston area, and then had gotten her Master's at Springfield College, a few hours back east on the Massachusetts Pike. She'd been an RD at Springfield, and had some security training and employment both as an undergraduate and graduate student. She came to Simon's Rock as an RD, and she came expecting something different than she found, at least as far as security was concerned.

To her surprise, security on the Simon's Rock campus, the kind of structured security she was used to, was almost non-existent. She sought out the security director, a man named Ron Ringo, and found that he was in agreement with her. In fact, he was having a hard time with his job because of the continual frustration he was experiencing. Every time he tried to put a new security measure in place he would be rebuffed by the college administration. Irvinia commiserated with Ringo, but little else happened until the Eddie Caruso incident.

Caruso was the kid in the Wayne Lo crowd who had been accused of making threatening gestures toward a female student. Irvinia took her concerns about Caruso to Bernie Rodgers and was more or less patted on the knee and told that everything would be all right. When she continued to express her concerns about security Bernie responded by offering her the position of liaison between the administration and the troublesome Ron Ringo. Irvinia had her doubts, since she was essentially in agreement with Ringo, but she did accept the position.

She had attended that 9:00 A.M. meeting on December 14, at which the package from Classic Arms was examined and discussed. She'd been adamantly against letting Wayne Lo take it back to his dorm. She remembered pointing out that it was against the law to have firearms on a college campus and that this package was from a firearms company and that it had been mailed to a college campus. She'd been overruled by Bernie Rodgers, and events had taken their course.

It was in her capacity as RD of the Crosby dorm that she had given Wayne the keys to the weight room after dinner on December 14, 1992. A month after the shootings, she was the person to whom the cleaning woman had given the live ammunition that had been found there. Knowing Wayne Lo had used the weight room a few hours before the shootings, she took the bullets to Dean Rodgers and asked what she should do with them. At our interview on the bench in front of Filene's, Irvinia repeated what she had stated in her deposition. She said that Bernie Rodgers told her to throw the bullets away.

She took the bullets to the police, and assumed that Bernie Rodgers would fire her for betraying him. But, according to Irvinia, Rodgers simply changed his story. He now claimed that he had told Irvinia to take the bullets to the police in the first place. On several occasions he made this assertion in her presence. (He stated in his deposition that he had even made follow-up efforts, to insure that the police had received the bullets.) She became angry, almost obsessively so, about what she considered to be Bernie Rodgers' lie. It also angered her that, despite the cogent and forceful points she'd made at the morning meeting, Wayne Lo had taken possession of that package. Unlike Andrew Jillings, she had a definite moral vision of these events.

Things went from bad to worse after the shootings. Ringo left his job in absolute frustration. Irvinia, who by this time was completely out of sympathy with Bernie, still had to work with him every day. She became increasingly isolated. The quality of her work was called into question. She was accused of being prickly and short tempered, of being aloof, of not fraternizing with her fellow RDs. ("All they wanted to do was drink beer and party." Irvinia told me, "I didn't have a problem with that, it just wasn't where I was at.") In addition, she was something of an instigator. She took it upon herself to educate minority students regarding minority issues, "How come there aren't more people like me here? I'm paying twenty thousand dollars to go to a place that doesn't observe Kwanzaa?" While this rather confrontational approach might not have been out of place at one of the urban campuses where Irvinia had gotten her schooling, it was, by her report, somewhat at odds with the more touchy-feely multiculturalism at Simon's Rock.

Finally, at the end of the 1994–1995 school year, Irvinia received a letter telling her there were certain problems with the way she was doing her job. The administration would be happy to work with her in solving these problems, and if she could make a commitment to solving them she would be welcome back.

She decided that she was not interested in solving those problems. That summer she went out and got another job. In fact, she got two jobs. She was working days at an automobile agency and nights at Filenes.

That was why we were meeting on this bench. She had an hour break between her day job and the night job.

None of the information about the college was new to me. It had all been covered in more or less detail, in her deposition and at the criminal trial. What did surprise me was her anger. It was fierce, and it was a feminine, intuitive anger that went right to the heart of the matter. There were no mitigating circumstances. In her opinion, Bernie Rodgers had lied. In her opinion, the administration had made mistakes in letting Wayne Lo get that ammunition, yet they were saying they'd done the best they could. "I don't see how those people can live with themselves," she told me, and her eyes flashed.

She didn't say so, but I guessed that there were other components to her anger. Some of it must have been frustration, or anger at herself. In a way she, more than anyone else, had seen trouble coming. She offered advice about the package from Classic Arms and was ignored. Had she done enough? I wasn't asking, but certainly the question must have occurred to her. Just as Jillings had volunteered his statement about the vagaries of memory, she told me explicitly, "I worked for those people. When they made a decision, the matter was settled. Bernie said the package was being taken care of and I assumed it was."

I wondered too if she wasn't angry about what this experience had stolen from her. She told me that, when she took the Simon's Rock job, she had hoped to pursue a career in the academic field, perhaps in Student Life; maybe she'd be a Dean one day or a Provost. The things she saw during her tenure at Simon's Rock and the treatment she received there changed those plans. If that behavior and those petty politics were the reality of small-college life, she wanted no part of it. So now here she was, working two dumb jobs eleven or twelve hours a day while she tried to figure out what to do next.

I liked her. I liked her energy and her drive. I had no doubt she could be difficult to work with. She was wrapped pretty tight, she liked control and she was stubborn. She could look bad in the wrong circumstances, and the shady groves of academe were definitely the wrong circumstances for her. But she was headed for bigger things than Filenes, and in time she'd mature a little and find the right situation for her talents. I told her that, and I told her it was time for her to move on, to get clear of her anger and to forget Bernie and the rest of them. Leave all that stuff to me, I told her. It was my job now.

That made her smile. Then it was time for her to get to work. We stood, I went to shake her hand and she said, "I'd like to give you a hug." I told her that sounded good to me, and that I thought she was quite something.

A hug from Jillings and a hug from Irvinia. I was on a roll.

I *was* on a roll. I felt it the moment she left. It was like seeing something pop from black and white into color, or from 2-D into full depth. I'd been working and working on the intricacies of the sequence of events of December 14; who was where, and who did what when, but the story still seemed disjointed, unconnected with itself. Now I thought I had the missing element.

Andrew and Irvinia could not have been less alike. Typically, Andrew was noncommittal, had little to say about Irvinia. Irvinia made it very clear that she had not liked Andrew from the first moment they'd met. To him, she had probably seemed like a troublesome individual, always butting heads, hard to get along with. To her, he was everything that was bad about a company man. He would go with the company and therefore could not be trusted as an individual. She was all moral and he was all social. Cat and dog, black and white.

What they, in their oppositeness, had given me was parallax, a measure. What I could see now was not so much the events of December 14 as the setting in which they had taken place; the ethos which was as much a cause as a context.

Simon's Rock was a small, comfortable institution, and it functioned with a culture particular to comfortable institutions. Despite its liberal tone, it was a good old boy atmosphere. It was fraternal, traditional. It was collegial. There were strictly observed loyalties. There was a strictly observed sense of the way things were done. And there was an insularity.

In a sense it was always Us and Them. The people at Simon's Rock were engaged in a very special mission and they, better than anyone else, knew best how to execute it. Most of this was typical, and most of it was reasonable. The politics of loyalty, and a common attention to the nurturing institution were sound principles for the efficient operation of a place like Simon's Rock. It had been going on since cave-times. A bunch of people would get together under the protective cover of a larger entity and do the bidding of that entity while the larger entity took care of them. They didn't question things and they didn't make waves.

I thought back to my navy days and it occurred to me that I had spent nearly four years of my own life in such an institutional setting, and that I had considerable familiarity with how the game was played. In both cases the structure was very good at keeping people in line and at handling situations for which it was designed. The navy was a hell of an outfit. Simon's Rock was an extraordinary place. The only dangers were complacency and unexpected outside occurrences. Complacency was hard to detect because the only people who might have detected it were the complacent ones. It was usually thrown into relief by an unexpected outside occurrence. In our 1960s military parlance, this was referred to as "the shit hitting the fan."

As I recalled the scenario, when the shit hit the fan you covered the institution first, then you covered your buddies and you covered yourself. When the institution and you and your buddies were secured, you tried to reconstruct the mission. I'm not talking about the Mekong Delta here; I'm talking about the daily politics of shipboard life, the institutional culture that extended all the way up to the Pentagon. So, things ran smoothly until that jetty suddenly appeared under the stern of our ship on the Columbia River. Then the good old boys had to do some scrambling.

Bernie Rodgers, it seemed to me, had followed this model in many respects on December 14. He was complacent and uncomprehending in the face of an outside threat (crazy Wayne Lo). In retrospect, it may seem hopelessly naive on his part to have thought that he could get to the bottom of Wayne's plans simply by asking him. But Bernie was repeating a procedure that had worked for him innumerable times. As I saw it now, he was too lulled by his sense of the norm, and by the liberal ideals his institution promulgated, to comprehend the threat Wayne actually posed. If he could not comprehend this, he could not use his powers of reason and his administrative abilities to their fullest. That was why he didn't nail down responsibility for checking on the contents of the ammunition package. That was why he accepted Wayne's word at their private meeting and did not take even the simplest steps (such as calling Wayne's parents) to check the story.

When the shit hit the fan he covered the institution by not summoning police in response to a possible crank call, and by not risking panic with a campus-wide warning. He covered his buddies by having Ba Win attend to the distraught Trinka and her children. But he never got to reconstruct the mission on that particular night.

Of course, in the navy our skipper lost his job when the ship hit that jetty. Even though it was really the helmsman's failure to understand or execute an order, it was the Captain's ship and he took the responsibility. Captain Bernie Rodgers denied responsibility for what had occurred on his watch. That disgusted me. That was what I had been so furious about for the past three years. Now I felt as if I finally understood the situation.

The feeling of clarity stayed with me the rest of that night on the road, all the way back to the Super Ramada City in Springfield, deserted now in the depths of winter, no dogs. It was late by the time I got there and most of the restaurants in the malls were closed. Again I negotiated Route 5 on foot, this time to Debbie's House of Wong where I treated myself to a sumptuous feast of yuk duck gai luk and several Tsingtaos. Then I crawled back to the motel to sleep the sleep of the just.

I knew I'd have to check all this out with Ron Ringo, but I felt sure I had it right. It was the negative aspects of the institutional culture that had let this Wayne Lo mess get away into tragedy. Bernie Rodgers had acted like an institutional soldier instead of an intelligent human being.

Just as I was dropping off I remembered Irvinia saying, "I'm afraid for those kids."

"You mean before the shootings?" I had asked.

"No. Now!"

That Irvinia ...

❧12
IN WHICH I STAND CORRECTED

He was all wavy, looked kind of soft, gestured a lot. There was a minister at the door trying to get out, but Bard College President Leon Botstein was having a hard time breaking off. He kept remembering one last thing. Then the minister's response would make him remember one more last thing. I stood just inside the entry with my hands clasped in front of me, a smile on my face.

The house was an ample Tudor-style stucco at the very top of Faculty Circle, just inside the entrance to Bard college. It was dark by the time I arrived, so I didn't get to see the campus. Botstein was a busy man. He'd squeezed me in after a faculty meeting and before whatever evening plans he'd made. I guessed he thought this meeting was important, or at least that it had better be dealt with sooner than later.

It had taken me months to get to this point. Things had slowed down after my visits with Jillings and Irvinia. The weather got worse and the world turned white and cold and slippery. Galen was dead. Each morning I'd wake and there would be that fact, as vast and unembraceable as the whiteness outside.

I went down to the video store and put in a special order for that old movie *Point Blank*. After a week or so it arrived and I watched it a couple of times with Brooks, who was home from college on his winter break. The plot was a bit different than I'd remembered it, but what struck us both on this viewing, thirty years after my first exposure, was how damaged the Lee Marvin character was. I remembered him being tough and relentless. In fact, he was relentless like a zombie. As long as he was going after the bad guys he was very efficient. But as soon as he got in a situation where he had to relate to a human being on some level other than violence or revenge, he practically drooled on his shoes. As Brooks observed, it wasn't as if he didn't have a reason. He'd been betrayed by his wife and shot by his best friend. Still, he opined, I'd chosen a hell of a dysfunctional role model. I shoveled snow and tried to keep the drool off my shoes. I worked on my case notes and mulled over everything I'd learned.

Toward the end of winter, when the snow was reduced to stubborn dirty piles, I bestirred myself and met with Ron Ringo and Maggie CapoNegro. Ron had been the head of Security at Simon's Rock and Maggie was the guard who'd been on duty with Theresa Beavers on the night of the shootings. Neither worked at the college any longer. Ringo had quit right after the shootings and gone back into the Marine Corps. Maggie had been fired from her Security job.

There was one other piece to the series of events that had made this tragedy possible and I was hoping Ron and Maggie could help me nail it down once and for all. Imagine a typical college campus. Imagine that some trouble occurs. Imagine that a frightened student runs to the phone and calls Campus Security. Shouldn't there be more than an answering machine on the other end? That was all Jeremy Roberts got the night he tried to warn college officials about Wayne Lo. I wanted to know why.

I reached Ron Ringo in the nick of time. He was being transferred from Norfolk, Virginia, to California and was just getting ready to make a trip back to New England to visit his kids from a first marriage. A few days after my call, we met in a shopping mall about an hour from my house.

He told me the college had hired him in the summer of 1992 to improve the Security Department, but that it had been a battle all the way. As soon as he'd tried to implement any standard procedures, such as checking the kids who went in and out of dorms after hours, he met with complaints that he was "too Gestapo." While these complaints came primarily from the residence directors, Ringo did not feel well received by other staff members either. An increased security presence was not going over well with any of the people who worked at the college. They were all used to a transparent security system and saw no reason to change. In response to complaints, Bernie inserted Irvinia Scott as a "liaison" between Ringo and the administration. It might have sounded sensible, but the effect of this move was to completely isolate Ringo. Bernie dealt with the problem Ringo and his security proposals represented by simply cutting them out of the loop.

In other words, just a few months before Wayne Lo's rampage, Simon's Rock had tried, and effectively rejected, an organized campus security policy. In December of 1992, there was only a collection of watch-people—Theresa Beavers, Maggie CapoNegro and a few others. And, according to Theresa Beavers, even these few were considered by the administration to be part of the maintenance staff.

Even taking into account the political situation at the time, Ron Ringo could not understand why Bernie didn't contact him as soon as that warning call came in. It galled him. Ron said he lived only five minutes from the campus and was available at all hours. With eleven years as an MP in the Marines and ten years as a Los Angeles County police officer, he, of any of the people there, had the knowledge and training to have dealt with the situation, and Bernie knew it. I asked him what he would have done and he said the procedure was simple: "Call the police. Detain Wayne Lo. Secure his room until a proper search could be undertaken."

No one in the administration saw fit to inform Ringo of the Wayne Lo incident as it developed. He was never told about the package in the morning. At the evening Security Staff meeting even Irvinia did not mention it to him. When the warning phone call came, he was not notified. It was too much for him. He quit the college in disgust.

Why had Bernie made the decisions he'd made? If anybody knew Bernie's thinking, it would be Mike Hogg, the college Business Manager. (I realized he was probably the college official who had so infuriated Howard Thomas about the unpaid tuition.) But Mike was gone too. Just up and left his kids and wife of twenty years, run off with a local woman. He was in Arizona somewhere.

Maggie CapoNegro had a slightly different tale to tell. Hers was of the political intrigue that followed Ron Ringo's departure. Being the senior watch person, she'd taken over as nominal head of the Security Department. But Irvinia still held the position of liaison to the administration and she badly wanted the job as department head. In the months that followed, according to Maggie, she did everything she could to undermine Maggie's position. Then Maggie broke her foot and had to stay home for six weeks. Maggie claimed that during this time Irvinia had rifled through her personal papers "looking for dirt" and had filed a dozen trumped-up bad conduct reports against Maggie. When she got back, Maggie pleaded her case before Bernie, who sided with her. Irvinia was removed from Security, her liaison position terminated. Meanwhile, an ex-Security staffer and an old friend of Maggie's, applied for a position on the staff. Maggie gave the application her OK, and this woman was brought back aboard. She didn't waste any time in going for the top spot herself, and she did it more efficiently than Irvinia had. She discovered that Maggie had been altering time cards. According to Maggie, all she'd been doing was letting people go home a little early, or giving them some extra time for personal business. Everyone did it, but technically it was against the rules. This infraction was brought to Bernie's attention, Maggie was fired, and the new lady was installed as head of Security.

Maggie believed there was another reason for her termination. It had begun to dawn on her that she'd been relieved at the guard shack by Theresa Beavers just minutes before Wayne Lo started shooting. The terrible realization that she might have been killed was just setting in. She was angry that the college hadn't told her or Theresa about Wayne having the gun. Being a vocal woman, she began letting them know she was angry. There had been one meeting, in particular, some months after the murders, at which she jumped up and said to Ba Win, "That's bullshit. You knew all along. Why didn't you warn us? Why didn't you do something?" Shortly after this outburst, she was fired. The timing may have been coincidental, but in Maggie's mind, there was a connection.

It might have been one big family at Simon's Rock, but after listening to Maggie CapoNegro and Ron Ringo, it was beginning to sound like one big dysfunctional family. I had the answer to my remaining question about the series of events leading up to the shootings. Jeremy Roberts got an answering machine when he called Security, because there was no Security.

As the events leading up to the shootings came into focus, I began to shift my attention to what had happened after the murders: primarily, the failure of college officials to transmit the facts of the case to the victims. Along with Bernie Rodgers' refusal to accept responsibility, this failure of communication was, I realized, a big part of the reason for my anger. It was why we were suing these guys. It was also why they were in hot water with the Beavers and with Richard Thomas' family.

The apparent stone wall that they had turned to the outside world had resulted in two lawsuits and a Workmen's Compensation hearing. This seemed like risk management of the most radical sort. I could imagine the creators of this policy deciding that it would be better to anger a few of the principals than to endanger the reputation and perhaps the very existence of their institution. To me, this indicated that they felt vulnerable about their role in the murders. They seemed to me to be acting like guilty people.

But who, exactly, were "they?" Who were the creators of the policy?

I mulled and stewed. Based on my conversations with Jillings, Irvinia and the Beavers, and on my own picture of the institution, I became convinced that the decision had been made at the highest level. Bard College, just across the line in New York state, owned Simon's Rock College. I became convinced that the policy had emanated from Bard College, the product of frenzied meetings of college officials, board members and consulting lawyers in the hours just after the murders. Nothing else I could imagine would account for the uniformity of this policy and the speed of its application.

By March of 1996, I had a plan. I'd go right to the top and ask a simple question. At first the question was going to be, "How come Bernie Rodgers still has a job?" But that was too cute. Instead I decided that I would ask why we'd had to learn about the Classic Arms package from the newspapers. This was, really, the first question I'd had about Galen's murder, way back in December, 1992. I called Bard College and made an appointment to see President Leon Botstein.

It seemed at least possible that he'd tell me the truth. I had shock value on my side. He'd be expecting the worst, and answering my simple question might seem the easiest way to get rid of me. In a sense, he didn't have anything to lose. We were still locked in a lawsuit, but that suit had little to do with the flow of information after the murders. Even if he lied, he'd be telling me something. Of course how could I tell if he was lying or not? It would be interesting to try to find out.

Finally the minister was gone and Leon Botstein and I were alone. He shook my hand (fleshy palm and fingers, vigorous shake) and offered me juice, coffee, tea or water. It was 6:15 P.M., cocktail hour for me. I'd spent a good part of my drive to Bard College wondering if I'd be served beer, wine or whiskey. I gritted my teeth behind the smile and declined.

He led me into a high-ceilinged front room, just to the right of the front hall. It contained a big black piano and some other ancient-looking long keyboard instrument. There were music stands bunched in a corner and the wall shelves were lined with what I took to be musical scores. We did a little small talk, like jogging an easy half mile before commencing the workout, and then Botstein started in.

"I can be a very blunt man." he said, "Very frank." His lips were soft like his hands and they made a big letter out of the B in blunt. I was starting to get nervous. I had not had good luck talking to people who tell me how frank they are. When Leon Botstein said, "I don't bullshit either," my heart sank. Here was a guy who didn't drink and who wanted first and foremost to tell me how honest he was. All I wanted was a drink and some information. The evening had bad news written all over it.

Perhaps Botstein caught something in my expression, or perhaps this was all part of the set-up. His next sentence was, "So I try not to bullshit anyone, except of course, when I have to, and you must realize that it is in the nature of a job like this that, occasionally, one is put in a position where one has to. Given that fact I try to make people aware of the realities of my situation." Was this a disclaimer?

"Are you saying that you're bullshitting or you're not bullshitting?"

He smiled. He liked the question. "What I'm saying is, that in a job like mine, well, let me give you an example."

And we were off on a wild conversational ride.

At least it was a wild ride for me. Maybe Leon Botstein had chats like ours every night. For all I knew he talked to his kids that way. He was a major-league talker. He was passionate, humorous, sophisticated, and learned. Those lips made lovely things of words. Within five minutes he was up in the middle of the room, not fluttering exactly, more like swooping and flapping, dancing on the carpet in front of his piano to the tune of what he was saying. The jacket came off and he was down to the red velvet vest, gold watch fob, floppy maroon bowtie and a torrent of stories, hypotheses, models, and examples for my edification. I could see how, as Andrew Jillings had suggested, this guy might be Bernie Rodgers' mentor. I could see in him everything Bernie aspired to. But where with Bernie it was just words, with Botstein it was the ideas the words made. It was conviction, it was life. He was very good at what he did.

That night, he mostly did the teacher, the counselor, the wise old rabbi; and he hauled up for our consideration the ageless wisdom born of the suffering of his people. Many of his family had died in the concentration camps. He had lost a daughter himself in the early 1980s, a five-year-old, beautiful child, hit by a truck, I think he said. He knew where I was coming from. He knew a lot about the country we'd both come through. And he was right, he didn't bullshit. He was way beyond bullshit.

The result of it all was that he did, in a sense, answer my question. The question, which I put forward in the first few minutes of our meeting was, "Why did we have to learn about the Classic Arms package from the newspapers? Was this failure of communication the result of an executive decision made by Bard College or was it Bernie Rodgers' personal decision?" The answer was no. And yes. And, well, let me give you an example.

I enjoyed it. He did most of the work, though I doubt it was work for him. I learned later in the evening that he was a music scholar, a violinist and a conductor, which explained his dynamic conversational style. The stories were good. There was the Polish Catholic aunt, a miserable person in daily life, who had acted like a saint in time of crisis, saving the lives of countless Jews in the ghetto. There was the grandfather who'd been a big man in daily life and who fell apart completely when the Nazis moved in.

He was laying a foundation for the first part of an answer to my question. The point was, that this Wayne Lo affair was so far outside the norm that it required exceptional behavior. Some people, like the Polish Catholic aunt were at their best in a crisis. Others, like the grandfather, who were at their best in normal times, could not cope with extraordinary situations. One of the sadnesses of the whole incident was that poor Bernie, much like the grandfather, did not possess the capacity for exceptional behavior under duress. Bernie was a good man, an excellent man, but he just didn't possess the equipment to deal with such abnormal events. And there was a tinge of something else in his depiction of Bernie's character. Botstein used the words "naive" and "naiveté" in reference to Bernie. I even stopped him and made him back up (image here of backing an eighteen-wheeler into a narrow alley) to be sure I heard him correctly. He stuck by the word. I gathered that in Botstein's view there was a certain inherent limitation, a lack of breadth or knowing, to Bernie Rodgers. This had something to do with how Wayne Lo had gotten past him, and something to do with why he hadn't been successful at communicating with me after Galen's death.

Botstein said he'd been at a restaurant in New York when he'd learned of the shootings. He'd gotten his daughter, a student at Barnard, and they'd driven right up to Simon's Rock together. She'd lived through the loss of his youngest daughter with him and she was good (as by this time I was to understand he was, too) in a crisis. There, the campus sealed off, they'd stood outside and Bernie had told them everything. Botstein regarded Rodgers' decisions prior to the shootings as "marginal but acceptable." What did marginal mean? Well, he wanted to give me an example. I didn't want an example. I wanted "marginal." It was complex. Would I accept, on a hypothetical basis, "A decision I might not have made but which I understood?" I would.

This condensation cannot do justice to the business of speaking with a man like Leon Botstein. The sequence I am reporting was just the

armature on which were hung bewildering thickets of examples, allu-
sions, cross-references and inspired inclusions that had nothing to do
with the matter at hand but which somehow fit. We traveled from the
Whitney Museum to nuclear physics to Beethoven's Vienna. His discourse honored the subtlety and complexity of reality by seeking to
replicate it. It was necessarily a highly sophisticated, highly intelligent
discourse. It also bordered on the incomprehensible.

I saw how this might be overwhelming; the preternatural energy,
the erudition, the conviction, punctuated by that assured earthiness.
He'd intimidate you, or out think you, or bludgeon you to smithereens,
or just outlast you, all in the most affable and civilized manner. I could
imagine people staggering out of their interviews with him.

But to hell with that. I'd already been bludgeoned, intimidated and
out-thought by men less able than he, and had staggered out of many
a conversation less challenging than this. Tonight I was here as a pure,
reduced product of human experience. I was a living question. Leon
Botstein understood this in some fashion, and he addressed it. He wasn't
going to make it easy for me, but he wasn't going to bullshit me either,
and when he did, he was going to let me know.

So no. Botstein, the board, and a bunch of lawyers did not get together
hours after the shootings and declare a stonewall policy on information.
However, some days after the incident, Botstein and Rodgers and the
boards of both colleges got together and decided they'd better retain
some outside counsel to deal with the criminal proceedings then underway, at which point one of the board members brought in Skadden and
Arps, the top-end New York law firm. At this time these outside lawyers
made suggestions as to what should and should not be done. These suggestions were about how the criminal case then underway should be
handled with regard to the media and the police. There was no suggested
policy about the Gibsons. Simon's Rock officials had their hands so full
wondering if the college would even survive that they did not consider

a policy about the Gibsons. Bernie's failure to supply me with information about the shootings was just Bernie's failure, not a policy decision.

Botstein went on to help me with my model of the event from an institutional point of view. He agreed that risk management is a dominating principle in the operation of an institution such as his. However, the people at Simon's Rock College, Bard's wholly owned subsidiary, were in this particular mess all by themselves. At no time prior to the shootings had Botstein or any Bard officials been informed of the ammunition package or of the threats. They were in no way involved in any of the decisions prior to Wayne Lo's rampage. Therefore the sound institutional policy had been to divorce themselves from Simon's Rock, at least officially, not to move in and take over. Yes, Leon Botstein conferred every day during this crisis with Bernie. Yes, Botstein lost a lot of sleep over it. But no, he was not making policy decisions for Bernie Rodgers. The prudent course in the days after the shootings, at least as far as media exposure was concerned, was to let Simon's Rock twist in the wind.

There was almost certainly more to it, and Leon Botstein wasn't saying there wasn't.

What else did I learn? His daughter's death had changed his life. Before she died, his career trajectory was going to take him to the presidency of the University of Chicago. Now he was going to stay at Bard until he retired. His focus had changed. Now, to fill the hole that his daughter's death had made, he wanted to make the world a better place. In this same way, the deaths of Galen and Ñacuñán had made better men of Bernie and Ba Win. They went back to their jobs with increased dedication and understanding, as they sought to repair the tragedy by trying to make Simon's Rock a better place.

In part, Botstein's vision was romantic, as might befit a musician and a conductor. The function of a college like Bard or Simon's Rock was to maintain a way of life that was becoming impossible in the world outside. Did they have their heads in the clouds, he asked rhetorically, did they ignore certain ugly realities that confront the rest of the world on a daily basis? Yes! That was what they were supposed to do! There was a certain standard of life and behavior and discourse that it was their mission to maintain and promulgate. And no. One did not cave in to terrorists. The fact that there were crazy people in the world should not determine how a college functioned. If we saw the world simply as a dangerous place full of lunatics, we wouldn't be doing what a college like ours is supposed to do.

Wonderfully, the explication of this doctrine flowed into a sympathetic analysis of Bernie's role in such an institution. If the institution existed to make the world a better place, what were the standards by which Bernie's actions were to be judged? I had my grief, certainly. I was entitled to it. But what about the greater good? What about the true function of the institution? What if ... and here followed a five-minute loop out into normative ethics and the psychology of grief and certain details of Leon Botstein's autobiography and even the hypothetical proposition of an extra marital affair, the gist of which was: what if Bernie and Ba Win acted the way they acted out of concern for the greater good, for the life of the institution? Could I see the difficulties of their situation? Could I see its tragic potential for those two men?

None of this was stated as overtly as I am reporting it. Some of these ideas found their way into my mind by virtue of what Leon Botstein did not say, as if his words, in this use, were to shade in a background against which the unstated truth stood, stark and self-evident.

While he was at it he disabused me of another idea. "If I had to be responsible for the safety and well-being of my students," he declared, slamming the table, "I'd quit my job." This astounded me, shocked me. It was harsh to hear, but I saw what he was getting at. No one in the world can guarantee anyone else's personal safety. Beyond a certain nominal degree of monitoring and care it is unreasonable to expect that such safety can be assured. While I believed that the college had an obligation to keep guns and ammunition off their campus, they claimed that they had tried as hard as they could. Our argument was over whether, in fact, they had.

Leon Botstein speculated that after the shootings, when the time came to talk to me, Bernie Rodgers was too confused, too upset, too at odds with himself to communicate effectively. It was just that the situation was so tragic, so extraordinary, that Bernie was unable to act efficiently, to thread his way between a humane response and the demands being placed upon him to protect his institution.

I replied that this was certainly a tragic and extraordinary situation, but that Bernie Rodgers was supposed to be a learned man in the humanities. What was the point of reading great literature, of looking at paintings, of listening to music, if these activities didn't prepare you in some sense, for tragic and extraordinary situations? What was the point of all that learning if it didn't help you in a situation like the one at Simon's Rock? Of all people, shouldn't the head of a liberal arts college be able to take the lead in such circumstances? How effective an administrator could Bernie Rodgers be if this particular extraordinary circumstance had left him too upset and confused to even keep in contact with the family of the murdered student? I told Botstein I didn't buy it. Bernie Rodgers failed to communicate because he was covering up, not because he was confused. Leon Botstein went off on another loop on that one. But this time the loop never really came back. There was no place for the loop to come back to except Bernie's essential failure. We both knew it.

The difference was, as the evening wore on and we moved into the kitchen and my new friend Leon finally got me to drink a fruit juice (it wasn't too bad), I saw Bernie's failure as a moral issue. He'd made a mistake and wouldn't admit it and tried to hide it. Leon Botstein saw Bernie's failure as a forgivable mistake, the result of a personal shortcoming. And whose personality didn't have shortcomings?

We had gotten down to the nub of it, and there we stood, all bloodied and smiling like at the end of one of those brawls in a John Wayne movie where Duke and the other guy fight to a draw and then become fast friends.

But Leon Botstein, President of Bard College, hadn't seen that John Wayne movie, and he wouldn't have related to it if he had. He was not a man of violence. He was the son of ghetto survivors and the parent of a dead child. He'd known suffering and had survived much. He'd seen a lot in this world. He reached into his cultural bag, way back this time, and came up with something very special for me.

It was the story of one of his concentration camp relatives, an uncle, I think. Years after the war, the authorities found one of the concentration camp guards, a brutal man, a bad man who had killed many Jews. They put him on trial, and they proved that he'd worked at this camp. Some friend of Leon's uncle was at the trial and he wrote a letter to the uncle. "They've got that guard," the letter said, "now they need to prove he was the one who killed all those Jews. You've got to write a letter to the court and tell them all the bad things he did."

Well, Leon said, the uncle thought on this long and hard, because it was very complicated. As it happened, this bad guard had loved to play chess, and when the Nazis came along for another trainload of prisoners to take to the ovens, the guard had kicked the uncle in the balls and chopped him on the neck and said to the Nazis, "Leave this one for me. He's mine." And the Nazis had chuckled and left the uncle there with the guard. The guard had saved the uncle's life so that he'd have some-one to play chess with. Now, years later, what was the uncle to do? Finally he wrote a letter to the court in which he said, "I can't tell you how to decide, but I must tell you that this man saved my life at the concentration camp." He told the court the whole story. In the end the guard had his sentence commuted.

What was the point of this tale? "It wasn't about the guard." Botstein said, slamming his palm on the kitchen table so the juice glass jumped, "Fuck the guard. He was a murderer." Leon used "fuck" very comfortably in his conversation with me. It was an urbane kind of use.

The point was that his uncle was a better man for having told his truth about the guard. The point was that violence begat violence and one always had to be careful about this. The point was that vengeance could come back and hurt you. The point was, he told me, "You could call Bernie Rodgers and Ba Win out in public for what you perceive to be their moral failures. They're the obvious ones to blame. From what I've seen of you tonight you could do a very efficient, very capable job of it."

"Like shooting fish in a barrel." I boasted.

What a stupid thing to have said! As soon as it was out of my mouth I regretted it. I'd been doing so well all night and now in one unguarded moment in the kitchen over a glass of cranberry-orange juice I'd let my anger show. Now I'd never learn anything! He was on it like a terrier.

"Well I don't like being shot." he said, and then again to be sure I had it, "I don't like being shot in a barrel."

Everything stopped for a moment and then he continued. "Bernie and Ba Win are too easy, too obvious. You could destroy them, sure. But what would you have gained? You'd have destroyed two careers, ruined two lives. And you'd be the worse for it, believe me. Then nothing positive would come of Galen's death, just more destruction."

My ears heard what he said. My mind took it in. This was wisdom. But my heart wasn't there for it. I was going to settle the score with those two guys, or try my damnedest, and I would not be better for it. He was right. It was a sadness.

That was the upshot of my evening with Leon. He pleaded for mercy for his hapless associates. He didn't deny their actions or defend their decisions. He suggested understanding and forgiving them. There were a lot of cynical objections I could have made regarding the self-interest informing his proposal, but they did not occur to me and I did not make them. He was not trying to change my mind as much as plant a seed. It wasn't a seed of doubt, exactly.

I had no idea if it would take or not. I wasn't kidding that night when I told him my walkabout was just a process. If the seed grew and blossomed into understanding and forgiveness for Bernie and Ba Win, so much the better. If I was too far gone and went ahead and efficiently and capably hauled what I perceived to be their moral failures out in public and destroyed two lives and careers, so be it and God help us all.

Weeks passed. I thought a lot about Bernie and Ba Win and Leon and Lee. For the first time since my walkabout had begun, I stepped back, just a hair, and looked at what I was doing. What I saw depressed me.

I'd tricked myself, or I'd been careless. At the very least I had failed to discriminate between getting information and getting even. Under the guise of discovering the redeeming story I'd been engaged all the while on a mission of revenge, in assembling a case against Bernie Rodgers and Ba Win. And look at my role models: Lee Marvin and Clint Eastwood gunning people down in the street; killers! I was just using them so I wouldn't have to face the emotional difficulties; the fact that my innocent boy had suffered and died, the fact that there was nothing I could do to fix it. Botstein had been right. There was no redemption in revenge, no peace.

Even worse was the realization that for all the digging and poking I'd been doing, for all the time and energy I'd put into my investigations, I'd only uncovered one part of the story. I'd really only been interested in the failure of college officials. The rest of it was still out there untouched, undiscovered. And precious time was ticking away. Facts were getting forgotten, evidence covered with dust.

Then it was May and the air took on that musky, spicy smell of life beginning once again. I was still thinking about my failure but by now

Botstein's message had begun to sink in and I was starting to decode the dense, rich stream of information that had come down to me that snowy day at Simon's Rock when I'd felt Galen's immanence.

I figured it was time to leave the college, time to graduate.

PART
THREE

❧13
SUPERIOR COURT

Some time in June of 1996 the completed transcript of Wayne Lo's 1994 murder trial was sent to Berkshire County Superior Court. This finalized the court's records of the case. These records were then "assembled" and sent on to the Supreme Judicial Court where Wayne Lo's appeal would someday be heard. I got the idea to look at these court records from talking to Gerry Downing, the Berkshire County District Attorney who had prosecuted Wayne Lo.

I wanted to learn more about the gun, and how Wayne had obtained and altered it, and I thought it would be helpful to look at some of the information the police had gathered. District Attorney Downing gave me to understand that public access to information used by the Commonwealth in their prosecution of a first degree murder case, particularly one which was currently under appeal, was a "gray area." However, he said, the court documents pertaining to the case were part of the public record. He suggested I start with these and see how much information they yielded. I agreed that this would be a sensible plan, and Downing then faxed me the docket sheets of the Wayne Lo case. These ran to thirty-six pages. They contained hundreds of individual items, which summarized thousands and thousands of pages. I drove out to Pittsfield, Massachusetts, and spent a couple of days in the clerk's office at the Berkshire County Superior Court reading through them.

The ladies who worked there were cheery and helpful. They brought out the whole case file, about a linear yard of paper, and piled it on a corner of the counter. I sat at a little desk underneath this pile and went through it item by item, checking each one off the faxed docket sheets to be sure I hadn't missed anything. By the time I was done, I had set aside about 250 pages of documents that seemed particularly interesting. These were carried away by the ladies to be copied, without a groan or a skyward glance.

Taken in its entirety that yard of documentation told the whole story of how the Wayne Lo murder trial had unfolded. Those papers showed how the prosecution gathered its evidence and how the defense contested the validity of some of this evidence. They showed that the defense several times asked for more money to prepare its case. (To protect his parents' estate, Wayne Lo was declared indigent and his case turned over to a public defender.) They questioned the effect of publicity on the defendant's chances of getting a fair trial, and they argued over the validity of certain psychiatric tests. It was a fascinating story in itself, though not exactly the story I was chasing. However, in resolving the general procedural issues, certain particulars were discussed, and specific pieces of evidence were introduced. These were the items that caught my attention.

The most interesting papers of all referred to the night of the murders. Shortly after the shootings the local police searched Wayne's room. They said they were looking for more victims, weapons or accomplices, and they may well have been, but they went in there without a search warrant. The defense contended the results of this search were illegal and should not be admitted in court.

The argument over the admissibility of the evidence from Wayne's room was carried out in these court papers, and in the course of this argument the events of December 14, 1992 and the search of Wayne Lo's room were reenacted before me.

Ultimately the judge agreed with the defense. He ruled that the results of the room search could not be admitted as evidence in the prosecution of Wayne Lo. As a result of the judge's ruling this vital evidence had been impounded and was not allowed at the criminal trial. Consequently, I had been trying to reconstruct events without knowing all the facts.

Based on the testimony given at the trial, on the depositions of Floyd and Trinka Robinson, and on my own conversations with Andrew Jillings and Irvinia Scott, I'd formed a scenario in which Wayne hid the gun and ammo in his closet in Kendrick House, then transported the gun, gun parts and bullets to the weight room at Crosby, which locked from the inside. There, I figured, he could have worked undisturbed to put on the plastic stock, load up the oversized clips and modify the weapon to accommodate them.

The court documents told a different story. In a fat sheaf of papers marked "Impounded" were all the police reports from the night of the murders and a summary of events leading up to the search of Wayne Lo's room. Sitting there in the busy Clerk's office on a hot summer day, reading those cold, precise statements was like deep sea diving; down and down to the remote tragedy of December 14, 1992, eerily lit, under the tremendous pressure of all that had come after.

I learned from the duty officer's statement that the first call had come in to the Great Barrington Police at 10:23 P.M. Given that Theresa Beavers was on the phone with her husband Bruce when Wayne shot her, and that Bruce had immediately called the Egremont Police, and that the Egremont police had immediately called the Great Barrington police, I guessed no more than five minutes would have elapsed between Wayne's first shot and this call to the Great Barrington police. That meant Wayne had started shooting at around 10:18, perhaps 10:15 at the earliest. The Great Barrington police were only minutes from the campus, and when they arrived, Wayne was still shooting. I knew from the criminal trial that Wayne's surrender call had been made at 10:33. That left, what? Fifteen minutes for the two murders and four woundings? Theresa Beavers 10:18; Ñacuñán Sáez, 10:20; Galen Gibson and Tom McElderry 10:24; Josh Faber and Ricky Thomas 10:28; surrender 10:33?

It seemed like an impossibly short span of time for so much to have happened. Somehow Tom McElderry drove onto campus, saw Ñacuñán's bloody body in its car, went past Wayne reloading outside the library, and ran in and cried for help. Somehow Andrew Jillings arrived on campus and started for Ba Win's just as Theresa and Ñacuñán were being shot, got to Ba Win's door as Wayne was shooting at the library, then ran back to campus. Somehow Rob Horowitz made his terrified escape from the library, from the side of his murdered friend. Somehow Simon Bromberg sat there in the Student Union with the killer, then left, then returned, unharmed. Somehow Wayne Lo wreaked all that havoc, spun off all those lifetimes of damage and pain in a few plays of a Monday night football game, one commercial to the next on *Murphy Brown*. Somehow Galen was dead.

The police reports, typed by various officers on various typewriters, formed a single narrative which proceeded from the guard shack to Ñacuñán's car, to the library, to the dorms and finally to the Student Union, where Wayne surrendered. The writing in their reports was terse and rough. These men, just local guys, had gone into the night after a lunatic with a gun, not knowing if he really did mean to surrender or if he had accomplices. I could imagine them back at their desks, in the early morning after the shootings, still high, still shaken.

This is the part of their narrative that interested me the most. It is from a report filed by Officer Merrit Heady of the Great Barrington police.

After Mr. Lo was taken into custody, and the dorms were checked for wounded students, it was brought to our attention by other students of Kendrick Dorm that Mr. Lo's dorm room was in fact in Kendrick Dorm (A2) bottom floor. At this point we felt it necessary to check his dorm room for weapons, other students, either hostage or possibly involved, or for that matter shot or wounded. Mr. Lo's dorm room was opened for us by a resident director, myself, Off. Sinico and Gardella entered the room. At first glance there was no one else in the room, the four-foot-high stand fan was on, blowing against the wall, all the lights were on in the room.

I first checked under the bunk style metal bed. There I located two large suitcases, both empty. In back of those suitcases up against the wall was a large, long brown box, the type of box a gun would be shipped in, I alerted Off. Sinico to what I had seen. I then pulled the bed away from the wall and Off. Sinico pulled the box on top of the bed and opened it. Inside I observed a Walnut colored stock which appeared to fit the gun used in the shootings, there were also numerous boxes of shells that were empty. Some paper work of where the shells and stock were bought from, and paid for with his VISA card. I remember looking at the dates to the order, noting it was ordered December 12, 1992 and it had arrived by Mon. Dec. 14, 1992, the day of the shootings. I did not remove any of the articles in the box, Off. Sinico took control of same.

So Wayne had altered and loaded the gun in his room. The trip to the Crosby weight room that night had just been to pump up. By 9:30 that evening he was back in Kendrick House for that dorm meeting, to argue with Floyd and then, perhaps, to hear Ba Win and the others moving Trinka from her apartment. Suppose this was about 9:45. He would have had a half hour. Probably this was not enough time for a novice to modify the gun and load six clips. Testimony at the trial had Wayne, normally a serious student, leaving his final exam in Sophomore Seminar early, at about 3:00 that afternoon. I guessed that, like a kid at Christmas, he could not contain his excitement. He left the exam to play with his new toy. On the evening of December 14, after the dorm meeting, Wayne had probably just gone back to his room, filled up his back pack, grabbed his newly modified gun and left.

The other documents that were useful to me were the several listings of potential witnesses. Under the rules by which trials proceed, the prosecution was required to let the defense know who they had spoken to and what evidence they had gathered. These documents contained the names and addresses of potential witnesses, lists of material evidence gathered, and lists of witness statements, including the date each statement was taken, and its length (though, except in the case of the room search issue, they did not contain the statements themselves).

I found, for example, the address of John Hernandez. I knew from the criminal trial that he was the man who had owned the SKS before Wayne had bought it. According to the Commonwealth's first Certificate of Discovery, filed January 5, 1993, John Hernandez lived right there in Pittsfield. I noticed that they had also recorded a one-page statement from him taken a few days after the shootings.

I thought it would be very interesting to get my own statement about the gun from Mr. John Hernandez, but I decided that I'd better do a little background work first. To be honest, I wanted to find out what I was getting into.

I had several preconceived notions about assault weapons in general and SKS rifles in particular. SKS rifles were the chosen gun of criminals, militiamen and drug dealers. These types wore fatigues and were angry a lot. Put all this together, and you can imagine the composite portrait that emerged from the Gibson crime labs—an angry drug-dealing Latino militiaman in fatigues. Not that I was deterred, I just wanted to be ready. So, after I was done at Superior Court, I went back to Dave's Sporting Goods to talk to Dave Benham.

Dave remembered me quickly and was as cordial as he'd been at our last meeting. This surprised me somewhat because he was under a lot more pressure now. Bruce and Theresa Beavers had instituted a lawsuit against him for selling the gun to Wayne Lo. They were also suing the mail order company that sent the bullets to Simon's Rock College. Their thinking in these lawsuits was analogous to idea behind the first lawsuits against bartenders for serving liquor to drunken patrons. Alcohol was deadly stuff. So were guns. Some responsibility on the part of the vendor was required. The Beavers hoped that, just as the courts had recognized this in the case of alcohol, their lawsuit would awaken a similar consciousness regarding the sales of guns and ammunition.

Dave's reaction to the lawsuit was interesting. We were back out on the porch at the entrance to the store, the same place we'd had our first talk. It was hot and sunny just like before, customers passed and greeted Dave just like before, but much had changed for both of us. He was silent for a moment, studying his shoes. Then he looked up at me.

"That guard, Theresa Beavers. They say she's got some permanent injuries from this."

"That's right." I told him. "She got shot up pretty bad."

"Well maybe the lawsuit money would be some help to her..."

He said he had insurance, so the battle was out of his hands. The lawyers were fighting it now. If he won or if the judgment against him were within the limits of his policy, things would go on pretty much as before. If the judgment exceeded his policy limit, he'd be ruined. Either way, there was nothing he could do now except try not to get too upset over anything before it happened.

We talked about the politics of the situation, and how Dave felt himself victimized by his local representative, Christopher Hodgkins, who he thought was using this issue just to gain votes. We talked about the recent history of gun control legislation, and finally the conversation got around to what I was doing now and why I was there. I asked him about that Hernandez guy who'd brought the gun in, the one Wayne Lo had then bought from him.

It turned out that John Hernandez was anything but what I'd expected. He was a professional man of some kind. Dave thought he'd worked for General Electric out here in the Berkshires, but had changed jobs and moved out of town. Dave had known him for years. He was a hell of a nice guy. His father still lived in town and John came back and visited often. He was an advanced gun collector, and active in the NRA and GOAL (Gun Owners Action League), too. As a matter of fact, the reason he'd brought the gun in to Dave's was that it wasn't up to his standards and he'd wanted to trade it up for a better model. It was, in Dave's words, "a real piece of junk." John had originally bought it from another gun dealer, perhaps Pat's Guns in Dalton.

We went back inside and Dave looked through a phone book and then in a Rolodex for Hernandez's number. He had a tough time with the phone book. He was either more upset by our chat than he'd wanted to let on, or a touch dyslexic. One of the other Daves came over to help and I recognized him from the criminal trial as the clerk who'd actually sold the gun to Wayne. I remembered Dave telling me his clerk had been having some trouble psychologically about the transaction. I introduced myself and told him I'd heard he'd had a rough time for a while. He said things were OK now. I told him I bore him no ill will. He smiled, mumbled a thanks. I shook hands with both Daves and left, Hernandez' new phone number in my pocket.

❧14
WHAT ABOUT BOB?

There was one other bit of information in that yard of documents that particularly caught my eye. From having gone over the case so thoroughly, from having talked with so many people, from having sat in that courtroom for four weeks, I thought I was familiar with all the players. Of the hundred-odd witnesses listed, and of all the names of people who had given statements, there was only one name I did not recognize.

According to the commonwealth's supplemental certificate of discovery dated March 30, 1993, a man named Robert Herring, Sr. had given two statements to the police on January 26, 1993. It was noted that one had been handwritten, the other typed. The address of Robert Herring, Sr. was in Lee, Massachusetts, just two towns over from Great Barrington.

I did not have the text of Robert Herring's statement, just a document that said it existed. When I got back home I did a word search through all my computer files, and even dug up the old newspaper clippings and my handwritten notes. Who the hell was Robert Herring, Sr. and what did he know?

By the end of July I was driving through Lee, Massachusetts, on my way back to Pittsfield to pick up the 250 pages of documents that the ladies in the clerk's office had copied for me. At the edge of town, right before the train tracks, I located Robert Herring, Sr.'s address. It was a strange little triangular shop at the corner of a building, which also housed a laundromat and a coffee shop. Herring's shop had a big awning out in front, and junk was piled on the street under the awning. It was somewhat more interesting than flea market junk, but it was still junk.

I found a parking place and walked back to the shop. It was called Bob's Corner Store. A wooden sign on the front door said, "Herring." The door was open but there was no one inside. Bob's Corner Store was an avalanche from the bottoms of decades of estate sales; of sorry box lots from country auctions; of cast off stuff from the backs of countless pickup trucks. There were old shop signs, iron farm hardware, fifty-year-old lighting fixtures, picture frames, costume jewelry, dinnerware, diplomas, humidors, knives, decoys, movie posters and, at the apex of the triangle, several shelves full of old books. My entree.

Twenty years in the old book business had brought me to many places like this. I knew exactly what to do. Without hesitation I dove into that sea of dust and petrified rat droppings. I no longer thought about Galen or the trial, or about Wayne Lo or John Hernandez or the gun both had owned, or the Berkshire County Superior Court, or even Robert Herring, Sr. I thought about nothing. I was just eyes.

The junk orgy came out better than I could have hoped. I was able to catch a box of sash weights just before it fell off the shelf and landed on my toe, and I found a Hampden County Atlas from the late 1800s, a second edition of Cozzen's *Yachts and Yachting,* and a stack of physician's permission forms to purchase opium, state of Maine, circa 1915. Satisfied weasel, I stood there grooming myself waiting for Bob to make his appearance.

After a while a man in a dark T-shirt came into the shop and regarded me and my pile of treasures in a noncommittal way. I asked him if he was Robert Herring. He said he was. He was solidly built, round shouldered under his T-shirt. He had a drooping moustache that matched a drooping quality to his wet brown eyes, just a bit of a hangdog look to him. I figured he'd been next door at the coffee shop, that he'd seen me enter and that he'd let me poke around for a while before he came in. I figured he spent a lot of time in the coffee shop.

I told him what I did for a living and showed him what I'd found. He knelt down over the pile and we got right to business.

"Ho, the atlas!" he said, "This is going to cost you a lot of money." I didn't say anything.

"These maps." He riffled through the pages. "They're fifteen each."

The atlas had about a hundred maps in it. It was worth $200, though by Bob's calculation I should have been writing him a check for $1,500. I didn't say anything.

Bob plowed ahead. He picked up the Cozzens book. The cover was a little worn, making it worth about $75. He said, "Twenty-five," and put it down. I didn't say anything.

Then he picked up one of the opium permission slips and looked at it like he'd never seen it before. "Hmm. Very interesting. Opium. A lot of people are interested in opium. These are going to be expensive. Twenty apiece."

That added another thousand to his total. More silence.

I said, "Why don't I write you a check for three hundred fifty dollars for the lot."

He was incredulous. "For all this stuff?"

I didn't say anything. He pawed through the items one more time, in disbelief. Then he said, "Make it four hundred. That's only fifty more."

I was supposed to say $375 and he was supposed to grudgingly accept, but instead I said, "That's fine. Now let's talk about what I'm really doing here."

I had his attention.

First he flinched, then kind of melted as he understood who I was. I must admit I liked the people who reacted that way. It showed they felt it, that they had some idea. Then the interview began, and it immediately went off on such a weird tack that I became disoriented.

He blurted out, "Of course it was a mistake. I'll be the first to admit that. It was a stupid mistake. I got too excited when I recognized them. It might have been a racist thing, I honestly don't know."

The eyes were doing something. He was rolling them as he became animated, and the whites were showing, like a spooked horse. "But I'll tell you one thing. I saw that kid. Nobody can say I didn't. And it took me about a minute to realize he was nuts. And dangerous. And I'm just Bob. The stupid junk dealer. There's forty people teaching at that college and thirty six of them are Doctors. Now if I could see it in this kid in one minute, and they claim they couldn't see it all year, what does that tell you, huh?"

What, indeed! I made him stop and dragged him back to the beginning, and after that we went over it another time, and then I understood.

One day, Bob thinks it might have been late fall because the sky was so deep blue and the sun so yellow, he came in from the coffee shop and Wayne Lo was in a corner of his store, looking at a big knife. He asked Bob how much it was, and Bob, suspicious, said it wasn't for sale. Then he asked the kid where he was from and the kid said Simon's Rock. He had another person with him, not Oriental, a white guy, who seemed nervous and was pacing out front. Then the kid, the Oriental kid, asked Bob if he sold assault rifles. Bob said he did not. The kid asked where he could buy one. Bob said he didn't know, maybe Pittsfield, but then asked more questions, got the conversation onto something else because he wanted to find out about this kid. Bob figured almost immediately that the boy was crazy and probably dangerous. But he felt that the other person, the nervous one, was keeping the kid under control. He seemed older, maybe a faculty member. Something had been said to the effect that they were both from the college. Bob thought maybe the second guy was a professor and that he was hitting on Wayne. This other guy walked in the shop during the assault rifle part of the conversation. Clearly he knew what was going on. Then the two of them left. They went next door and had a cup of coffee, and Bob never saw them again. He went home and told his wife that very night about the kid and the rifle. And he told her the kid was crazy, dangerous, and that something bad was going to happen. I could ask her myself if I didn't believe him.

So you can imagine how he felt when, a few days after the shootings, he opened the local paper and there was the kid. And there, he thought, was the other guy too, the professor. He put it all together. The queer who'd been hitting on the kid. And now the kid had got the gun and murdered him. The other dead one, he was probably involved in it too, somehow. He went to the police and told them his story.

Wayne Lo had been in Bob's shop looking for a gun. And he'd been there with another person.

I'll say this about Bob. For every shop like his that I've been in, I've known a Bob like him. They're all missing something, some essential piece. Maybe some are drunks or strung out on drugs. Maybe some have that self-destructive mechanism that keeps derailing them. Maybe some are just too nice. Whatever it is, it's why they're all selling headless Barbies and broken trains instead of sitting in the front row at a Christie's auction in London. But they're all smart in their own fashion, street-smart. They're good at understanding people and motives in a short-term way. They have to be good to make livings selling junk. So I did not doubt for a moment the accuracy of Bob's diagnosis of Wayne Lo, or that he'd been able to make it so quickly. His assessment was supported by a lifetime of survival experience. It had at least as much weight as the opinions of those two-hundred-dollar-an-hour psychologists they'd trotted out at the criminal trial. Wayne Lo was sending his message and Bob had picked it up.

Where Bob had failed, and maybe where he failed all the time, was that he put the whole story together too fast. He was a little too impetuous.

Imagine how the cops must've felt! Here they had a guy who could prove Wayne Lo's actions were premeditated. But the rest of his story was nuts. If they put him on the stand the defense would have eaten him alive. Ñacuñán Sáez was Wayne Lo's homosexual lover? Uh huh. Tell us more, Mr. Herring …

Whoever this other person with Wayne had been, Bob had confused him with Ñacuñán's picture in the paper. It made a tighter narrative that way, but it was absurdly, sadly mistaken.

So Bob's name had been on the witness list but the police had never called him.

Then something else fell into place for me. That story about the other gun dealer. The rumor that Wayne Lo had gone to another gun dealer and been thrown out of the store. I could never verify it. Derek Gentile, my newspaper pal, had checked every dealer in the area. None of them had seen Wayne prior to the shootings. But Robert Herring, Sr. had. I was sure he'd been the source of that rumor about the other gun dealer.

I pressed him for details about the other person with Wayne. He said there'd been two pictures of Ñacuñán in the papers, and one made it look like he had somewhat lighter hair and skin, and that was why Bob had been confused, because the other guy with Wayne was fair skinned. The rest was hazy. This other guy had been taller than Bob, maybe six-foot-one or six-foot-two, maybe he'd had brown hair, lean not fat. Seemed older. Bob had assumed he was a faculty member, though this was never stated. Just something weird about the vibe. That was why he'd thought it was a gay thing. And nervous. Kept pacing outside the store. But he'd been concentrating on Wayne and it was hard to remember. Hard to remember more …

It was hard to keep him on this track. I could see that dragging these matters up was bringing his own feelings up too, and that they were on the verge of overwhelming him. The murders made him very sad and mad. He was angry that the college had not stopped Wayne. He told me several more times about the forty professors and thirty-six doctors and why couldn't they see what he'd found out in a minute? He was convinced there was a cover-up. He was convinced there was some relationship between Wayne and Ñacuñán that the college was hiding. He was convinced that Wayne waited for Ñacuñán expressly to murder him.

I told him how Ñacuñán had been already on his way home, and had turned around and gone back to get something he'd forgotten when he was killed; that his death was the cruelest kind of accident; that there was no way Wayne could have known Ñacuñán was going to be there. This hardly slowed him down at all. The college was covering something up, damn it.

Worse still was the way the police had treated him. He'd fingered Wayne Lo. He'd known. He'd even told his wife. She'd testify to that. But just because of that confusion over the second guy, the cops had dropped him like a dirty Kleenex. He was insulted. He'd wanted to help.

The poignancy of Bob's situation did not escape me. He had been on the outside all his life. Now he had an important piece of information and he wanted to do something with it. But the system wouldn't let him in.

I wrote him his check and picked up my booty and we shook hands and I said I'd be back some day, but he still had something to tell me.

"That kid. It was like a train going through here."

I could ask his wife ...

I went on to Pittsfield to pick up my photocopies from the smiling clerk ladies and then over to the District Attorney's office to see Gerry Downing and the assistant DA, David Capeless. They were skipping their lunches to talk to me, but sitting there in their rumpled white DA shirts, they acted as if missing meals was their favorite thing to do.

We talked about what I was learning from the Superior Court records and then I asked them about Bob Herring.

"You went to see him?" Capeless sounded surprised.

"Got the whole story. The whole gay murder conspiracy angle."

Downing and Capeless grinned the same rueful grin at one another. "Well, you can see why we couldn't use him." Downing said, "Fortunately we didn't need him."

"I can see that, and I can see why he wasn't much use from your point of view. But for me, his story is important. He could be as nutty as a fruitcake. He could think Wayne Lo killed JFK. That doesn't matter. What matters is that Wayne Lo was in his shop asking about an assault rifle. And there was another guy with him."

Downing and Capeless looked at one another. Capeless looked at me.

"This is true," he said.

He wasn't smiling anymore.

✣§15
THE COLLECTOR

We were standing at the white Formica island in John Hernandez' white kitchen. The SKS was laid out on a piece of heavy brown paper that John had brought up with the gun and spread out to protect the counter. At first it seemed there were going to be no difficulties with the procedure. John simply announced, "I know you're curious about how Wayne Lo modified the rifle, so I'll take this one apart for you and show you what he did." But almost immediately, he got stuck.

There was a little button, right at the base of the trigger guard that was supposed to be pushed. This, John explained, would cause the trigger mechanism to pop out. He pushed on it with a retracted ballpoint pen, and then with a fork, but it wouldn't budge. Then John disappeared downstairs for more tools.

It had been delicate getting to see John Hernandez. He'd moved to Rochester, New York, or at least that was the area code of the phone number Dave Benham had given me. I called it several times, got no answer, and began to wonder if I'd been led astray. Finally, on a whim, I phoned him late one Sunday night and got through. He'd just gotten in the door from a trip to Detroit.

He asked me if I'd used the BATF records (Bureau of Alcohol, Tobacco and Firearms) to locate him. I told him I'd gotten my information from the gun dealer, Dave Benham, who'd spoken well of him. He chuckled, told me he worked in the collections department of a telecommunications firm and that right now they had him commuting between

Rochester and Detroit. It was running him ragged, but he expected it would only last a few more months.

Beyond that he was guarded. I told him who I was and what I wanted, and he told me he was sorry for my loss. He was a father himself and he couldn't imagine anything worse happening than what had happened to me. He could grasp the value of what I was doing and he understood the strange irony of our lives being linked by a gun. But he wondered, really, if there was anything he could do to help me. He'd only owned the gun for a short while, had never even fired it, and was in no other way connected with Wayne Lo or the murders. Besides, his time was really at a premium right now. Perhaps we could get together later when he was visiting his Dad in Pittsfield.

I told him I'd spent the past seven months working on understanding the college's true role in the murders, and that now I was starting on the gun issue, but not necessarily just from a political standpoint. I told him how, in the source of my gun studies, I'd noticed that "collectors" were always mentioned. I told him I'd never met a gun collector and was most anxious to learn more about collecting from him. I told him I also wanted to learn something about SKS-type weapons. What was their history? Where did they come from? How did they work? I told him about Wayne's gun repeatedly misfiring and how, but for that failure, there might have been fifty dead on the Simon's Rock campus instead of two. I told him the theory about the magazine not fitting all the way into the body of the gun. I told him there was a chance I might some day get to examine the murder weapon and that when I did I wanted to be familiar with it so I could understand exactly how and why the malfunction had occurred. I told him I wanted to learn how long it took to add a folding stock and a thirty-round magazine to an SKS so I could know more about the chronology of the evening my son died.

There was a moment of silence while I was catching my breath and while John was realizing I had finished. Then he said, "You've got some real questions there, don't you?"

"Yes I do. I need someone with knowledge to help me answer them. That's why I'm calling you."

I think Hernandez understood then that he wasn't going to be sitting in mourning with a grieving dad, feeling vaguely guilty about something that wasn't really his fault. If we did get together we'd have something concrete to talk about on a level he could relate to. And if there was just a tinge of guilt on his part, helping me would expiate it.

We made a tentative date that I was supposed to verify by telephone as the day drew near. I did this and he had to cancel our meeting. He was very apologetic about it. He said he was going to a motorcycle race with his son. It was their only time to do something together. I think he never really expected me to call back and had made other plans. I told him I understood perfectly, that there was plenty of time, that I had no intention of giving up on this. We made a date for the end of July that I was again to confirm by phone. I did, and this time it was a go, and that was how I found myself in John Hernandez' spotless white kitchen, over a greasy SKS.

Of course John didn't just go get the gun. When I first arrived we went through an expectable but slightly uncomfortable searching-out process, to get to be able to intuit how much we could say to each other.

For my part, I got a pretty good initial reading. John Hernandez was slight of build, olive skinned with a precise moustache, brown eyes and dark, graying hair; mid-forties, not a trace of fat on him. Not a speck of dirt, either. The first salient fact I gathered about John was that he was a neat freak. He lived in a development that couldn't have been more than two years old. The houses were large, and of a curious mongrel Georgian-Palladian-Cape Cod design that managed to stay on the good side of tacky, but just barely. Each house was different, but they all looked the same. They were all spotlessly maintained. Inside, if John's house was any measure, they were comfortable, roomy and light. And clean. Very clean.

When I'd knocked on his door this Saturday morning, John had just been finishing up some paperwork at that white Formica kitchen island. Expense accounts, he told me. Because of the Detroit assignment he had a lot of commuting to do, a lot of expenses to keep track of. They all went in folders that went in an envelope that went in a box. We talked about the motorcycle race he and his son had attended. In fact, they'd actually raced in the event together. The boy was sixteen, so he and John competed in the beginner's class, in which there were no age limits. We chatted about sons and we chatted about motorcycles. Then, when John felt like we'd had enough chat he said, "Well, are you going to write a book?"

I had to admire the question. It was intelligent, perceptive, and it established a certain intimacy between us. John had decided that we might possibly be able to have a conversation, and now was giving me an invitation as well as a challenge. I told him I hoped to write a book, and that I'd been keeping written notes, but that I had a realistic attitude about the difficulty of getting such a thing published, particularly a book about a dead son. My main intention was to try to understand as well as I could everything that had happened. If a book resulted, so much the better. That seemed to satisfy him, so I proceeded in my search for understanding by asking him about gun collecting. How had he gotten into it?

John Hernandez had not started as a collector. He and his brother-in-law had been target shooters. Hunting had never appealed to him. He had done some hunting a long while ago and actually had gotten a deer. (He made a small face that told me the death of this animal had been distasteful to him. I got a quick image of spotless John up to his elbows in deer-gore.) No, hunting wasn't for him. But shooting, that was fun. He told me how, when people stand in the Berkshires and look west, they think they're seeing the Taconic range. When they stand in the Taconics and look east, they think they're seeing the Berkshires, but actually there are hills in between. Somewhere in these hills between the two mountain ranges, John and his brother-in-law found their ideal shooting spot. It had been a National Guard training site and was now abandoned. It was in a valley with hills all around out in the wilderness, perfectly safe. They'd go up there every weekend with lawnmowers and rakes and garbage bags and after a while they turned it into a nice little range. They shot pistols mostly, but some rifles too. It had been a lot of fun, and it had gotten John into collecting. He began by acquiring new firearms to shoot and then got interested in them for their own sake, as pieces of machinery or examples of engineering.

The assault rifle part of all this had started sometime in the late 1980s, maybe 1987. He had been collecting for a while but hadn't yet acquired any assault-style weapons. He decided he should add one to his collection and selected a German model, the Heckler-Koch. This was one of the weapons used by NATO troops and it was at the other end of the spectrum from the kind of gun Wayne had bought. It was finely designed and manufactured, a sort of Mercedes of assault rifles. It had cost, even in 1987, something like $1,100. However, just after John had put his order in with Dave Benham, something strange happened. One of those crazy guys, maybe it was Purdy out in California, the one who killed the kids in the schoolyard, went on a spree with an assault rifle. Public opinion erupted and President Bush ordered a temporary moratorium on the sale of assault rifles. Dave Benham got word that John's Heckler had arrived, but Dave was not allowed to receive it and John was not allowed to purchase it. This annoyed John, but more importantly, it got him thinking.

He lived in America. How could a presidential edict tell him what he could and could not buy? He began studying up on the gun issue and its history. He soon realized that the politics of guns involved his rights as a consumer and a citizen, and he began looking into these matters as well. They led him to a study of our Constitution and an immersion in political philosophy. What form of government were we supposed to be living under? How, in contrast, were we actually governed?

I got the impression that he had not been politically aware prior to these inquiries, and that, for this reason, he felt he was approaching the issue with an open mind. He described his subsequent political education as a process in which one discovery drew him on to another. What he learned surprised him. The true conditions under which we lived were not at all as the media had described them, nor were they as the framers of our Constitution had envisioned them. John Hernandez had come to believe that the federal government was very probably engaged in an effort to invade every aspect of the lives of the citizens of this country. Modern information technology and high-level conspiracy would enable the government to exercise more and more control over each citizen, to deprive citizens of certain of their constitutional rights, and eventually to establish a totalitarian regime. Once this regime was in place it would merge with the One World Government into a global dictatorship. The so-called gun control movement was just a part of this general trend, but typical of the way it proceeded. Under the guise of public safety, the government was attempting to negate one of our basic constitutional rights. Our freedoms would erode, one by one.

John Hernandez was not a frustrated redneck who'd bought hook, line and sinker into some NRA polemic. He was not a survivalist, or a militiaman or a stone crazy Bircher from the set of *Dr. Strangelove*. He was an earnest, honest man who had started out trying to get some answers and now found himself confronting a whole new reality. It had not been a comfortable process for him. There had been losses along way. Even his family was having a hard time with his discoveries.

As we talked, or as he talked and I listened, I became aware that we had something more than a gun in common. We were both on journeys of discovery. I was in search of a story, and the world that contained it. I was headed away from the isolate hell of grief and rage. John was in search of answers about his government, and this search was leading him away from his old comfortable world into a strange new one. We were each trekking through a wilderness and our paths had crossed.

His was not a pretty place. It was a place of continual struggle, a place of conspiracies, of secrets and lies. It was a war zone of dark against light that dwarfed my own perception of our ongoing cultural battles. I think a part of him sincerely regretted being there, but the vision of it occupied him with an obsessive intensity.

It occupied him so much that he had actually moved beyond his gun collecting phase. At one point I told him I had no sense of guns as collectable objects. Did they hold their value? Were they good from an investment standpoint? What would his collection be worth when his children inherited it?

"Nothing." he said, "There probably won't be anything for them to inherit."

There would be nothing left of his collection because the government would have confiscated it all. Gun registration was a perfect way to create a database of the people who owned guns, so that when the government was ready to seize them, they'd know right where to go. The same thing had happened in Nazi Germany. Did I know that the Nazis had instituted a strong policy of gun control so that they'd be the only ones with weapons? If you want to establish a totalitarian regime, one of the first things you have to do is disarm the citizenry. Didn't it make me wonder what all these gun ban campaigns were really about?

Or the terrorism thing. There was a perfect example. The bomb goes off at the Olympics in Atlanta (this had happened the night before my visit with John and reports of the catastrophe were all over the news that morning), and right away the government declares it a possible terrorist act. They do that, he asserted, because then the FBI can step in and suspend all the normal constitutional rights of citizens involved in the investigation. Didn't I see what was going on?

Or the Oklahoma City bombing. This was a perfect current example of the government not being honest with us. Did I know that the 4,500 pounds of ammonium nitrate explosive in that rental truck could not possibly have caused the damage, or the damage patterns, that resulted? It was a simple calculation that any engineer could do. There had to have been more explosives purposely placed in very specific parts of that structure to have caused the damage that resulted. He cited specific examples of inconsistencies in the damage and blast pattern, and explained how these could only have been caused by additional explosive charges. And if this was a plot against the ATF by Nichols and McVeigh, how come no ATF agents were injured in the blast? Had the feds done this themselves? What other people or groups, or countries might have been involved? And didn't I think it was odd that they'd been in such a bloody hurry to tear that building, the Murrah Building, down? Usually, in a case like this, they analyze every shred of evidence. Here, they could hardly wait to get in with the wrecking crane and bulldozers.

This was hardly what I had driven eight hours to hear, yet I was fascinated. The immensity of John's implication was truly, deeply frightening, but I tried hard to stay open, to let it keep coming, because I had an idea where he was headed.

Sure enough, after a few more minutes, his conspiracy theorizing led him back to guns; and sure enough, he believed that an armed populace was the one guarantee that the People could maintain their sovereignty in the face of this insidious federal takeover.

"People wonder what good small arms would do against a government supplied with tanks and helicopters and missiles and planes. But look at Afghanistan or Vietnam or Chechnya, or a dozen other places in the past few years. History has shown that a determined indigenous population, even lightly armed, can be effective against a mechanized occupying force."

Then I realized something I had overlooked until now. John already had the gun on his counter and we were discussing these things relating to it like medical students over a cadaver. He had not yet begun his attempt to dissect it.

"So this kind of gun ..." I said, pointing to the SKS.

"Exactly! That kind of tactical situation is what this kind of weapon was designed for. A population armed with these could very effectively thwart any attempts at a government takeover."

How strange it is to say this. I felt a tremendous satisfaction. I was giddy with it. Ever since Galen's death I had been looking for just one reason, other than selfish bang-bang pleasure, why anyone might think rifles like the SKS were necessary or useful to our society. Finally, thanks to John, I had it; even a shred of a possible excuse why these guns proliferated in such numbers. In the minds of people like John Hernandez, they represented a public reservoir, an ever-present arsenal with which as yet unformed citizen militias might protect themselves and their rights against the encroachment of a totalitarian regime. The very knowledge that such a reservoir of weapons existed would be a strong inhibition to any government or group of individuals in a government trying to seize absolute power.

I thought about the gun magazines I'd read during the course of my research, and all those strange ads they carried for watertight storage boxes. Another piece snapped into place. Those boxes were for burying rifles. When the feds came to confiscate them you'd bury them out in your back yard or in the Berkshires or wherever, for when you really needed them. That was why John thought these damned guns were important. They were like an insurance policy for the continuance of the republic.

Could he himself envision such a takeover scenario actually occurring? He didn't know. But it was black, somber. He didn't like the way things were headed. It was, he said, like being in the grip of a boa constrictor. With each law, each regulation, the coils just got tighter.

John came back up from his basement with a small cardboard box of 7.62 x 39 mm. cartridges, the standard ammunition for the SKS. He removed one from the box and showed it to me. "These are what they call full metal jacket." he said. "Unlike soft nose or hollow point bullets, they're meant more to wound than to kill. This is military ammunition. The thinking is that it would be better to wound an enemy than kill him. If he's wounded you've tied up three of the opposing forces; the wounded man, one man to move him and one to patch him up. If he were dead, you'd only have taken one man out of commission."

Galen had been killed by a bullet designed to wound.

To my surprise he took the bullet, a shiny brass and copper thing, and jammed the nose of it right into that little depression at the base of the trigger guard, and pushed like hell. The gun started sliding on the brown paper, so I helped him hold it. It was covered in a layer of brown preservative goop called cosmoline. Soon our hands were covered with cosmoline. John stopped for a moment to catch his breath and rest his cramping fingers, and then resumed pushing. The entire weapon, he grunted, was meant to be field-stripped using no tool other than a cartridge. He wanted to do it the "right" way so that I'd see how simple the process was.

However, it wasn't simple. The button behind the trigger guard went in, reluctantly, and the trigger assembly moved a bit away from the stock. We could see that the cosmoline was acting as a glue as well as a protective coating. Now, he said, the entire metal part, the gun itself, should slide out of the wooden stock. But the metal gun-thing wouldn't budge. I tried to steady it while John pushed and pulled. The trigger assembly finally came free, but everything else stuck fast.

The exertion had made John's hands start to shake, the way one's muscles react to unaccustomed stress, and he had begun sweating profusely. His wife had joined us. She was small and pink. Her name was Shirley. As the tableau at the Formica island developed into a man-versus-gun struggle, Shirley started bringing sheets of white paper towel over to John. John would wipe his brow, and then wipe the brown cosmoline off his hands, put the expended towel on the edge of the Formica counter, and start again. After a few minutes, the pile of sweat-dampened, cosmoline-stained towels spilled off the counter and Shirley had to collect the whole mess and throw it away, then wipe her hands with a fresh towel, then get another one for John.

We continued talking while he worked. When he finished explaining about the reason for the existence of these kinds of guns, he explained why he'd returned that first Chinese SKS he'd bought, the one that Wayne had then bought used from Dave. The workmanship on that first gun had been lousy. They were all made from the same design, but on that first one the place where the barrel had gone into the breech was just a flange and a pin instead of being smoothly machined. The gas return had just been a pipe. The trigger guard, instead of being cast, was just a bent piece of sheet metal. It was real junk. He'd taken it apart once, refinished the wooden stock, and then sold it to Dave, who had then gotten him this SKS, which was of better quality. It was identical to Wayne's weapon in every respect, just better built and machined.

John remembered there was a lever in front of the magazine that had to be flicked, and again, with the nose of the bullet, he pushed on it. It didn't flick, but eventually it dislodged from the brown goo and moved grudgingly 90 degrees. Then we went back to pushing. The metal part of the gun moved inside the wooden part, but then stuck again. John was starting to get embarrassed. He said he didn't remember having this much trouble the first time, and that maybe it was time to consult the instructions.

He disappeared again, and Shirley and I chatted briefly. She'd spent her whole life in the Berkshires and she missed them. When they went back home, she said, it felt like the mountains embraced her.

Then John was back, and this time he had half a dozen stapled-together sheets of paper. The lettering on the pages was blurry, as if the text had been photocopied many times. I asked him if Wayne's gun had come with instructions. He said it had not.

Slowly, step by step, we sorted the procedure out, John naming each gun part now. The gas return tube, a metal pipe over the barrel, had to come off first. Then the receiver cover, the part over the bolt where the empty shells came out. John had forgotten about that. It was held in with a pin that had to be jiggled in just the right way, then the thing could slide free. Once that was accomplished, the bolt assembly separated into two parts and came out. Finally, after removing a pin in front of the trigger assembly, the metal guts of the thing slid out of the wooden stock. It must have taken us a half hour to get this far.

After we washed, John could show me how Wayne had replaced the wooden stock with a plastic one. Even more importantly, he could show me the magazine assembly and demonstrate his theory about why the gun had misfired.

The original ten-round magazine, as it came from the factory, slid front end first into the bottom of the gun, then the trigger assembly was inserted behind it. When the trigger assembly clicked into place, a pin in the front of the trigger assembly slid into a receiving notch at the back of the magazine, locking the magazine into place. This was the pin we'd had to remove to disassemble the weapon. On the outside of the trigger guard, there was a little metal projection that fit over a lip at the back of the magazine. John theorized that because the mail-order thirty-round magazines that Wayne used were removable, there was no way the notch-and-pin device could be used to secure the magazine. You'd have to remove the trigger assembly each time you inserted a new clip, which obviously Wayne did not do. So these mail order clips must have relied solely on that outer projection and lip to secure the magazine in place. It was a very imprecise fit, particularly on such a poorly constructed weapon. In John's view it was quite likely that Wayne had not been inserting the magazines with sufficient force. The lip on the magazine was just jamming against the metal projection on the trigger assembly, rather than clicking under it. This would have produced sufficient misalignment to cause the cartridges to misfeed after a few rounds.

When I had digested all of this, John reassembled the gun, put it in its original wrapper, and replaced it in the original cardboard mailing box. Then he wrapped brown paper around the box and sealed it with tape. The guns retained a higher value, he told me, if they were kept in their original shipping cartons. All his guns were kept in boxes. I took this as a hopeful sign. John Hernandez wasn't completely resigned to a totalitarian regime confiscating all his guns. He was still protecting their resale value.

I could not get from him precise information about how many guns were in his collection. I got the idea that he owned something like twenty assault rifles of various kinds. There were certainly other guns as well. He didn't display his guns, and he didn't talk about his gun collection in public or at work. He was concerned about the chances of his collection being stolen, and anyway it was sometimes "difficult" for people to understand his particular collecting interest.

He asked me if I'd like to see some other examples of the assault rifle type. Perhaps he could explain something about the evolution of the gun while he was at it. He brought up an old Kalashnikov in its wooden stock, with the Soviet designations stamped in the metal. It was a real collector's item, he said. He showed me its primitive features and then it went back in its box and downstairs, and up came a German rifle, the equivalent of the Heckler he'd first tried to buy, the gun that had started all this off. Compared to the other guns it was indeed a fine piece of machinery, heavy and smooth. The last gun he brought up looked more like a Star Wars weapon than something soldiers used today, but in fact it was one of the current models employed by European forces, and when I looked at it closely, the major features were the same.

John explained how such weapons had evolved at the end of World War II, to fit changing theories of battlefield warfare. The strategists no longer envisioned one man shooting accurately over a distance. They began thinking more in terms of the number of bullets that an individual soldier could throw at the opposition. The guns became shorter and lighter and easier to point, and they became faster, much faster. The bullets became smaller. Infantrymen no longer needed to be highly trained marksmen. Even the poorest shooter now had the capability of spraying a tremendous amount of lead at the enemy.

Each of the guns in John's collection varied from its military counterpart in only one respect. The fully automatic function, in which bullets came out rapidly one after the other as long as you kept the trigger depressed, had been disabled. The gun that Wayne or any of us could legally purchase would be disabled in the same fashion. You had to squeeze the trigger each time you wanted to fire a bullet.

I asked him again if he was still collecting any types of guns. He said no, that he hadn't bought a gun in the past two or three years, that he doubted he'd buy any more. The other quest was occupying all his attention now. We talked about Oklahoma City some more. We talked about the sudden lack of interest in the John Doe character, the other guy who'd supposedly been with McVeigh. Why had the feds stopped searching for him? We talked about the possibility of McVeigh being no more than a dupe for others. We talked about how interesting the McVeigh trial would be, assuming McVeigh survived to attend it.

John brought me a copy of the John Birch magazine *The New American*, which summarized the information about the disparity of the explosive used and the blast pattern and damage at the Murrah Building. He gave me two other issues of the same periodical, which linked McVeigh to German security under the Kohl regime, and described how America was rapidly becoming a police state. He gave me a copy of a publication issued by Jews Against Gun Control outlining the Nazi takeover scenario. He gave me a back issue of *Shotgun News,* which contained all the information I could possibly use about which gun modification parts were currently available on the open market. He gave me a copy of an article entitled "Dial 911 and Die" which let citizens know that the police were under no legal obligation to risk their lives protecting the citizenry, and that we'd better protect ourselves. He gave me a paperback book called *The Insiders* about the architects of the New World Order, and he gave me a catalog of books published by the John Birch Society. Finally, he gave me the name and date of an *Atlantic Monthly* article on guns by a man named Erik Larson.

We went out and stood on the front porch while Shirley snapped a picture of us, smiling like fools. He thanked me for keeping an open mind and hearing him out. I thanked him for being so generous with his time and information. I felt like he had given me as much as he could. But we never did get down into that basement, or wherever he kept all his guns, and I could only imagine them down there in their original boxes in the dark, wrapped in brown paper and taped tight, against the dreadful day they'd actually be needed.

16
MY OWN JOHN DOE

I did some sorting on the ride back. The country east of Rochester was large and rolling, and there was lots of room, big fields of hills with tree clumps like grazing elephants in the afternoon sun. My mind wandered around out there and probably made itself up before I reached Albany, but I held off a conscious decision till I'd had time to read all the material John had given me.

Ultimately I decided that John's world view was too relentlessly secular. Aside from the fact that the founders considered our rights God-given, there was no spiritual connection at all in the literature I perused, no escape, no uplift. John's gang of freedom fighters was as drab and hopelessly political as any bunch of Soviets or Brownshirts ever were. I didn't see any room in his New America for the likes of Thelonius Sphere Monk, or myself, for that matter. Anyway, I was a stone-liberal who'd grown up thinking Arthur Clarke's *Childhood's End* was great literature. The idea of a one-world government sounded just fine to me. How else were we going to get this poor sick planet together?

There was something sentimental about the way John wanted his America to be. He had a nostalgia for a simpler world in which one thing led directly and perceptibly to the next; a kind of mechanical, Newtonian universe. Perhaps this world had existed in the eighteenth or nineteenth centuries, but now we were all networked up and we moved around at the speed of light. Brown once told me, "It wasn't democracy that brought the Soviet Union down, it was the fax machine." I liked that idea. It went right to the heart of what was wrong with John's view.

As far as guns insuring the continuance of the republic, the concept had a sort of rough and ready appeal to it, real American. But it was John Wayne's America, not mine. The idea of firearms preserving individual freedoms was as gone as the America of 1800, as plowed-under as the Wild West. It had become essentially a Hollywood legend, important in who we were and how we saw ourselves, but having as little else to do with reality as most of what Hollywood churned out. Would I keep a gun in my home if I lived in a rough neighborhood? Maybe. Would I carry a handgun if I felt my personal safety continually threatened? Maybe, yes. But if the Republic needed saving, I'd save it with guile, a monkey wrench in the machine or a samizdat publication, not by standing in my front yard with an SKS while an Abrams tank rumbled down my street. That was Rambo bullshit. It was the kind of imaging that had gotten into the head of a sick kid and resulted in my son's death.

I was thankful to John, and I wished him well in his quest, but I was bound in a different direction.

Perhaps I should say I was bound in a different *wrong* direction, because I was certainly headed off on a toot.

Analyzing John Hernandez' world view wasn't the only thing I did on my return from Rochester. I'd gleaned an important fact out there, and was busy working it into a theory about the murders. That SKS had been damned hard to take apart and reconfigure. There was nothing intuitive about the operation. Either you knew which pin to remove and which lever to turn or you were in for a lot of experimental fiddling around.

When I got home there was a fat manila envelope on my desk. It contained the Case Report of the State Police officer who'd been in charge of the Wayne Lo murder investigation. It also contained the witness statements of about a dozen people, including Robert Herring, Sr. and Wayne

Lo's pals at Simon's Rock College. I worked this new information in with what I'd learned from John Hernandez and my theory sprouted wings.

I'd found out about this Case Report from the documents at Berkshire Superior Court, and was finally able to get access to it thanks to Downing and Capeless in the district attorney's office. At our first meeting, as I've already mentioned, Downing told me he felt it would set a bad precedent to have a private citizen rummaging through the files of a first degree murder case which was still under appeal.

He then asked me what kind of material I thought my lawyer had accumulated in preparing for our civil suit against the college. He mentioned that lawyers often request case files from the state police, and that often these requests are granted. These state police files contained much of the material that the DA had used in preparing his case, including the witness statements I was so eager to see. Capeless told me he thought that my lawyer had, in fact, requested these files from the state police.

They didn't exactly give me a big wink, but they had managed to tell me how I might be able to get the material I needed without giving it to me themselves. It was one of those happy occasions where the niceties of a prosecutor's logic chopping and the ideal of public service coincided. I consulted the lists of witness and police statements contained in the docket sheets, and faxed my lawyer a request for the dozen or so that I considered most important to my inquiry. Sure enough, he had obtained these from the State Police long ago. When I got back from visiting John Hernandez they were waiting for me, mailed first class and copied in triplicate to give the package a nice lawyerly bulk.

There was a statement from a kid named Robert Schork, who claimed that in the spring of 1992, six months before the murders, Wayne had tried to borrow his car to buy a gun. "The next day he (Wayne) approached me again and asked if my offer to drive him was still good. He asked if Kevin Wolak could come along. I asked him where he

wanted to go and he said Pittsfield. I asked where specifically and ...
he finally told me that he wanted to go to Pittsfield to buy a gun..."

Robert Herring's written statement contained essentially the same
story he'd told me. It established that Wayne Lo had been thinking about
an assault weapon at least since the fall of 1992. It also established that
there was someone else with him when he went gun shopping at Bob's
junk shop. This person was slender and stood six-foot-one or six-foot-
two. Herring stated that this person knew Wayne was looking for an
assault rifle.

According to what I'd learned at the criminal trial, and from various
statements by Wayne's pals, Wayne only had two opportunities, totaling
about three hours, in which to have assembled his SKS and loaded the
ammunition clips. Was this enough time for him to have done the job?
If he hadn't known what he was doing, maybe not.

According to John Hernandez, Wayne's gun had not come with any
instructions. In the lists of what had been confiscated from Wayne's
room after the murders, contained both in court documents and the
Case Officer's report, there were mentions of sales slips, and invoices,
but no mention of instructions.

I began to believe that someone had helped Wayne with that SKS.
Either they'd stood there with him and showed him how to do it, or
they'd mentored him; described in much the same way as I described
John Hernandez' efforts, how to take that gun apart. This would have
been known only to Wayne and the mentor. After the murders Wayne
said nothing about how he'd accomplished the crime. He was not called
to testify at the murder trial. The accomplice, having nothing except
possible criminal charges to gain from speaking out, had kept his silence.

Like the feds after the Oklahoma City bombing, I had my own John
Doe. Their John Doe had vanished in the mist, but mine was still around.
He'd gone to Robert Herring's shop with Wayne, and he'd probably
helped Wayne, in one way or another, with that SKS.

I remembered the reaction of Downing and Capeless to Herring's story. There had been a certain frustration, a dissatisfaction. Part of it was that they couldn't use his testimony, but the rest, I figured, was because there was still a loose end. One of Wayne's friends—and we talked about this possibility—might have known more about the gun that he'd let on. We hadn't named any names but we didn't have to. I knew what the choices were.

As days went by, I became more and more certain that Wayne had an accomplice. I became more certain of his identity. It was, perhaps, typical of people in my mental state. I had rejected the Lone Gunman theory in favor of a Conspiracy.

Back in December when I'd been on the first part of my walkabout, Rob Horowitz told me that his theater teacher had been convinced that a kid named Kevin Wolak had helped Wayne with the gun. I had decided back then to talk to Wolak. I wanted to hear from someone who'd known Wayne, who might be able to give me some insight into the kind of psychological changes that had turned an alienated kid into a killer.

I had called the family home a couple of times, and eventually reached Kevin's father. To my surprise Wolak senior refused to let me speak with his son, or even to tell me where Kevin was living. It was over now, he said. Done. Settled. There would be no point in dredging the awful business back up. Kevin had made a statement to the police. That was all he had to say. Mr. Wolak was cold, adamant and unsympathetic. I was shocked. I called again and got the same refusal. I wrote a letter and received no answer. It was most strange. Of all the people I'd approached, Wolak was the only one who refused to even speak with me. Certainly he'd been hiding something. Now I had a pretty good idea what it was.

I found the witness statement to which Kevin's father had referred, and I read it closely. In this statement Kevin said, "I've known Wayne since the beginning of school ... We got to be very good friends ... Wayne and I are both pretty far to the 'right' ... Wayne often spoke about getting an automatic weapon and going into the cafeteria and shooting people at random. He would target African Americans one time then Jews or homosexuals another time ... (The day of the murders) I saw Wayne around 3:30 P.M. in the cafeteria. We were taking a test so we didn't talk then. After the exam we met outside the cafeteria. He said, 'I got it, an SKS!'"

Then Kevin Wolak went on to admit, "I have an SKS myself. It is a 7.62 mm. Chinese semiautomatic rifle. My SKS is at my home in Connecticut."

This kid lived west of Hartford, not too far over the state line from Great Barrington and Simon's Rock College. It was easy to imagine him getting a car for a weekend and driving around with Wayne looking for guns. It was easy to imagine the two boys driving to Kevin's home and spending some quality time with Kevin's SKS.

There were dozens of inexpensive weapons available on the open market. Was it just coincidence that Wayne chose to purchase the same type of Chinese SKS that Kevin owned? Was it just coincidence that Wayne had told Robert Schork he wanted to go gun shopping with Kevin Wolak?

Ever since the murders I'd known that Galen and Brooks had been friends with a girl named Kara Jessen, who'd been friends with Wolak. It was one of those small-world coincidences that linked our family, sort of through a back alley, with Wayne Lo. I told Brooks I wanted to talk to Kara and he got her number for me. I called her in Manhattan, where she was staying for the summer.

It was an interesting conversation, to say the least. Kara and Kevin had been friends as teenagers, and she had spent her first year of high school with Kevin before he'd transferred to Simon's Rock. She'd been a sophomore when Galen was killed. She told me that both Kevin's parents were very restrictive, and "sort of weird." Kevin had always been really angry, often for reasons that were not clear to her. He'd been a skinhead in high school, but had not been as ardently racist as he now seemed to be.

She told me he'd changed a lot after the shootings. He'd moved away from his parents but was still in Connecticut somewhere. She thought maybe he'd gone to a local community college for a while. She knew he'd had a job, but had been fired for incompetence. She said, "I don't really know him anymore ... Now he just gets drunk all the time and bitches about the world." In her opinion Kevin went off the deep end after the shootings, into some kind of redneck, white-trash mode. "I pretty much think this is it for him. He's over the edge. I don't really understand him anymore."

Might Kevin have showed Wayne about guns? There was no doubt in her mind. He'd always loved guns and had great interest in them. She remembered when he got his first gun, how excited he'd been ...

According to her physical description Kevin was six-one or six-two, skinny but muscular, with dark hair.

That pretty much clinched it for me.

Now I had the little son of a bitch. I'd go down to there and get a motel. Stake the house out, check the city directories and find out what old man Wolak did, where he worked, nose around at the cop shop, see if Kevin had ever been in any trouble, get the goods on the whole family. Then I'd confront the old man. Tell him I knew all about his dirty laundry, that he couldn't hide the truth from me.

Then I'd go after the kid.

First, however, I had to go after some more money. Bills were piling up and my book business was showing signs of neglect.

I was always complaining about this to Annie, how my bookselling activities took me away from working on the Galen story. In this case, however, I was damned lucky to have something to take me away from the Galen story, because I was right on the verge of making a serious mistake; one that would certainly have proved embarrassing, possibly harmful.

I began assembling the materials I'd collected for my next rare book catalog, and immersing myself in them. I had accumulated some wonderful stuff over the summer. There was the manuscript journal of a clipper ship captain's first command, full of his own nervousness and worry. There was a large group of letters from an American trader in China in 1842, just as the Opium Wars were heating up, in which he described the political and military situation in detail and told his brother back home that they ought to think of getting into the opium business. There was a rare coast pilot for California waters, written at the height of the Gold Rush. In all there were a couple of hundred manuscripts and books to study and catalog so that I could eventually sell them. They took me out of my own troubled days, back to a rich and varied past that was already securely in place. It was from this nineteenth-century vantage point that I looked up at my own life in the twentieth century, and realized I'd almost committed a blunder.

It occurred to me then that I was not going to solve the Wayne Lo murder case. Somebody had already done that. They'd had a trial, proved Wayne Lo guilty, and locked him up. This Wolak obsession of mine was nuts. It wasn't going to fix anything. It wasn't going to bring Galen back.

So what if Kevin had been interested in guns with Wayne? So what if they'd talked about his gun back home? So what if they'd even gone to see it and Kevin had showed him how it worked? In his statement, Wolak had also said of the shooting, "I couldn't imagine why on earth he would actually have done it. This was the most senseless thing I'd ever heard of." Should I believe the rest of his statement and not believe this?

Sure I was angry at old man Wolak for refusing to talk to me. Sure I was angry at all Wayne's friends. But what could I possibly gain by launching a vendetta against the Wolak family? The mechanics of assembling that gun and Kevin's possible involvement in it were no more than an interesting sidelight to the case, one that I might pursue later. It certainly wasn't what my search was about.

Then another theory presented itself to me. There was no doubt that old man Wolak was hiding something. But what if the secret he was hiding was just that his son was a mess? What if he was simply ashamed that his boy had become an alcoholic who couldn't hold a job or stay in school? He wouldn't want me to discover this, with my own murdered, perfect son making Kevin look so much the worse. And suppose the murders really had sent Kevin close to the edge? Maybe Mr. Wolak really did think that talking to me would upset the boy. Maybe Kevin was hanging in the balance and the old man was terrified of making him worse.

Bernie Rodgers and Ba Win, the insurance companies and Leon Botstein, and now Kevin Wolak. Did I detect a pattern here? Something like slamming myself against the wall of my padded cell, collapsing on the floor, then getting up and charging the wall again?

This was difficult! There was probably some therapeutic value in the process of getting angry at these guys, recording what I learned in the course of getting angry, and then realizing there was nothing to be gained by being angry. But it was a pattern that could repeat itself forever without getting me anywhere.

On the other hand, where did I think I was going to get? I wasn't going to fix anything. Galen wasn't coming back.

Failure was a part of the job.

❧§17
WAYNE'S GUN

Until about 1865 bullets and their propellants were loaded into guns by hand, usually from the front end of the barrel. After the Civil War, breech-loading firearms came into dominance and soon these new weapons gained another dimension by becoming repeaters. Winchester, Spencer, Mauser, Chassepot and other arms manufacturers around the world designed a variety of systems for getting cartridges to feed, one after another, into the firing chambers of their guns. By the end of the nine-teenth century the typical military rifle was bolt action and magazine-fed. It weighed ten or twelve pounds, measured about fifty inches in length, and was accurate over distances of a thousand yards or more. It was fed by a magazine which contained a few bullets that came out as fast as the soldier could work the bolt.

Inventors were struggling to introduce the concept of automatic oper-ation into small arms design. The idea, as it was developed, employed either the recoil of the rifle or the gas released by firing to eject the spent cartridge and load a fresh cartridge into the breech, thereby eliminating the time-consuming manual accomplishment of these actions. The engi-neering required was too complex to produce a reliable automatic rifle for the onset of World War I, but the great powers were able to adapt automation to slightly larger "machine" guns. Notably, the American genius (and I do not use this word ironically) Hiram Maxim invented a machine gun based on the recoil principal. It was adopted by both the Germans and the Allies and it dominated the War to End All Wars. In many ways a weapon that has never been equaled, Maxim's machine gun weighed just under fifty pounds, was modular in design with read-ily replaceable parts, and could fire ten thousand rounds per hour indef-initely. It has been estimated that this weapon was responsible for ninety percent of World War I's thirty-one million dead.

By World War II a number of self loading rifles had been designed. Some of these were semi-automatic. Each squeeze of the trigger delivered a round, ejected the spent cartridge and loaded a new round into the firing chamber. Others, such as the famous Browning Automatic Rifle, could also fire in the fully automatic mode, which delivered bullets con-tinuously as long as the trigger was held down. Weighing in at about twenty pounds, the BAR stood on the cusp between a rifle and a light machine gun.

Continued experimentation with automatic small arms and a fuller understanding of the way soldiers might use them ultimately resulted in the evolution of a new type of weapon, the so-called assault rifle.

An assault rifle, while it still fires from a locked breech like the battle rifles of World War II, is shorter and lighter. It utilizes a less powerful "intermediate" cartridge, larger than pistol ammunition but smaller than a full-sized rifle cartridge. It is capable of firing in both semi-automatic and fully automatic modes and it employs large capacity detachable magazines. As John Hernandez had told me, this type of rifle was developed in response to a change in tactical thinking; away from single shot high accuracy, toward increased firepower and high mobility. With this new kind of weapon a soldier could carry twice as much ammunition, and deliver it faster if need be. However accuracy limits were in the hundreds, not thousands of yards.

The Germans produced the first true assault rifle. Near the end of World War II the Wermacht fielded a gun called the StG-44, which was designed with the new tactical considerations in mind. The concept was picked up by the British and the Russians after the war, with the Russian version, the Avtomat Kalashnikova Model of 1947, or AK-47, emerging as the most successful of its type. In its standard configuration this gun was about thirty-four inches long. It weighed a little over ten pounds, employed thirty-round magazines and was capable of firing six hundred rounds per minute.

The United States was slow in recognizing that the battle tactics of the Second World War were obsolete. As late as 1958 we were still promoting the M-14, a full sized infantry rifle. Bad experiences in competition with the AK-47 in Vietnam prompted the U.S. to accept the assault rifle concept, and the result was the M-16. After some early development problems our M-16 became the standard military assault rifle outside the Soviet bloc. Meanwhile, countries like Finland, Israel and Belgium were improving upon the venerable Kalashnikov design. The results were second-generation weapons such as the Finnish Valmet and the Israeli Galil. We are now in a third generation of weapons design, with the French FAMAS, the British LIW and particularly the Austrian AUG dominating. These new guns continue to grapple with the basic problem of how to make the weapon as light and compact as possible without significantly reducing barrel length and accuracy.

For all the technological innovations that have been introduced since World War II, the reliable AK is the most widespread design, with over fifty million having been manufactured. In 1956 the Chinese produced their own version of the AK. These found their way into the Vietnam conflict and were quite successful in competition with the more sophisticated M-16. After the war the Chinese military continued producing these guns. As with other descendants of the AK, their simplicity, cheapness and reliability have made them the preferred weapons in dozens of third-world conflicts.

Contrary to what you might have gleaned if you had been reading newspaper accounts of Galen's murder, Wayne Lo's gun had little to do with any of this.

His gun was an SKS Chinese Type 56 Carbine. This weapon, an evolutionary predecessor of true assault weapons, had been developed in the 1930s and 1940s by a Russian named Simonov. It was a carbine, which by definition is a short rifle. It was configured like a battlefield rifle and it was about ten inches longer than the AK-47. Although it was gas operated like the AK, and although, like an assault rifle it employed intermediate-sized ammunition, it was capable only of semiautomatic fire. The first models were in the hands of Russian troops by the end of World War II but it was not mass-produced until 1946. In 1956, just as they had done with the AK, the Chinese began making their own copies of Simonov's rifle, engineered so that they could be manufactured quickly and inexpensively under relatively primitive conditions. The Chinese stamped out millions of them, and their continued production has provided Communist China with considerable revenue.

After Galen's murder the confusion of this Chinese carbine with the Chinese version of the AK assault rifle was rampant in the media. For example, a couple of days after the murders the *Boston Herald* called Lo's gun "an SKS assault rifle" and stated, "The SKS is very similar to the better known AK-47 military rifle." A *Boston Globe* article from the same day was illustrated with photographs of AKs and M-16s. It is easy to imagine NRA activists and gun-savvy collectors like John Hernandez gnashing their teeth over such spectacular and exploitative displays of misinformation. The AK, with its big, curling clip and pistol grip looks nasty and lethal. The Chinese SKS, with its ten-round magazine looks exactly like what it is—an undersized rifle.

Military guns have always found their way into America's civilian marketplace. In 1934, after Machine Gun Kelly and the Tommy gun had amply demonstrated the hellish potential of the new automatic weapons, the federal government prohibited the sale of any "full-auto" guns on the domestic market. No rifle sold over the counter to civilians today is capable of fully automatic fire. The AK or any so-called assault rifle may look and feel like its military counterpart, but if you squeeze the trigger of one of the domestic models, only one shot will come out for each squeeze, rather than a burst of fire that continues as long as the trigger is held down.

In that their full-auto function is disabled, none of the deadly looking rifles currently on the market are truly "assault rifles." The NRA is absolutely correct that this terminology has been abused by the media and by anti-gun interests. However, it is also a fact that, in terms of their ability to do harm, there was no difference between the SKS Wayne bought and the AK the newspapers made us think he'd bought. This is because both kinds of guns accept thirty-round magazines. The thing about these high-capacity magazines is that they are replaceable. You can load them up ahead of time and slap in a fresh thirty-round clip when the old one is expended. In other words, it made no difference whether Wayne had an AK or an SKS. Both were limited by law to semi-automatic fire, but both accepted detachable thirty-round magazines. Such magazines are the last vestiges these weapons bear of their intent as military tools. They were not designed as hunting rifles. They were designed to kill or maim enemy forces, and to do it as efficiently as possible.

The proliferation of Chinese weapons in America is probably an issue that NRA people would rather not discuss in great depth. John Hernandez' first SKS cost him something under $200. When Wayne Lo bought it, used, it cost $129. His 200 rounds of imported Chinese ammunition cost him, via Classic Arms, about $25. In contrast, Ruger's sporting version of the 7.62 x 39 carbine, their "Mini Thirty Rifle" would have cost Wayne about $580 new (and it would only have come with a five-round magazine). The scary-looking Colt version of the M-16 would have cost him $1,000. The Chinese SKS is plentiful and cheap, and the story of how it got here has more to do with sloppy foreign policy than with Second Amendment ideals.

In 1980, the People's Republic of China was granted most-favored-nation status. This allowed them to export goods to the US under the lowest possible tariffs. In 1983, according to ATF statistics, China exported seven rifles, two handguns and 1,300 rounds of ammunition to this country. Then in 1987, as our relations with China warmed, State Department bureaucrats approved an agreement that allowed The People's Republic of China to export light industrial products to the US. Along with typewriters, bicycles and barbells, these goods included the AK and SKS rifles that were still being produced in factories controlled by the Chinese military. This trade agreement was never reviewed by Congress or widely publicized, it was just part of a softening of our larger foreign policy regarding Communist China. American firms were already selling weapons and weapons-related technology to China, and the Chinese demand for access to the U.S. market was seen as fair reciprocity. After the 1989 Tiananmen massacre, President Bush stopped U.S. weapons sales to China, but their weapons sales to us continued.

By 1991 China was sending twenty-five percent of its exports to the US, including 100,000 rifles annually. Because its most-favored-nation trade status kept being renewed each year, it continued to pay low tariffs. As the trade door opened wider, the Chinese saw their opportunity and seized it with vigor. In 1992 Chinese rifle exports to the U.S. jumped to 1.42 million (they were accompanied by almost one million handguns).

Our permissive culture soaked these guns up as fast as they could be shipped. They were marketed as hunting or target rifles; but to reiterate, the concept behind the SKS tends away from marksmanship, toward portability and firepower. You could go deer hunting with an SKS, and many people have, but if you want to hit your target, rather than riddle it with bullets, there are better guns to use.

A lot of the SKSs thus marketed got used a few times, then wound up in closets or attics, or buried in the backyards of people awaiting a government takeover. Some of them got modified with folding stocks, muzzle brakes and other after market accessories, and dragged to target ranges by grownups with Rambo fixations. Some were used in the commission of crimes (again, the NRA is correct. These weapons are *not* the favorite of criminals). A very few fell easily into the hands of dangerous individuals. Wayne Lo shot up Simon's Rock with his SKS, while Patrick Edward Purdy massacred school children in California and Mir Aimal Kansi shot motorists outside CIA headquarters in Virginia with AK-47s or variants thereof. These rifles may not have been the chosen weapons of drug lords, but the crazies liked them. Why? Probably because they were available and cheap.

If I were a Chinese Communist leader, I couldn't imagine a better way to destabilize American society than to flood it with inexpensive weapons and ammunition. And, if I were to get paid in useful hard currency for doing it, so much the better.

Congress tried to control the problem in 1994, after the nut-case shootings had started to pile up. Following Galen's murder there was a series of television news shows exposing a big Chinese import company with bases in the US for the importation of light industrial products from mainland China, including guns like the SKS. A man named Eftimiades who worked for the Pentagon showed that some of these Chinese export companies were also centers of espionage in the US. An import ban on Chinese rifles was passed by Congress in 1994, and by 1995 the shipment of these weapons from China had been reduced to a trickle.

We had closed the barn door but the wolves were already inside. Added to domestic guns and imports from the former Soviet Union (a story in itself), there are millions of Chinese firearms circulating in this country today. Many thousands were shipped before the ban and remain in warehouses, whence they continue to be sold.

There's one other aspect to all of this that NRA types don't discuss much. Back when the Second Amendment was written, guns were still made one at a time, and Americans were using single-shot flintlock muskets for the most part. Here's what Carl P. Russell, in his book *Guns on the Early Frontiers*, has to say about the operation of such weapons:

> The process of loading the piece entailed placing the hammer at the half cock, opening the pan, removing a cartridge from the cartridge case which the soldier carried at his side, carrying the cartridge (in the right hand) to the mouth, and tearing the paper with the teeth. A priming charge was then poured from the broken cartridge into the open pan and the steel was pulled back, shutting the pan; the butt of the musket was dropped to the ground; the powder was poured from the cartridge into the muzzle and the ball was inserted; the ramrod was drawn and turned end for end and inserted upon the ball and the wadded cartridge paper; these were rammed home with two forceful blows. The ramrod was then withdrawn from the bore, turned with its small end to the first pipe, and forced down to its place under the barrel. The piece was then ready for cocking and firing.

The rate of fire for an expert marksman was four or five rounds in two minutes.

What would the authors of the Bill of Rights have said about the rights of city dwellers to bear concealable weapons that fired bullets as fast as the trigger was pulled? How about Ingram M-10s, spitting out entire thirty-round magazines in an eye-blink, or inexpensive, semi-automatic, military-style rifles with high-capacity magazines, available at your local sporting goods store for about the price of an hour with a shrink?

The "arms" that the founding fathers thought about keeping and bearing didn't need defining in 1800.

They do now.

❦18
THE AWFUL TRUTH

You would think this business of telling one gun from another should be fairly simple, but some people have more trouble with it than others. The Massachusetts State Legislature, for example, found it impossible. The result was the Assault Weapons Ban debacle of 1996.

This round of legislation had been in the works since 1995, when a package of petitions for gun control laws was introduced by State Attorney General Scott Harshbarger. He had been a consistent gun control advocate and had enlisted the aid of like-minded state legislators to help pursue his agenda. As it also happened, Harshbarger was thinking of running for governor because Governor William Weld was thinking of running for the U.S. Senate. Gun control was an issue that resonated with the public and Harshbarger knew that successful passage of some kind of gun control legislation would be a good thing for him to accomplish.

The petitions were referred to the Committee on Public Safety, which was headed by the same legislators who, in 1991, had approved the change in residency laws that had enabled Wayne Lo to buy his gun. They scheduled a public hearing on the proposed legislation at the Massachusetts State House.

I got there early and watched the auditorium fill up. The pro-gun people outnumbered the anti-gun faction by 5 to 1, easily. The gun guys tended to have bushy beards, baseball caps and camouflage clothes or fatigues. If it wasn't beards and camo it was flannel shirts or down vests, big belt buckles, not many suits and ties. They all wore buttons that said "Crime Control, Not Gun Control." They all carried informational leaflets that explained the several proposed bills, and had very clear instructions about how to testify before the committee. This information was disseminated by the Gun Owners Action League, a Massachusetts lobbying group.

Admittedly, the people at that hearing were only the zealots from both ends of the issue. There must have been millions of reasonable, pro- and anti-gun citizens out there with real lives and moderate, sensible, not very dearly held ideas on the matter, who looked nothing like the guys I am talking about. However, they weren't going to be at the State House this morning. They had jobs to do, kids to raise. There was nobody at this hearing but us fanatics.

In contrast to the pro-gun guys, the anti-gun faction was in disarray. Some were against all guns, some were specifically against handguns, and some were only against assault weapons. They were uncertain how the hearing was to proceed, or of the exact content of each petition. They wore white ribbons on their lapels.

Eventually the crowd settled down. The politicians stopped hobnobbing up front, people found seats, the chairman brought the hearing to order, and witnesses began giving testimony. Because the committee was hearing statements on several aspects of the gun control package, the witnesses cited statistics or related anecdotes that supported or invalidated any one of these several aspects. The overall effect was one of passionate confusion.

A septuagenarian ward-heeler and career politician got up before the Committee and proceeded to tell the audience how these two scumbags waved a machete in his face, *right in his own driveway* ... and the other guy had a portable weed whacker ... coulda taken my face off ... and I reached for my Piece and told him, I'll blow your head off. That was the only thing that saved me ... I'll tell you. This country is coming

apart from the inside ... Right, rights. All they want is their rights ...
I'd like to give them their *last* rights ... har har.

He brought the house down, a whole auditorium full of gun guys
roaring their approval in a single angry male bellow.

Up stepped Michael Kennedy, Bobby's son, serving his political
apprenticeship, paying his dues addressing the Committee on Public
Safety. He told us that there were more guns in the United States than
there were people, and that a new gun was being manufactured every
twenty seconds. He thought this was an insane situation. There was
scattered applause from the few who agreed with him, but the clapping
was drowned out by an intimidating round of boos. It must have been
frightening, or at least disheartening, to have been a one-hundred-thirty-
five-pound Quaker, let alone a one-hundred-seventy-pound Kennedy,
in that room full of bearish gun-toting galoots. But, maybe Quakers
were used to that sort of thing. Certainly, Kennedys were.

Mostly, it was politicians and people from inside the system who
spoke. The chief lobbyist for the Gun Owners Action League gave a
concise, witty, fact-filled presentation. He pointed out inherent flaws in
the proposed gun bans and told us of the welter of regulatory laws
already on the books that went unenforced.

A doctor got up and said that guns kill people. They are a public
health hazard that should be much more controlled, if not eliminated
entirely. It was all well and good for us to toss around these facts and
figures, but if we worked in an emergency room and saw the carnage
that guns produced on a daily basis, we'd think differently.

But we didn't all work in emergency rooms. We each thought whatever we thought and we knew we were right. It made us angry, pro and
con, that we weren't getting what we wanted.

By 2:30 that afternoon, the committee chairs, not having had lunch,
began to vent *their* frustrations back at the witnesses, saying how hard
they had been working to get some consensus on an effective legislative

course, and all they were getting was impossible demands. To the physician one legislator said, "So what you want is the elimination of all guns, is that right?"

"Yes."

"Well, we can't *do* that!"

Finally, near the end, I got up and told them how Galen had been murdered by a boy who'd made an entirely legal purchase. I told them that if the proposed legislation had been in effect then, Galen would still be alive today. This having been noted, I went home.

After listening to all the witnesses and considering all the facts at their disposal, the Committee on Public Safety recommended that the proposed legislation be "held for further study"—in other words, disposed of.

Later in the legislative season, despite the recommendation of the Committee, the bill was brought to the floor. In February of 1996 the Massachusetts House passed a bill banning twenty-five types of so-called "assault weapons." By June the bill was in the Senate, and under threat from pro-gun forces. First they succeeded in passing an amendment that reduced the number of named weapons from twenty-five to fifteen. Then they came up with a proposal to strip the ban entirely and replace it with "Crime Control, Not Gun Control" legislation. It looked momentarily bad for the weapons ban, but help was on the way. Governor Weld, also lining up his political ducks, came out in favor of an assault weapons ban. Enough support then existed in the Senate so that, on its final reading, the proposal to ban assault weapons was approved.

However, the senators, in their wisdom, could not agree which specific weapons should be banned. They resolved to pass a weapons ban and leave it up to an otherwise undefined special committee to decide at an unspecified later date which weapons would be included in the bill. This was the measure that finally passed the Massachusetts legislature in July of 1996.

Polls showed that the public favored some kind of gun control, but there was no consensus on what kind. Harshbarger saw it as an area where he could define his position, and many of the urban legislators were under a public mandate to act on this issue. This was enough to get some kind of legislation started. But what about the rest of our duly elected Solons up there in the State House? The public wanted some kind of gun control, but nobody knew what kind. What should they do about it? Simple! Just vote for gun control, but don't say what *kind* of guns you want controlled. Let somebody else decide that later.

It was brilliant. It was awful.

Eventually, I came to understand that the Assault Weapons Ban debacle was about money and power, not necessarily about right and wrong. According to the American Shooting Council, the firearms industry contributes $20 billion and 690,000 jobs to the nation's economy each year. This statistic was intended to show how important the gun business is to the national economy, but it also demonstrates that the industry is big enough to wield considerable political clout. Hundreds of millions of dollars are spent annually at national and local levels by pro-gun organizations, the NRA being chief among them, on advertising, lobbying and direct political contributions.

As long as it is guns versus no-guns in the legislative forum, the pro-gun factions will have enough political power to protect their interests. The result will be gridlock or gutless legislation of the sort I saw in 1996. Despite the posturing of politicians on the gun control issue, there doesn't seem to be much hope for legislated bans of specific weapons as a solution to gun violence.

However, there is another way to approach the problem.

In 1992, the year of Galen's murder, 37,000 Americans died from firearms. Only about half of these were murders, and half of those murdered knew their killers. Fewer than one quarter of those who died lost their lives to that stranger in the dark alley, the nameless thug that the "Crime Control, Not Gun Control" people put forward as the cause of most gun violence.

It is a simple fact that access to guns increases the chances of being killed or wounded by a gun. From a public health point of view, the gun is a potentially dangerous consumer product, as much as it is a symbol of one of our constitutional rights. Seen in this light, firearms are simply another product that needs to be regulated—not banned— like booze or automobiles or any similarly hazardous item to which the public has access.

The public health argument makes sense from an economic stand-point as well. Accidents, suicides and gun violence cause an annual health care bill in the billions of dollars. Add the totals of lost wages and rehabilitation expenses, and the final cost neutralizes any economic benefits proposed by the American Shooting Council. Wayne Lo's $129 gun cost society many millions of dollars in legal fees, medical bills, insurance payments and prison expenses.

Pro-gun ideologues have joined with the domestic firearms industry to fight this approach tooth and nail, usually under the banner of our inviolable constitutional rights.

As far as I was concerned, the very fact that it made the NRA nervous spoke well for the public health argument for firearms regulation. How-ever, the thing that clinched it for me was a study released in 1997 by the Centers for Disease Control. Their research showed that American youngsters were about five times more likely to die by gunfire than young people in the rest of the industrialized world.

If this is the price our children must pay for a freedom their elders enjoy, we need to re-examine the contract.

❦19
THE UN-GUN

Suddenly Celia was five-foot-nine.

It wasn't really sudden, of course; it only felt that way to me. Deep in the winter of 1996–1997, I was sitting in the kitchen drinking my bourbon and reading the paper, in just the proper retrospective mood. She was in the living room with the music on, stepping through the choreography for one of her figure skating routines. I glanced out at her and all at once she seemed to fill the room. She wasn't a baby anymore. She was a willowy thirteen-year-old dancing around out there in the aura of her own uniqueness. She was smart, funny, self-assured and right on the edge of being a woman. She was going to be just fine.

She'd been too young, too unformed, when Galen died, to take it all in. Her process of dealing with his death had been gradual, unfolding as she matured. This was a progress Annie and I followed anxiously. In fact, we were concerned about both Celia and Brooks. We could never be sure that the trauma of Galen's murder hadn't planted a time-bomb somewhere inside them. Brooks coped bravely and visibly, though mostly in silence, every day. Celia seemed largely unaffected by any of it and then, two years after the shootings, she had her crisis. She'd just turned eleven.

Annie and Celia and I had gone fishing at a little cove over in Rockport. It was a beautiful summer evening, the air was soft and sweet and Celia had made up a song to all the fish in the ocean to come to her hook and get caught. She sang it over and over, and in that drowsy ending of the day, against the warmth of the rocks, it put us all in a trance.

On the way home she was strangely silent and removed, and then she became hysterical. It took hours to calm her down and discover the problem. Celia explained that she had been singing to the fish to come onto her hook and that she then realized that meant the fish would die. She'd been singing to them to come and die. Then, gazing into the great wide ocean, she thought about Galen being dead, and about how badly she missed him, and she realized that if she wanted to see him, all she'd have to do would be to die, too. It seemed so simple and gentle and possible at that moment, under the velvety dusk. It called her, just as she'd been calling the fish. Then she became terrified. She didn't want to die! But it was calling, calling ...

In the immediate aftermath of this incident, Annie and I feared that perhaps Wayne Lo's evil and the college's ineptness had claimed another innocent victim. Yet in the long run we saw that this had not happened. Celia had realized Galen's death, and the possibility and terror of her own death. She had confronted these things, and survived them, and was beginning to work them into her own understanding of the world.

It felt good to reflect on Celia's success, and I needed something to feel good about, because I was stuck deep in my bad season. This started each September 27th, with Galen's birthday, ran through the December anniversary of his murder, then through the misery of the holidays, and on into mud season. I had little interest in the outside world, little interest, to be honest, in life. I drank too much. I gained weight. My knees were giving out.

I visualized my place of refuge during these bad seasons as a little circle of light with utter blackness all around. It was as if I lived in a bunker, in a hole in the bottom of the year. And, as I hunkered down there through the winter of 1996–1997, that strange place was rendered stranger still because of what was in there with me.

Once again, I wanted to get a gun.

I was drawn into it step by step, each increment of which seemed no more than a logical extension of what had preceded it.

In the spring of 1996 I had switched the focus of my investigation from the college to a study of firearms, their history, and their place in our society. This proved to be a vast and fascinating topic. Despite my firm belief in the necessity of gun control, I actually began to get interested in guns. As time went on, my focus narrowed from firearms in general to military weapons, then to assault rifles, and finally to Wayne Lo's gun in particular.

Each step of the way, I found ample information to fuel my interest. There was the internet, of course, with its gun company home pages, and all sorts of chat rooms for Second Amendment zealots, survivalists, militiamen and gun freaks. There were libraries, with shelves of gun history, and book stores full of glossy paperbacks and magazine racks overflowing with the latest publications on new generations of firearms. My rare-book hunts now became research trips, as I scoured the shops of New England for old gun manuals. My information gathering verged on frenzy. I was learning new things every day, and soon, I thought, I would have sufficient material for a complete understanding of the gun Wayne Lo had used in the murder of my son. This intense node of activity produced a lurid glow. I saw it as a circle of light.

As soon as I narrowed my researches to SKS rifles and their operation, I recalled the miraculous malfunction of Wayne's gun. Each time he had inserted a new clip of ammunition, the gun had fired a few shots, and then jammed. This repeated failure had saved many lives on the dark night of December 14, 1992. In the darkness of 1996, it occurred to me that the logical extension of all my information-gathering should be a scientific experiment. Using the knowledge I was accumulating, I could purchase a gun and ammunition identical to the gun and ammunition Wayne had used. Then I could buy the same plastic stock and oversized ammunition clips and modify the gun exactly as he had. Finally, I would test fire the gun and see if I could duplicate Wayne's results. I would find out, once and for all, if that malfunction had been a fluke or the predictable result of using those cheap components; if Galen's death and the salvation of others had been God's Will or just a mundane event.

I was excited about this new plan. It seemed a hopeful sign that, even in my bad season I could have such a *useful* idea, and it was a relief to finally have something concrete and vitally important to do. This felt like the key to my whole investigation, and I bustled happily about my bunker making preparations to carry the plan forward.

I went to the archives of the Boston Public Library and found copies of the several magazines that, according to the prosecution at the criminal trial, Wayne had used to help him order his gun parts. Sure enough, in the back of one of them I found the ad for Classic Arms. I wrote for a catalog and was delighted when, several weeks later, it showed up in my pile of mail, a cheap cut-and-paste, photocopied and stapled thing. To me it was an object of fascination. There, in its pages, was my plastic stock, the one that would make my SKS look and feel more like a real assault rifle. And there, wonder of wonders, was the same cheap imported steel clad 7.62 mm ammunition Wayne had ordered. I was surprised because I thought these kind of bullets had been outlawed. Unlike the malleable copper cladding on more expensive bullets, the steel cladding on the Chinese bullets was prone to shatter on impact, causing more damage. The physical characteristics of these bullets must certainly have added to the severity of Galen's injuries, but this was not the issue for me now. The main thing was that those cheaper steel-clads were manufactured to a different standard. If I was going to run this experiment correctly, it was vital that I have them, and there they were! Still available from Classic Arms. It was as if the fates were conspiring to insure the success of my plan.

When I went to the Police Station to obtain my Firearms Identification Card, it seemed like the most natural thing in the world, just a part of my "research." I received the questionnaire that asked if I was crazy, a drug addict, or a felon. I answered these questions, in ball point pen, in the negative. Then I paid a few dollars, waited a few days, and picked up my FID Card without skipping a beat. Things were cracking right along. Now I could legally purchase any gun anyone could legally sell me. That felt good.

I encountered only a momentary roadblock in Annie. We'd just lit our woodstove for one of the first times in the season, and we were standing around it, congratulating ourselves on not being cold. I mentioned to her, in what I thought was an off-hand way, how exciting it was that soon I'd be purchasing and test-firing a gun just like Wayne Lo's. She didn't say anything. She just looked at me, through the shimmering heat the fire was sending up, then turned and went over to the counter and began working on dinner. She didn't have to say anything. After twenty-two years of marriage, I knew that look. It meant, "You're crazy. It's a stupid idea. But you're so stupid anyway that the more I try to argue you out of it, the more you'll want to try it. So I'm not going to argue about it." I realized that she didn't understand the importance of what I was trying to do, and that because of her faulty understanding, she'd been hurt by what I'd told her. I knew then that I would have to keep the whole experiment to myself.

Across the street from our house was an old building, scarcely more than a chicken coop, that we referred to as "the shop." This was where I stored my bookselling supplies, and where I housed books that were for sale on the internet. There was a work bench in the back of this building and it was there that I planned to modify my SKS. I worked on my books over there all the time. No one would know if I happened to spend a few hours working on the gun while I was at it.

Then I realized that getting the project out of my house wasn't enough. It wouldn't do to have a military rifle and ammunition laying around the shop, especially after my experiment had been completed. So I removed a ceiling panel from over the work bench and examined the space up in the rafters. It was tight and dry, and once the ceiling panel went back, no one would ever discover my hiding place. Who knew? If we ever did have John Hernandez's government takeover, I might need my SKS again.

My old friend Brown came up to spend Thanksgiving with Annie and Brooks and Celia and me. We had a lovely celebration, just us and Brown, and a few extra kids from the old gang who'd drifted in. Brown told me that his mother was doing better, and that he was still going on those prearranged dates, but that now there was something new in his life. He was playing the stock market. He'd had considerable success so far, more than with the women he'd been dating. His was an innovative approach. He explained it in detail over a bottle of Knob Creek bourbon, but as vivid as his explanation seemed at the time, the only words I clearly remembered were, "idiot savant."

We rested on Friday and then on Saturday Brown and I went out to lunch and, fortified with martinis, meandered up coastal Route 1 into New Hampshire, stopping at two gun shops on our way, inquiring after, and finding, SKS rifles. I let him in on my plan before we started out, but if Brown had any questions about the nature of the research for this particular chapter, he kept them to himself. The excursion was as matter-of-fact as getting my FID card. It was just Brown and Gibson out on another of their jaunts, just as we'd been doing since we were seventeen years old.

The first place we stopped was Big Al's, a distinctly fuck-you-if-you-don't-like-guns sort of a place, rambling and woodsy, with racks of miscellaneous longarms up and down the floor, and gun racks on the walls behind counters full of side arms. There were two SKSs on the rack there, cheap looking little things with beat-up wooden stocks.

The second place was a few miles farther up the road, and it was as unlike Big Al's as it could have been. The only thing I can think to call it is a gun boutique. It was aimed at another segment of the market than the backwoods guys who patronized Al's establishment. Seacoast Firearms was selling guns to middle class people, professional people; for home or self-defense, for recreational or target shooting, for family enjoyment. The store was clean and crisp and the sales people were offering customer service as well as firearms. Their one SKS was in much better condition than those at Big Al's.

In no time the clerk had me on the telephone with their SKS expert. This gentleman explained to me how one SKS was distinguished from another. Each was made in a certain armory in China, and the armory number was stamped on the left side of the receiver, the place at the back of the barrel that housed the bolt. All SKSs were essentially the same, except that some armories turned out a better product than others. If I knew the armory number of the SKS, he could search for it over the internet. He could probably find me just the gun I wanted.

The Armory number! I'd missed this bit of information in all my research, and having it now sent me into such high excitement that I couldn't look at any more guns. We drove for a bit, and then stopped for a beer as I chattered on about the importance of this data for the successful completion of my experiment.

Then we continued up the coast to Wallis Sands, where, years before, my mother and father had rented an apartment for a few weeks each summer. The place was still there, but it was boarded up now. We stopped the car and took a walk on the beach where I'd spent my childhood summers. The tide was out and the ocean lapped gently on the edge of the gleaming sand. We started reminiscing about the old days, and then somehow Brown got me talking about my family, and the fun we'd had here. It had been a safe and happy place for us, a refuge from the forces that seemed to be tearing our family apart, and revisiting this spot helped me recapture some of the good things from those difficult years. However incapable my mother and father and sister might have been of coping with the stresses and demands of family life, each had given me all the love they knew how to give. That gift had helped me survive them, more or less intact, and it was helping me survive Galen's loss as well.

"That's a good story, Gibson."

I knew what he was doing. He was trying to slow me down. He didn't really understand the importance of my plan, and he was trying to ground me, to keep me from going overboard with it. Well, that was all right. It was a caring gesture, and it felt good. But I was not about to be distracted.

After Brown left, I called Sgt. Steve DelNegro of the Massachusetts State Police. Sgt. DelNegro worked at the office of the Berkshire DA and it was his responsibility to keep track of all the evidence required by the District Attorney to prosecute his various cases. The way I first got to know him was as the case officer assigned to coordinate the State Police investigation of the shootings at Simon's Rock College. In the first horrible days after Galen's death, Steve DelNegro was the one who relayed to us what little information leaked out. He was a witness at Wayne Lo's criminal trial, and he was present throughout the proceedings to assist prosecutors Downing and Capeless. Annie, Celia and I soon established a rapport with him.

I had relied on his support and advice earlier in my research, and I did not hesitate to call on him for help now. I needed to learn the armory number of that gun and I wanted to do it through irrefutable channels rather than by rumor or second hand report. He told me he was certain that the Bureau of Alcohol, Tobacco and Firearms had done a trace on the weapon because the State Police had requested it. He did not have a copy of the document in his files, but he gave me the name and telephone number of the local ATF agent, a guy he'd worked with on other cases, through whom this trace had been requested.

This agent's name was Ken Varaille and he was as helpful as Steve said he'd be. He told me that he thought he recalled performing a trace on the gun at the request of the Massachusetts State Police but that, even if he did have a copy of the trace in his files, he could not simply turn the document over to me. In careful detail he told me where to write to request a copy of the trace, and exactly what to say. I was to write to the Disclosure Branch of ATF and I was to tell them that, under the Freedom of Information Act, I was requesting a copy of the trace on the gun that had been the weapon used to murder my son. I was to explain the circumstances of the murder and to state that my request was in no way related to any legal action pending in my son's or my family's behalf, Finally, I was to make it clear that I would be willing to pay any fees or costs necessary to produce the document.

I mailed my letter, and within two weeks I received a reply from Joyce A. Thomas, senior disclosure specialist at ATF. She told me that they were processing my request, and would have my results in a couple of weeks. I was so excited that I let those weeks pass with no word, certain that the senior disclosure specialist, who'd been efficient enough to send me a letter telling me she was working on my request, was trying her hardest to accomplish this difficult task of retrieval.

Christmas came and went and the gun thing and I were still hunched down there in that little circle of light.

In January I paid a visit to Sgt. Phillip Langton, a ballistics specialist for the Massachusetts State Police, and an important witness for the prosecution at Wayne Lo's murder trial. Sgt. Langton was cordial on the telephone and when I went to visit him at the State Police ballistic labs in

Sturbridge, Massachusetts, he was even more accommodating. I got a tour of the firing range and lab, and I even got to look through the split-image microscope that had enabled him to match shell casings test fired from Wayne Lo's gun with those found at the scene of the crime.

We talked about guns and crime in general, and about the Lo case in particular. The defense had tried, unsuccessfully, to embroil Langton in an argument about how close Wayne had held the gun to the car window when he'd murdered Ñacuñán Sáez at the guard shack. Apparently, they were trying to establish a scenario in which a crazed Wayne was shooting randomly—as opposed to the picture of a malignant, purposeful Wayne who put his gun up to the car window and fired.

Langton had test fired Wayne's gun in part to establish that it was the murder weapon, but also to collect samples of gunpowder residue and patterns of this residue at various distances from the muzzle. At the criminal trial he had shown that the chemical composition of the residue from test firings of bullets found in Wayne's possession matched the residue found on Ñacuñán Sáez's clothing. Sgt. Langton had also produced white cards into which he'd fired Wayne's gun from distances of six inches, a foot, a foot and a half, etc. The particular patterns of residue dispersal established by these repeated firings, when matched with residue from the crime scene, demonstrated that Wayne had shot Ñacuñán at very close range.

This line of argument was interesting but it was the sub-text of Langton's testimony that was more important to me now. In the course of these experiments Sgt. Langton had fired Lo's gun repeatedly. Had he experienced the same failure that Wayne had experienced? After a few shots had the gun misfired?

Yes.

It hadn't been a misfire in the sense of the primer not igniting the charge or of the propellant failing to send the projectile up the barrel. What was happening was that the magazine was improperly seated. After a few rounds it would slip down a bit and the bolt would be unable to feed a new cartridge into the chamber. Sgt. Langton found that if he pushed the magazine back up into place and cycled the gun by hand, manually working the bolt, he could get another round into the chamber.

I asked him if he thought this failure was characteristic of SKSs and thirty-round magazines in general or if it was confined to this particular gun and clip. He replied that he didn't know. This was a poorly made gun, and a cheap aftermarket magazine, but he had not tested enough SKSs in this configuration to make any generalizations.

I told him how I had been struck by the realization that the repeated failure of Wayne's gun had saved many lives at Simon's Rock College, and I told him how, lately, I had been wondering if this was a one-of-a-kind occurrence or the predictable result of combining a cheap gun, cheap ammo and a cheap clip. Had it been a "miracle" or merely the result of using bad equipment?

I told him I was interested in obtaining the same kind of SKS and the same kind of bullets and clip, and seeing if I could duplicate the experiment. Sgt. Langton did not respond to this, other than to look at me and nod his head, taking my statement in.

I told him I knew what kind of ammunition and magazine Wayne had ordered, and that now I was focusing on the SKS. I told him what I'd learned from the expert at Seacoast Firearms, that SKS rifles varied in quality and that the quality of their manufacture depended on which armory had produced the gun. I told him I had applied to the Bureau of Alcohol Tobacco and Firearms for a copy of the trace that had been done on the murder weapon, in hopes that it would provide me with the serial and armory numbers of Wayne Lo's gun, but that my request was at least temporarily stalled in red tape.

Sgt. Langton said, "Wayne Lo's appeal hasn't been heard yet. That gun is still being retained as evidence. Why don't you just go over to wherever they're keeping it and take a look at it?"

It was getting to seem like an awfully long time since I'd heard from the senior disclosure specialist. Finally, on January 28, 1997, I received another letter from Ms. Thomas. She wrote, "We were unsuccessful in locating information pertaining to a firearms trace. However, if you could provide us with a serial number and the approximate date of the trace ... we can conduct a more conclusive search."

I admit to having been disheartened by this response. The blackness was pressing hard upon my shrinking circle of illumination. I was desperate to put my gun scheme into action and she was making this impossible. Then, from I know not where, inspiration came.

The senior disclosure specialist needed the serial number of the gun so that she could furnish me with the trace so that I could learn the serial number of the gun. Very well then, I'd been in the military, I'd read *Catch-22*. I knew how to do this. I called Sgt. DelNegro.

"Wayne's gun is still being retained as evidence, isn't it?"

"Yes."

"And it's still in the vault over at the courthouse?"

"Yes."

"Do you suppose we could go take a look at it sometime?"

"I don't see why not."

So, a few weeks later, Steve and I went over to the Berkshire Country Courthouse, to the same office where I'd sat and read through all that trial evidence the summer before, and got the gun out for a closer look. Actually, the Clerk of Superior Court got the gun, since no one, not even Sgt. DelNegro, was allowed around back where the smiling ladies guarded the evidence.

It was not very big, not much longer than my arm, and it was not very heavy. One of the ladies placed it gingerly on the counter. Sgt. DelNegro picked it up, pulled the bolt back and checked that the firing chamber was clear. The magazine was not in place so I could see up into the bottom of the gun. In fact, when Steve drew the bolt back, I could see right through it. For a moment it seemed an oddly insubstantial thing to have displaced so many lives. That, however, was the last I thought of the gun in its context as a killing machine. Steve and I were soon drawn deep into its essential thingness.

On the right side of the receiver we found the serial number, and some other letters stamped into the metal. We flipped the gun over to read the armory number but found no such designation. We were shocked. We squinted and gaped. We held the gun at various angles to the light and looked up and down the length of it. Finally, right at the edge of the plastic handgrip we saw an indecipherable marking. It was clearly part of a symbol that had been stamped in the metal, but it disappeared under the handgrip and not enough of it showed to be legible. From what I'd learned on my gun trip with Brown I knew that the armory number was printed in stylized type inside a triangle. What we were looking at was the top portion of the triangle.

Wayne had replaced the original wooden stock with a plastic stock that made the SKS look more like an assault weapon. On this particular aftermarket stock, the folding shoulder piece was just a framework of plastic. A pistol grip extended down from behind the trigger guard, and the fore-end extended up to the front of the gun, a few inches short of the muzzle. This was all a single piece of molded plastic and it was intended to replace the single-piece wooden stock that held the metal parts of the SKS. It was somewhat larger than the original wooden stock and hence it obscured most of the armory number. We would have to disassemble the gun.

Steve removed the cleaning rod from the front end and, harking back to my session with John Hernandez, I remembered there was a retaining pin at the back of the receiver cover that slid out, allowing disassembly of the bolt mechanism. Soon the parts of the bolt mechanism were spread over the counter and we were busily trying to figure out how to separate the plastic stock from what remained of the body of the gun.

We did not lack for advice and counsel. Court officers, cops and lawyers went in and out of the Clerk's office on business of their own. Many of them knew Sgt. DelNegro, whose office was just a few blocks away. Several, sensing our increasing bewilderment, regaled us with gun jokes. A few offered to help. One kind soul, after watching us poking and probing with ballpoint pens and paperclips, loaned us his Swiss Army Knife.

It was a frustrating situation. I'd already struggled through this with John Hernandez, and in the course of my gun research had found magazine articles containing step-by-step instructions for field stripping an SKS. I knew there was a button at the base of the trigger guard, and another one up front somewhere. I just couldn't remember the sequence of what and how to twist, push and remove. It was equally awkward for Steve. He was a cop, for crying out loud. Here he was out in public with a bearded civilian, waving an SKS around the office of the Clerk of Courts. Finally we were reduced to standing there like a couple of baffled chimps.

"This is really stupid." I said, "I've got detailed instructions for stripping an SKS. It would've been so simple to have brought them."

Suddenly Steve brightened. "That's it! Wayne's instructions for replacing the stock are back in the evidence files. I'll have somebody bring them over."

He went off to make a phone call and in a few minutes two young, husky, crew-cut state troopers appeared, carrying between them a single sheet of paper on which were printed instructions for how to disassemble the gun and install the new plastic stock. In three minutes the thing was apart.

That put to rest once and for all my theory that Kevin Wolak had been Wayne Lo's armorer. Consultant, maybe. Armorer, no. The printed instructions were all anybody would have needed to alter that gun, and, although no instructions had come with the gun, they had accompanied the plastic stock. These instructions had been in the cardboard box that the cops had found in Wayne's room when they'd done their illegal search. They'd been part of the impounded evidence, and I'd never heard about them.

I recorded the armory number, 906, then turned the gun over. Stamped into the metal in small block letters was the designation, "CAL ST ALB VT." I knew from my research that this was routing information. The gun had been manufactured at armory 906 in China, transshiped to California for delivery to a depot in St. Albans, Vermont. From there, I knew, it had proceeded to a smaller distributor, a company named Camfor in Westfield, Massachusetts, from whom the first gun store had purchased it. John Hernandez had purchased it from that store, and then sold it to Dave Benham. Dave had sold it to Wayne Lo. Now I had the whole story, the first part of it stamped right into the gun itself.

That routing information also made it clear, in case any additional evidence was needed, that the gun was in no sense military surplus. It had been intended, from the time of its manufacture, for use in the United States. It had been made in China for someone just like Wayne Lo.

Now the gun had to be reassembled, and with the arrival of the two crew-cut troopers, we had sufficient manpower. After several trials we managed to recombine the pieces of the bolt assembly in proper sequence and stuff them back into the guts of the gun. Then it was time for the metal part to go back into the plastic part. Since all that was required in this operation was to distinguish the front of the gun from the rear, the four of us were able to accomplish it with little delay. This left only the trigger assembly which, we knew, fit into place just forward of the pistol grip. According to the instructions, upon application of suitable pressure the trigger assembly would, "snap into place."

Well, it did not snap. The gun slid across the counter and the trigger assembly stuck. The crowd of spectators did not diminish. Steve suggested we put the gun on the floor so that we wouldn't scratch the Clerk's counter. I knew he wanted subsequent operations farther removed from public view.

Laying there on its back on the floor, its skeletal shoulder-piece and pistol grip sticking into the air, it looked like a big dead bug. In a moment of minor but perfect synchronicity, one of the crew-cut troopers murmured helpfully to Steve, "Why don't you step on it?"

I knew how the rest would go. I could picture myself down in my hole at the bottom of the year, in that little circle of light, bent over my bench in the shop, reconfiguring that SKS so it was exactly the way Wayne had his. That circle of light would become the lamp under which I worked. The darkness around it would be dark only by contrast. I'd move easily through it on my way to the firing range. I could imagine the eerie feel of the weight of the gun and I could imagine the gun itself, cold steel and dark metal. There would be the harsh bark of the bullets firing, the kick of the cheap folding stock against my shoulder, the smell of gunsmoke, the adrenaline rush, the power surge, the chill of death. I could imagine it all.

But at that moment in the Berkshire County Clerk's office, looking at that gun on the floor, something changed for me. My whole orientation shifted, as surely as if I'd just sweated out a high fever.

In fact, I had done such a splendid job of imagining what I'd do with the gun that my imagining had become its own reality. There was no need for me to buy an SKS. I'd already accomplished what I'd set out to do. I had confronted the most frightening aspect of Galen's murder, the killing tool itself. I had confronted the idea that this vile piece of machinery was designed to destroy life. I had studied it, handled it, and by some transformative magic my mastery removed this evil charge.

I was ready for Wayne Lo.

PART FOUR

❧ 20
DEPARTMENT OF CORRECTIONS

It was as astonishing as if the money truck from the Publisher's Clearing House had pulled up at our front door. One morning after breakfast, Annie put her book down and said to me, "I'm tired of sitting around the house all day watching you work. I'm going to get a job."

By some method unknown to me, she had completed that deep, careful, sorting and turning that had held her attention since Galen's death. She didn't articulate it, and I no more thought of asking her about it than you'd think of asking someone how they digested their food. The grieving wasn't over; the grieving would never be over. But she was moving again and that was the important thing. She went back to the hippy health food store where she'd worked twenty-five years earlier. It was much bigger now, more like a department store. They hired her to manage their clothing boutique.

The change felt wonderfully odd to me. I was still in my study, making noises, slogging through the last of the gun business, trying to figure out how to figure out whatever it was I had to figure out about Wayne Lo, and all of a sudden Annie just got up and went off to work. I felt like yelling after her, "Hey! You can't do that! I'm the one who's supposed to get out of here first." But I knew she'd just keep going, and that made me happy.

Then Danica called.

Danica and Galen had fallen in love in the fall semester of 1992. Annie and I could remember the way it felt the first time each of us had fallen in love (not with each other) and we knew that was how it was with them. There was no telling where their relationship might have gone, however, because it was cut short at its first, intense flowering. One of the results of this was that when Galen died, Danica was nearly destroyed.

Always a quiet girl, she was now submerged in silence. She hung on at the college for another miserable year, trying to collect herself and complete the requirements for her bachelor's degree. Finally, mercifully, she was able to hobble through a sufficient number of hoops to graduate. When this was accomplished, she traveled for a while in Europe, then came back to the states and held a succession of menial jobs. We'd see her from time to time, up here in Gloucester or down in New York when we were visiting Brooks. We loved her because she was a sweet girl and because she'd loved Galen, but that whole Galen part of her life seemed to be an area of such pain for her that we couldn't bear to dwell on it. I never interviewed her in the course of my walkabout, and though we occasionally talked about Galen, we almost never talked about him in the context of Simon's Rock College. Annie and I worried about Danica. She seemed to be drifting through life, unable to catch hold of anything. We were afraid she'd become a permanent casualty.

Then we got that call from her. She was leaving the country again, she said, traveling to Poland. She'd gotten a teaching job there. It was going to be a great adventure. Her other trips had been escapes, evasions, but this time as she described her plans, there was something different to her voice. There was life back in it, and humor and joy. It wasn't a very long conversation, but it was sufficient to convince us that we were talking to a different Danica. Like Annie, she had found her way back to the world of the living.

Galen had long been a fan of the rock musicians Sting and Bono. Even now, whenever one of those old Police or U-2 songs came on the radio his presence returned to me so strongly that it was, for a moment, impossible to understand how he could not be alive. This presented a serious difficulty in planning my approach to Wayne Lo. If I still had trouble comprehending the fact of Galen's murder, how would I ever be able to understand his murderer?

What could I hope to learn about Wayne Lo's motivation? He was either crazy or he was a very bad person. Or, there might be a third reason, one which had occurred to me almost immediately after Galen's death. It presented itself as an image of pure evil, just a little black sphere of it, moving around in this world. One day it had landed on Wayne. How could I expect to discriminate craziness from badness from possession by evil? What were the distinguishing characteristics of such states? Where would I go to learn about them?

There were other difficulties as well. In the first parts of my walkabout, the people with whom I'd spoken had been sympathetic and supportive. I knew that I might get a different reception from Wayne Lo, his lawyers and his friends. Even if I did some day manage to sit down with Wayne Lo himself, what could I expect from him? He'd already told his story to the police and to the psychiatrists. For the few weeks during his criminal trial in 1994 he'd had the attention of the entire country. What made me think he was going to tell me any more than he'd said then?

Finally, there was the problem of method. I had gathered information about the college and about the gun in a more or less linear fashion. The facts piled up, evidence mounted, and certain conclusions were drawn. In Wayne Lo's case, things were going to be different. I had been thinking about him, in some background way, more or less continually since Galen's death. I already knew much of what I needed to know about him, and had already formed approximate ideas of the things no one could ever absolutely know. What I needed was not new evidence, but a way to organize the evidence I had already accumulated—a way to think of Wayne Lo that seemed true and real, and that would answer the questions I had about his actions. In order for such an imagining to be possible, it was necessary first to understand the full significance of things I already knew. This was not the first time in my life such a condition had obtained. However, I was slow to grasp it, and spent quite a while thrashing about, trying to get the "facts."

Initially, it seemed that the most direct approach, if not the simplest or the easiest, would be to talk to Wayne himself. To this end I scheduled a meeting with Liz Keegan, the victim assistance lady at the Berkshire County DA's office, and asked for advice on how to arrange a meeting with Wayne Lo.

Liz had done much to facilitate my walkabout. When I first embarked on it I went to her, and she gave me encouragement and some general suggestions. Later she helped me gain access to District Attorney Downing and Assistant District Attorney Capeless, and to Sergeant Steve Del-Negro. I think she was intrigued by my response to Galen's death, and somewhat amused by me personally. For my part, in those harsh first days of the criminal trial, I had imprinted on her the way a baby duck imprints on its mother.

She knew, when I came to her with my questions about visiting Wayne Lo, that she could be honest and direct with me, and she was. She suggested that I not bother trying. Visiting Wayne Lo, she informed me, would not be possible.

I asked her if she could help me devise an alternate approach. I told her that whether or not I'd ever be allowed to visit Wayne, it seemed important to me to learn something about his life in prison, perhaps even take a tour of whatever hell-hole was currently his home. Obviously, his behavior in prison would tell me a lot about him. If he seemed sane in prison, the notion of Wayne as victim of mental illness would be called into question. If he was a behavioral problem in jail, or if he bragged about the shootings or continued the antisocial behavior he'd evidenced at college, it would suggest that everything the prosecutors had said about him was true. More than this, I had an unaccountable desire simply to see the jail in which Wayne Lo would spend the rest of his life. I did not know why this was important to me. At the time of my conversation with Liz Keegan, I'm not even sure I understood that it was distinct from my desire to learn about Wayne Lo.

Liz told me that any dealings with Wayne or his jail would involve contact with his jailers, the Massachusetts Department of Corrections. She helped me fill out some forms that would register my name and address with the DOC. I would be notified if Wayne escaped from prison, if he were scheduled for a parole hearing, or if he was to be transferred to a less secure facility. She also gave me a 165-page book entitled, *In the Aftermath of a Crime: A Guide to Victim Rights and Services in Massachusetts,* published by the Massachusetts Office for Victim Assistance. Despite its hopeful title I couldn't find much in there about the right of fathers to speak with the murderers of their sons, or even about the rights of victims to visit prisons. The closest I could get was a paragraph that began, "In some cases, criminal justice agencies are also authorized to provide you with 'evaluative' or mental health information about an offender." The book went on to say that information was released at the discretion of the agency holding it, and that release of information was generally reserved for cases in which the information had some bearing on the "victim's security or well-being." That wasn't much, but it seemed like a place to start.

At Liz's suggestion, I called Judy Norton, the Director of Victim Services in Massachusetts. She, too, was very sympathetic, but I gathered from her frank disclosures that I was heading into a bureaucratic stone wall. The Massachusetts Department of Corrections was in business to "service" offenders, the people who committed the crimes. The victims of these crimes, and their particular needs, were something of an afterthought. This didn't surprise me. I was annoyed, perhaps, at the disparity between the promise of a name like "Victim Services," and the actual services delivered. The major service seemed to be that they would try to notify you if the person who had victimized you escaped from jail and was coming after you. While such notification would indeed be a valued service, I didn't see that it merited a 165-page book.

Actually, in the course of my business with Judy Norton, one surprising event did occur. I told her, apologetically, that I knew my irrepressible desire to see Wayne's prison must seem odd. She told me that it was not odd at all.

"What you're trying to do," she informed me, "is to keep being the best father to Galen you can be. This means insuring that the proper people are punished, and that their punishment is real. You're just being a good dad."

Until that moment it had not occurred to me that my efforts might have been inspired by a desire to continue to care for my son. I liked that notion; I liked it a lot.

Judy Norton sent me along the line to Stephanie Connolly, Director of Victim Services for the Massachusetts Department of Corrections. In the course of a lengthy telephone conversation, she was able to answer many of my specific questions about Wayne Lo and the DOC.

At the conclusion of his murder trial on February 3, 1994, according to Ms. Connolly, Wayne Lo had been sent to MCI (Massachusetts Correctional Institution)-Cedar Junction, in Walpole, Massachusetts. He had remained there until November 10, 1994, at which time he had been transferred to MCI-Norfolk, in Norfolk, Massachusetts, where he has remained. Cedar Junction, she explained, was essentially a place for inmates who might pose security risks. It was the state's only maximum security facility. Inmates were kept in their cells twenty-three hours a day and there were few programs for them, other than menial house-keeping jobs. Because it was limited in size, inmates who showed no behavior problems would soon be transferred to one of the state's medium security facilities. This had been the case with Wayne.

She told me not to be confused by the terms "maximum" and "medium" security. At a medium security facility like Norfolk, there would still be the same amount of isolation from the outside world. However, inside the institution, the rules were a little different. There were more programs, and more opportunities for work. Based on good behavior, inmates could obtain passes to go out to the yard or to participate in programs. Also, inmates could begin to obtain a few personal possessions, such as televisions. However, life in a medium security facility was still highly structured. Under the pass system, authorities would know at any time where each inmate was, and there were still a number of times each day when inmates had to be in their cells to be counted.

She told me there were about 1,300 inmates at Norfolk. None of them left the facility other than by reason of transfer, death or escape. The only exception to this rule involved the death of a family member. In this case the inmate might be allowed to view the body. The viewing would be private, and the inmate would be "in restraints" and accompanied by two guards, one of whom was armed.

There was no telling how long Wayne would be at this facility. He might be transferred for any number of reasons. He might develop a medical condition that could not be treated at Norfolk. He might get into problems with other inmates and be transferred for security reasons. He might exhaust the few programs at his current facility and be moved to another location. He would never be transferred to a less secure facility. If he was transferred to another medium security institution, I would not be notified.

As far as information about Wayne's actual prison life, there was not much she could tell me. A Classification Report on each inmate was filed twice yearly, and this document was Stephanie Connolly's main source of information about Wayne Lo. According to Wayne's January report, he had not been subject to any disciplinary action during his incarceration. Currently he was a "house man," or janitor, at Norfolk. At Walpole he had worked in the kitchen. He had been enrolled in a music appreciation program at Norfolk. She had no documentation of his being involved in any other programs. Stephanie Connolly did say that there was an exercise yard and a gym at this facility, and that, if inclined, Wayne might have participated in baseball, basketball or weight lifting. She did not have specific information about any of these activities. She told me that an inmate's behavior was also monitored, and that Wayne consistently got good evaluations in this category.

I asked her if, as a victim, I was entitled to receive a copy of Wayne's Classification Report. She told me that I was not. I asked her about the paragraph in the manual about Victim Rights and Services which said I might be provided with evaluative information. She reminded me that, "decisions about releasing evaluative information are made at the discretion of the agency." In this case, DOC's discretionary decision was that no information would be released, other than a single page summary of the inmate's status called a Key Issues Sheet. I asked her why the manual didn't just say that. She told me she didn't know. I asked her if I could obtain a Key Issues Sheet. She said she would be happy to mail me the forms to fill out to apply for eligibility to receive a Key Issues Sheet.

We then moved on to my request to visit Wayne's prison. The answer, again, was no. There was currently no program for victims to meet with the inmates who had victimized them, or for victims to tour facilities in which their offenders were housed. Could I imagine the chaos that might ensure if an offender and a victim were accidentally to meet in this setting? I told her I could not imagine any chaos and I asked her if she were implying that DOC could not control their inmates. She replied that the motivating factor in DOC's policy was "security," and that they felt they were protecting victims by keeping them away from institutions in which their offenders were housed. I asked her if any outsiders were allowed to tour prison facilities. She told me that, occasionally, on Media Day, television camera crews toured the facility. I asked her about the chaos that would ensue when the images of offenders were broadcast to hundreds of thousands of Boston-area homes? If they could manage camera crews securely, why couldn't they manage visits from an occasional victim? She reiterated, very patiently, that the reason victims were not allowed in prisons was that victims were not allowed in prisons. I lapsed into dumbfoundedness.

Sensing that, for whatever reason, I was too dim to grasp this simplest of explanations, she confided that she was working on a plan that might alleviate my frustration. She emphasized that this new, radical approach was just in the planning stage, and she specifically requested that I not mention it to other victims, if I were in contact with any, because she did not want to jeopardize her scheme in its infancy.

Her plan was to take a few photographs of each facility, Norfolk and Walpole among them. Perhaps there would be a photograph of the yard, and one of a typical cell, and maybe one of a work area. There were problems of course. No specific inmates could be pictured, and the facilities could not be made too look too pleasant. Nobody could appear to be enjoying themselves. There were the complex political manipulations that would be needed to steer this plan through the bureaucracy, but Stephanie Connolly was sure these problems could be overcome. Then, whenever a request like mine came in, she could photocopy the pictures and send them out.

She was proud of her scheme, and proud of herself for having conceived of a Victim Service which lay so far beyond the scope of DOC policy. Trying to hide my despair, I asked what I could do to help move her plan forward. She told me the best thing I could do would be to write her a letter. In this letter I should explain how useful it would be in my healing process if I could see a picture of the institution in which Wayne Lo was housed. She could then use this letter to obtain support for her plan.

Perhaps she felt we were beginning to establish a rapport. She told me there was something else I could do, another course of action I could take that might help me satisfy my needs in this difficult situation.

I asked what she had in mind.

She told me that I could drive past Norfolk Prison and look at it. I could take Route 1A to Pine Street and see both Bay State and Norfolk prisons in the same drive-by.

My despair congealed and quickened into anger. She was informing me that I, a citizen of the United States, might get in my car and drive on a public road. Nor had she finished sharing information about Victim Services.

"I want to be honest with you," she told me.

There was a pause. Stephanie Connolly was struggling with something. "Please do." I replied.

"I want to be honest," she repeated, "When anybody, like you, expresses interest in a particular inmate or a particular institution, I am required to report it to that institution. I don't have to tell you this, but I want you to know." There was another pause, another internal struggle to find the right words. "Don't try to get in there and see him. You'll get in serious trouble."

That did it for me.

There were local, state and national politicians to mobilize. There were two national parents-of-murdered-children organizations, and one victim reconciliation group with strong connections among liberals and conservatives alike. There were many, many letters to write. There was the *Boston Globe*, always ready for a little muckraking, and the *Boston Herald*, with a permanent soft spot for victims of gory crimes. And how would the *11 O'Clock News* like to try to tour Walpole from a victim's point of view? Stephanie Connolly was going to rue the day she ever uttered those words to me. I'd make mincemeat of this dame and her dimwitted policies.

All this came in a heartbeat, an anger surge as instinctive as the red flash that welled and broke whenever Galen, always testing, pushed me past my limit. Then the picture flipped, and in the next instant I had a vision of my follies with Bernie Rodgers, Great American Insurance, Kevin Wolak and the ATF. If I went to war with this lady, I might beat her and her bosses or I might not, but the war would surely consume me and all my energies, and I would be as much a prisoner of it as Wayne Lo was of the DOC.

So, I thanked Stephanie Connolly for her advice. I told her that, for her own benefit, she should consider rephrasing the DOC's "security" explanation. (I am afraid I used the words "reeks of bureaucratic para-noia.") I complimented her on her courteous and professional manner in dealing with me, and thanked her for spending an hour on the phone.

As for the anger, it turned to dust.

All this scheming and telephoning was but one phase of a failed attempt to amass new information about Wayne Lo. Another approach, equally unsuccessful, began in February of 1997, when my book business took me on a two-week trip to the West Coast.

While I was there, I spent some time with Taj Moore, who had been one of Galen's best friends at Simon's Rock College. Taj was living in San Francisco, saving his money and getting ready to continue work on a degree in economics at University of California, Davis. I was exhibit-ing at the 30th California International Antiquarian Bookfair, which happened to be in San Francisco that year. I called Taj, and he and his girlfriend paid a visit to the bookfair. While she wandered around inside, Taj and I sat in the sun outside and talked.

Taj and Galen had spent two years together at college. They'd both gotten interested in fencing and rock climbing, and those activities had been a bond, but more importantly, their personalities had just seemed to mesh. Galen had brought Taj home to stay with us over the Thanksgiving holiday in 1991, and after Galen's murder, Taj had been at our house for the funeral and the sad days around it. I knew he was intelligent and observant. I thought he'd be a good source of new information about Wayne Lo, but he was not. He was something else instead.

Taj couldn't remember much about Wayne or his circle of friends. He and Galen and their friends had little contact with Wayne and his friends. Wayne had not seemed especially frightening or repugnant. It was more that he had been uninteresting. At the worst Taj and Galen had detected something strange about Wayne and avoided it.

"I mean, we were *all* weird, but Wayne was weird in a different way. So many people did crazy stuff with their hair, but Wayne had his buzz-cut with the initials USMC shaved in the back of his head, like he was consciously trying to go in the opposite direction than everybody else."

There were more fragmentary recollections of a similar nature, of no particular use in themselves, perhaps helpful at a later time. He also gave me names I hadn't heard before. There was a Brian somebody, Taj couldn't remember the last name, who'd been on the edge of Wayne's crowd. Brian was a maybe-gay weightlifter who used, it was rumored, to pop Wayne's zits. There was a kid named Zack who knew the weight lifter, and a kid named Willy, who'd been Taj's roommate and had been the only other Asian on campus.

It was all scattered, inconclusive and imperfectly recalled. As he rambled on, trying his damndest to be helpful, I began looking at Taj, comparing him with my memory of our meetings five and six years before. He was still lean, but had acquired a man's musculature. Because he'd come from a racially mixed family he had coffee-toned skin which, combined with his angular features, had always given him a somewhat exotic look, but now the pimples were gone, and with them the awkward dreadlocks and all the teenaged shyness and uncertainty. Taj Moore had become a good-looking young man, just moving into his prime, just beginning life's journey in earnest.

His girlfriend joined us and we went across the street, out of the sun, and sat in the cool darkness of an overpriced cafe. We ate a gourmet lunch and drank micro-brewed beer and made small talk, and I kept looking at Taj and the attractive girl beside him and I kept thinking, "There's Galen. There's where he would be right now, not specifically, but in this place in life, in this vigor and youth, and all its possibility, all its beauty."

The thought stayed long after they left, not as a sadness, but as a measure of some kind, or a counting; as a term in mathematics beyond my comprehension, but no less perfect for being so.

$21

THE BATTLE OF
THE SHRINKS

I already had quite a bit of information about Wayne Lo.

At his criminal trial in the first days of 1994, much testimony had been given about Wayne's life, and much had been speculated about his mental and emotional condition.

The prosecution spent the first two weeks of the trial stating its case: that Wayne Lo had knowingly and willfully planned to murder people on the Simon's Rock Campus, and that he had carried out his plan. This portion of the trial had been of greatest interest to me in the earlier parts of my walkabout. It was based almost exclusively on eyewitness accounts and on physical evidence of the sort Sgt. Langton had given about the gun. Prosecutors for the Commonwealth of Massachusetts intended to prove that Wayne Lo was the shooter, that his shooting was premeditated or planned and that Wayne was aware of the wrongness of his acts. To this end witnesses were questioned, documents and material evidence were produced, and a chronology was developed. However, the commonwealth made almost no effort to deal with Wayne's motivation. This was beyond the scope of what they needed for a conviction.

Then Wayne Lo's lawyers presented their defense. They called family members, teachers, friends and professional psychiatrists to the witness stand to talk for hours about Wayne. They did not contest that he had done the shooting. They were concerned with his mental state. They wanted to show that the murders were not premeditated, and that

Wayne Lo was not in sufficient mental health to understand that what he was doing was wrong. They wanted to show the jury that he was not guilty by reason of insanity.

Finally, after the witnesses for the defense had testified, the prosecution countered with their own mental health experts who disputed the opinions of the defense psychiatrists. It was these latter portions of the trial that interested me now, the defense's description of Wayne Lo's mental state and the prosecution's rebuttal. If there was a "how" or a "why" to Galen's death, I thought I might have a chance of finding it here.

With this in mind, I began to review the thirty-six pages of single-spaced notes I had taken at Wayne Lo's criminal trial. They wakened in me an intense recollection of the dark weeks we'd spent in that courtroom. All the anger, confusion and sadness that Annie and I had experienced came back once again, scarcely dimmed by the passage of time. This immersion in the past was punctuated by moments of clarity from the present, as I'd suddenly understand, in the course of my review, the strategic reason for the appearance of a certain witness or a particular piece of testimony. Thus, as my recapitulation of the trial proceeded, I found myself in a curious internal back-and-forth between the text of 1994, and the analysis of 1997.

After the physical facts of the case had been established, Wayne's attorneys began laying the foundation for their insanity defense by calling on two clinical psychologists who had examined and tested their client. David Smith, a long-faced psychologist from the Berkshire County House of Correction, told us that Wayne had reported receiving commands that related to the Book of Revelation. These "voices" were not auditory commands, but were directly perceived. They ordered Wayne to purchase the gun and do the shooting. Smith told us that Wayne had requested a second interview, several days later, to report that the commands had come again, this time to tell him "It is done."

This seemed credible to the psychologist, and he made it seem credible to us. He said the most convincing aspect was Wayne's "presentation." The voices came only at specific times, rather than continually, as malingerers usually reported. Wayne gave no indication of trying to convince the psychologist of anything. Most tellingly, at the end of their interview he began to disavow his hallucinations. Smith told us, "I'm assuming that nobody malingering a psychosis would back off."

The trial took place fourteen months after Galen's murder, and we were still so emotionally wrought-up that we could only understand it in the simplest terms. To us it seemed that the defense and all their witnesses were Bad Guys. We regarded everything they said with suspicion and mistrust. Wayne Lo had murdered our son, and his lawyers were trying to get him off the murder charge; to send him to some psychiatric country club from which, if were ever "cured," he'd go free!

So I was angry at these technicians, Smith and the even more boring Aneregg who followed him, sitting up there, reeling off their jargon-laden opinions. I have in my notes, and could tell you if I had to, what WAIS R, Wechlesler R, MMPI 2, TAP and Rorschach tests are, what they predict, how they are administered, and how Wayne registered in the crazy zone in all of them. What could the prosecution say to refute them? The kid aced his tests, and in 1994 it filled me with anxiety, lest these bland clinicians be taken at their word by the jury. They came and spoke, and their numbers proved Wayne Lo was crazy.

After the first round of clinical information, Chia Wei Lo, Wayne's father, was called to the stand. His bearing was erect and military. His speech was curiously stiff and lacking in spontaneity. I assumed that every line of his testimony had been rehearsed with Wayne's lawyers, to put his son in the best possible light.

We learned that C. W. Lo had joined the Taiwanese Air Force thirty years before, when he was seventeen years old. Although his military career afforded the Lo family considerable contact with the US, Wayne and his younger brother Ryan had both been born in Taiwan, and even now the family spoke Mandarin around the house. Finally, in 1987, Mr. Lo left the air force, and took up residence in the United States. The situation in Taiwan was uncertain, he said, and he knew the United States would provide the best future for his sons. There followed years of hard work as Mr. and Mrs. Lo struggled to make their Chinese restaurant the best in Billings, Montana. Much was expected of young Wayne during this time. He came home from school, cleaned the house, cared for Ryan, who was five years his junior, fed them both, put Ryan to bed, then did lots of homework to get As. Also there was Wayne's music. Mom had been a Suzuki teacher in Taiwan, and Wayne had started violin lessons at four years of age. The defense established that C. W. was always working and never spent any time with his sons. He was something of a martinet who always demanded complete respect and held his sons to the highest standards of performance. We learned that Wayne was fifteen years of age and working at the restaurant before he ever talked back to his father.

C. W. Lo told us there had been no warning, no hint that anything was wrong with Wayne. Then the shootings happened, and the very next day C. W. flew out and visited Wayne in jail. "His body was there but a different soul inside," the weeping parent reported.

I was unmoved.

Wayne's best friend from Billings, Casey Stessman, was called to the stand to reinforce C. W. Lo's testimony. Casey told the court that he'd spoken with Wayne the day before the shootings, and that nothing had seemed wrong at the time. They'd even made plans for the forthcoming Christmas vacation.

From my vantage point in 1997, I could see that the defense had structured the appearance of their witnesses with a definite purpose. They wanted to show, first, that Wayne was crazy in a medical sense, and secondly, that he was unaware of this—hence blameless. The testimony of Stessman and several other witnesses was aimed at demonstrating that Wayne had planned to go on with his life; that the day before the shooting he had no idea of what was about to happen.

In 1994 this had been a low point for me. During the early stages of the trial, while all the forensic evidence was being presented, defense and prosecution had simply been jockeying for position. Now they were arguing about Wayne's mental state, the key issue before us, and all the chips were on the table. The defense seemed to be making their case in a most convincing way, and the prosecutors had been letting this damaging testimony roll on unimpeded. I was getting antsy. If the DA's people weren't up to it, I was ready to jump out there and take on the defense myself.

The defense called Michelle Mattix, Wayne's English teacher at Central High School in Billings. She articulated and enunciated with stiff perfection. She spoke with pride about the dress code at Central Catholic High, about the modesty required of girls, the decency of boys.

Defense Attorney Eisenberg made the most of this teacher who had liked Wayne—"He was one of my favorite students"—this poor stifling, wooden creature who was somehow enamored of the wooden, stifled boy. She spoke of the "banter" she exchanged with Wayne at the beginning of each class. They bantered about sports. Wayne liked Larry Bird and he was an ardent Yankees fan.

There was a problem with baseball for Wayne. Michelle Mattix and all the other Billings witnesses told this story. Casey Stessman and Wayne, the sports buddies, started playing a lot of baseball together. They wanted to try out for the local American Legion team. Wayne tried out for a day, then his father wouldn't let him play baseball any more. C. W. was afraid Wayne would hurt his violin hands (as he himself had, years before) and ruin a brilliant musical future. Wayne took it hard.

He even told Michelle Mattix about it. Michelle reported to the jury in her simpering tone, "I wasn't aware that baseball was a dangerous game. Especially when one wears a glove."

Wayne's schoolwork deteriorated his last semester at Central Catholic High. Much to Michelle's distress, he'd revel in his bad grades. One day just before the Easter break he made a point of saying over and over that this would be his last class, that Michelle could keep all his English papers, and so forth, and Michelle was terrified that he was going to commit suicide. Instead he stole his mom's car and drove to Oregon to see a girl.

That evening Channel 40 *Eyewitness News* had it all figured out. Over our nightly drinks Anne Marie and I learned that the demands of an overbearing father had driven Wayne around the bend. He went crazy and killed two because his dad wouldn't let him try out for the baseball team.

We were terrified that the jury might find this convincing, and at the same time it seemed so utterly dumb that we couldn't imagine anyone believing it. We didn't know whether to laugh or cry, so we did both. Then we washed our faces and went to a Lebanese restaurant the landlady had recommended.

In 1997 I recognized that, despite its absurdity, the facile two-minute evening news gloss had done a perfectly adequate job of summing up the defense's argument to that point. Wayne was crazy and he didn't know it, so he couldn't be blamed for it. In some obscure way, it was his family's fault, hardworking and honorable though they were. Witnesses came and went, each reinforcing one or another aspect of the defense's portrait of Wayne.

The most memorable of these character witnesses was Gary Gaudreau, a big hulking guy, a lay Franciscan. He had been one of Wayne's teacher at Billings Central Catholic High. Like Michelle Mattix, he spoke slowly, with clear articulation. He told us that Wayne didn't fit in any group or clique, and didn't seem to have any friends.

Gary was faculty advisor for the chess club, of which Wayne had been a member. Wayne's sole ambition in those days was to beat Gary, and when he finally did, he demanded that Gary announce it over the loudspeaker at school, which Gary did. This testimony produced a *huge* smile from Wayne Lo over at the defense table, and much confusion for Annie and me. The kid was a murderer, yet here was this teacher, member of a religious order no less, trying to win us over with fond reminiscences. Those were the good old days, eh Wayne?

Gary Gaudreau chronicled Wayne's slide to ruin. Everything was OK his freshman year at Central High, and in Gary's Christology lectures first semester sophomore year Wayne did very well. But then in the second semester during Sacraments and Morality class, Gary became concerned about a "buildup in Wayne of tremendous stress, tremendous anxiety." He went to the school counselor, Sister Barbara, and told her he feared suicide. Sister Barbara didn't follow up. Neither did Gary. Why, the defense wanted to know, didn't you speak to Wayne's parents? Gary confessed that it would have been "professional suicide" to have challenged the hierarchy at Central and gone directly to the parents.

According to Gaudreau's testimony, he then wrote a letter recommending Wayne for admission to Simon's Rock College. He did not mention any of his concerns about Wayne because of a tacit school policy not to undercut any student's chance of success. Gary told the court he felt "guilt" and "responsibility" for not pursuing what he knew were accurate observations of Wayne's mental state.

Even then, recording the proceedings in my battered state, the awful wrongness of this situation had not escaped me. Here was another cause among the skeins of causes that led back to our son's death. Here was one the first places something could have been done differently and was not. Reading my notes in 1997, that image of Gary Gaudreau, the bearish Christologist, the teacher of Morality, lit me on fire.

Gaudreau felt "guilt," did he? Well, there wasn't enough guilt in the world for him or his pious, hypocritical kind. And, speaking of the world, why blame just Gary Gaudreau? Why not blame Red Auerbach for drafting Kevin McHale? Hadn't he and his duck hunting buddy Durand started this whole thing? Why not blame those cynical politicians and the gun nuts they catered to? Why not blame them all, the bastards?

For a moment the rage was with me again. But it was no longer the steady, smoldering ally that had propelled me through the earlier stages of my walkabout. Since my telephone session with Stephanie Connolly, Director of Victim Services, the anger had seemed more of a hindrance than a help.

Why not blame them all? Because now I had something more important to do. I was going to get to the bottom of my son's death. I was going to understand it, and then I'd be clean of it. I sentenced Gary Gaudreau to eternal after-school detention in an overheated study hall in the nether reaches of my psyche, supervised by a nasty gym teacher with a hangover and bad breath. I made him sit next to Stephanie Connolly.

Perversely, Gaudreau had been a strong witness for the defense, in that he extended the culpability for Wayne Lo's actions. Now the high school guidance counselors could share some of the blame. Building on this, Wayne's lawyers upped the ante. They called their Arch Shrink to the stand. His name was Erik Plakun and he was Director of Admissions at Austen-Riggs, a high-class mental hospital in Stockbridge, Massachusetts. He had conducted four interviews with Wayne, totaling a little less than eight hours. He also relied, as his primary document, on *DSM-III-R*, the *Diagnostic and Statistical Manual of Mental Disorders* (third edition, revised), which was the most up-to-date classification of these sorts of diseases—in his words, "the premier diagnostic instrument."

I had a clear recollection of this well-groomed psychiatrist, the linchpin of the defense's insanity argument. Dr. Plakun was like a commercial.

He was wonderful at explaining abstruse concepts without seeming to patronize. To further validate himself, he introduced this book, with a title that sounded like a wonder drug or an experimental airplane. As the trial went on, *DSM-III-R* would appear again and again.

I didn't catch on to what Dr. Plakun was doing until the defense attorney asked him if he was familiar with the Massachusetts laws on insanity and criminal responsibility. "Oh, sure." he cheerily responded, and then went on to recite the law verbatim, using precisely the same language that the trial judge and both lawyers had used when they recited it to us—only Plakun recited it for us *as if he were making it up.* He used hand gestures, pauses, facial expressions, all the mannerisms of a man searching for each appropriate word. The defense hadn't just snatched some cloistered academician from his study to render a learned opinion. Dr. Plakun had done this before. He was smooth. He was a professional.

It was no surprise that, based on his training and professional experience, and on the materials he had examined and tests he had administered, he had an opinion within a reasonable scientific certainty that on December 14 Wayne Lo was suffering from a "psychotic disorder with command hallucinations and paranoid delusions of grandiosity." And, in Plakun's estimation, he did indeed lack capacity to appreciate the criminality of his acts. "The paranoid schizophrenia interfered with his ability to appreciate the wrongfulness of his acts. Mr. Lo was not criminally responsible."

We then went into definitions of the terms Plakun had used, and their diagnostic guidelines according to *DSM-III-R.* Wayne met all the criteria for Plakun's diagnosis.

Next Dr. Plakun told us about the result of his interviews with Wayne. These established the defense's version of why Wayne was the way he was. It seemed that Wayne liked the disciplinary beatings administered by his father. Plakun asserted that a pattern of "transgression, punishment, purification" had established itself in Wayne's psyche, and that this determined Wayne's behavior in the shooting spree.

Plakun related what Wayne had actually told him about the night of the shootings. The "voices" came and commanded Wayne to read Revelation and find out what to do next. They also told him to keep his mission secret. In his ensuing study of Revelation, Wayne found that there were sinners at Simon's Rock. He realized he must punish, and then he ordered the ammunition and bought the gun. Then the feeling came to him and said, "It is time." So he went out with his gun after dinner and, "shot at anything that moved ... I felt no anger or terror."

"It was quite a night," Wayne confessed in the course of their interview, "It was a climax." Plakun said Wayne seemed to feel he'd accomplished something.

Sitting in that courtroom, Annie and I became more miserable with each word, as the certainty mounted in us that the jury would be persuaded by this learned testimony. Wayne was mentally ill and the jury would send him to a hospital for a while. The rest was too awful to contemplate.

Fortunately for us, the proceedings kept moving at such a pace that we had no time to indulge our gloom.

Now the question was how the defense would support their star witness. To their credit, attorneys Eisenberg and Janet Kenton-Walker did something quite unexpected. Instead of immediately weighing down Plakun's argument with more professional testimony, they staked out their own claim on the emotional side of things. Wayne Lo's mom, Lin Lin Lo, was called to testify.

She seemed small, frightened, and very much alone up there on the witness stand, as she led us, in her halting English, through the same history Wayne's dad had given us. Even the specific anecdotes were the same. Did so little go on in this poor kid's life that every time they told the story nothing changed? Finally she came up with a new tale. Mom asked Wayne what he wanted for his fourteenth birthday and he said a vacuum cleaner so he could clean the house better. So she got him … *a vacuum cleaner* for his fourteenth birthday present!

Mrs. Lo testified that when Wayne was leaving for Simon's Rock she filled out a student information form stating that English was Wayne's second language. She had every expectation that this important fact would be duly noted by college officials, and later, no indication that they had even been aware of it.

Then to the shooting. Lin Lin had called Wayne on December 12th. Nothing wrong. On the fourteenth they got the news, the call from Bernie, and she couldn't understand. At first she thought Wayne had been shot. She cried as she narrated that horrible day, and C. W. sniffled in his seat at the back of the courtroom. She told us that after she realized what had happened she didn't cry at first, she just kept cleaning and cleaning. Next morning they still hadn't told Ryan. He was sitting there at the breakfast table while she called Ryan's school and told them something had happened and Ryan would be absent. (I wondered if this was a cultural difference or simply an abysmally low level of communications skills within the Lo family.) Finally Ryan asked what was going on. She told him what had happened and they both cried and cried. Ryan ran up to his room. Neighbors came over.

We were moved, finally, by her story. We remembered that awful December 15 in our house and we could imagine the same day in theirs.

Then back to the medicine of it all. The defense Called Dr. Albert Gaw, a psychiatrist who worked at the Bedford, Massachusetts, VA hospital. He told us, "Mr. Lo is suffering from a delusional disorder." And that, yes, that was one of the psychoses listed in *DSM-III-R* and did constitute, in Mr. Lo's case, "a mental disease or defect." Interestingly, he

261

interviewed Wayne in both English and Mandarin, in order to cross-check meanings and nuances of what the defendant told him.

Of all the shrinks, I liked this Dr. Gaw, despite the fact that he was testifying for the defense. There was a realness to his presentation. He was using his mind, not just a textbook. He told us, for example, that at first he thought Wayne's gang of pals at the college were just the misfits or troublemakers who'd banded together. But that then he had discovered something else. They were the Conservatives on the campus, and that it was their shared Conservative beliefs, even down to them all watching Rush Limbaugh regularly, that held them together.

His portrait of Wayne's psychosis was very convincing. He asked Wayne in Mandarin Chinese about the "voices" and the answer he got back led him to diagnose the commands as somatic hallucinations. These were perceived directly in the body, "like a charge of electricity." Dr. Gaw gave us an exegesis of Revelation and of the shootings from Wayne's perspective. "He's misjudging reality at this point, engaging in illogical thinking that only makes sense to him. For example, Revelation was written to the churches in Asia. Wayne says, 'I am Asian, therefore Revelation is being written to me.'" Gaw testified that Wayne Lo was very much encouraged by the failure of Trinka Robinson and Bernie Rodgers to intercept the ammunition, and by their failure to thoroughly search his room. This convinced him that God was paving the way for his special mission. Not only did the inaction of college officials passively aid Lo, it fed his disturbed fantasy.

After all this, "Does Wayne Lo believe he is mentally ill?" "No. To this day he does not believe he has a mental illness." Gaw's common sense analysis reinforced the textbook thumping of his colleagues. Wayne Lo was crazy.

As their last witness the defense called Ronald Schouten, a psychiatrist at Massachusetts General Hospital. Oddly, Annie and I were feeling better by this time. Perhaps the humane Dr. Gaw had relaxed us. Perhaps he'd convinced us. Perhaps we'd given up hope. If we had, Dr. Schouten's testimony restored it. We learned, after the long recitation of his credentials, publications and sources used in arriving at a diagnosis (including *DSM-III-R*), that after nine interviews, Wayne Lo did not fit neatly into any specific category. At the time of the shooting he was suffering from a "psychotic disorder not otherwise specified." This category, he told us, was also listed in *DSM-III-R*.

This struck us as ridiculous, and we could not believe the defense wasn't sensitive to the borderline absurdity of it. They had paraded three psychiatrists before us, who told us Wayne was suffering from schizophrenia, or delusional disorder, or psychotic disorder not otherwise specified. It was as if these learned doctors were reading right out of the book and each had chosen a different diagnosis from the same page. Annie and I began to suspect that all was not lost for our side of the case.

Reviewing this material years later, surrounded by the reassuring clutter on my desk, it was even more obvious that the defense's argument was not as airtight as it had seemed at the time. They'd sent Dr. Schouten up to the witness stand to do damage control; to shore up the edifice they'd been trying to construct.

Schouten began with a disquisition on delusions and how someone can suffer from a delusional disease and appear normal to everyone else.

"And where," asked defense lawyer Janet Kenton-Walker, "do delusions come from?"

"Delusions form to fill a hole in a person."

Schouten harked back to Wayne's self-esteem problem, suggested the boy needed a sense of fulfillment to patch a hole in his person, and to explain his life experiences. Why a religious dimension to his delusions? It was brought on by his course work in college. All those dangerous thinkers this radical institution was cramming into the minds

263

of its innocent and unprepared students. The infamous AIDS paper, in which Wayne proposed a pogrom against homosexuals, and for which he had been so heavily criticized, gave him material for his persecution delusion. His past difficulties, the AIDS paper, the Thanksgiving argument with Floyd and Trinka Robinson—all these "stressors" helped the delusional state develop.

According to this argument, Simon's Rock College was also partially responsible for Wayne Lo's disintegration. In developing a line of failure from parents to high school to college, the defense was trying to show that Wayne's mental disease or defect had a long history. This testimony reinforced what Gaw had said about the failure of the college to intercept the ammunition, and what Mrs. Lo had said about their failure to recognize that English was not even Wayne's primary language. In that it was a criticism college officials, this should have cheered us.

Instead, we were confused. Our simplistic way of relating to the proceedings was breaking down. First, Dr. Gaw had half-convinced us that Wayne was indeed crazy. Now we were seeing that, in their indictment of Simon's Rock College, the Bad Guys on the defense were aligned with us. This was a mere hint of the complexity of the case; something I would spend the next three years trying to unravel. In 1994, alas, the only things unraveling were Annie and me.

Finally, to complete his job as damage control specialist, Ronald Schouten proceeded to explain how Wayne could be crazy and still capable of rational-seeming acts. He asserted that there was a "supervisory ego function" intact in Wayne during his delusional period, and that, crazy as he was, some part of him could stand back and cast a sane eye on what was transpiring. This flowed into a model of Wayne with his psyche on two parallel tracks, one delusional and one normal. All the crazy orders from god were on one track and all the normal things he did immediately before and after the shootings were on the other track. The two could coexist, but the delusional track ruled. Thus hiding the ammo was sane behavior in the service of the delusion. Plans for the future were an expression of the normal track. All his behavior, in the defense's view, was explained by their model of the "supervisory ego function" and Wayne's delusional state.

Therefore he could not conform his behavior to the requirements of the law. "He was psychotic and suffering from a delusion at the time of the shooting. By reason of the delusion he believed that what he was doing was not at all wrongful."

As contorted as this argument sounded to me on my later reading, it was most convincing in the context of the trial. Schouten seemed a reasonable, credible witness, and his presentation of this final wrinkle in Wayne's diseased psyche was no more difficult to accept than any of the others had been. We knew we were now at a critical point. The momentum had been swinging back and forth throughout the proceedings, and at the conclusion of Schouten's testimony it was suspended, almost a palpable thing, in that open space that separated the lawyers from the judge and jury.

The prosecution needed a definitive rebuttal of Dr. Schouten's theories, and they got one from the assistant DA, David Capeless. I give it here as I recorded it in 1994.

Then to the cross-examination, in which Capeless immediately set to work, hammering away at Schouten's description of the shooting as impulsive. "He told you the voice came to him and said, 'It is time.' Did that voice tell him to walk from his room across the frozen field, to take out the communications center at the guard shack, to hold his gun to the window of that car? He was armed and ready when that voice came."

"Were you aware that the defendant already knew how to get to Dave's Sporting Goods in Pittsfield, that he knew it would be crowded and that he'd have to wait in line? Did you know he knew the gun was already at Dave's?"

"Did you know he had to reassemble the gun (to use the over-sized clips)? You described the ammunition as a common type. Didn't you later learn it was specifically for this kind of weapon? Did Wayne tell you he bought this ammunition through a magazine ad that was specifically marketed for an SKS? Did you consider that he bought this specific type of ammunition *prior* to purchasing the weapon?"

"He told you he shot at no particular target. Don't you think the guard shack was a very specific target, since all the college communications went through there?" (Capeless walked to the map of the campus that was tacked up at the back of the courtroom and showed the path Wayne had taken that night, out of his dorm, across that big field to the road that lead back onto the campus.)

He continued in this manner, using his rhetorical questions to contrast Wayne Lo's actions and statements with Schouten's hypotheses. Finally he reached this climax.

"You said he felt no criminal responsibility for his acts, but why, when he was finished shooting, DID HE CALL THE POLICE?"

Until that moment in the trial, I had never considered Capeless's point. You call the cops when you know something bad has happened. As I then imagined, if I were Wayne Lo in the grips of a delusional state, and the voice told me it was done, I'd just stop. I'd lay the gun on the ground, hunker down, and maybe drool a little. I'd be crazy. I wouldn't call the cops and carefully negotiate my surrender.

I thought it was a brilliant, telling point, and was so overcome with the elegant simplicity of the logic that I wept.

The defense rested.

For their rebuttal, the prosecution produced two of their own psychiatrists, Wesley Profit and Michael Annunziato, who asserted that Wayne was suffering from a "narcissistic personality disorder" rather than a mental disease or defect. Drawing on Capeless' line of argument, these men told the court that Wayne's hiding the bullets and lying to college administrators proved that he knew his actions were wrong. They argued that he had the mental capacity to deceive, and that, if he had this capacity he could equally have used it to conform his conduct to the law.

By the time of my 1997 review, it had occurred to me that there was a deeper level to their attack, one that had more to do with the evidence itself than with testimony about Wayne's mental state. Again and again in my notes I had recorded that the prosecution made a point of asking us what *kind* of evidence we were going to believe. Would we believe the theories of hired professionals and their tests and books, or would we believe the evidence of what Wayne Lo actually did and said?

In Plakun and Schouten we had two people who the defense contended were expert at interpreting texts and who had seen Wayne Lo through these texts. In the prosecution's psychiatrists, Doctors Profit and Annunziato, we had men who knew texts but who the prosecution wanted us to believe were experts at interpreting people and their actions.

Dr. Wesley Profit, a large black man with a James Earl Jones voice and a relaxed manner, saw nothing really remarkable in Wayne Lo's past, certainly no sign of mental disorder. During the clinical interviews he had conducted, he found that the defendant was cooperative but that he wanted to control the examination process. He wanted to tell his story and not be interrupted. When confronted with contrary information, Wayne would take exception to any suggestion that what he was saying was not the truth. His affect, thought processes and expression were normal. Profit found no sign of suspicion or paranoia, no sign of major mental illness.

He did, however, find indications of a "personality disorder," a rigidity and centeredness of thinking, and a habitually maladaptive way of solving problems, best described as narcissistic. "Mr. Lo sees himself as the center of things. He sees things referring to him when in fact they do not. He tends to think less of other people and their feelings."

Profit was using the same kind of language his colleagues had used, but what he was telling us seemed more a matter of common sense. People with personality disorders of this kind had difficulty in their social relations. Because of the way they perceived themselves and others they tended to be disagreeable to the people around them. Because of the way they solved problems there could be violence.

He was followed by Dr. Michael Annunziato, who spoke with a distinct south Boston accent, and who looked like he might have been a longshoreman before moving on to medicine and psychiatry. In his opinion, there was no evidence that Wayne Lo was suffering from a major mental illness. He harked back to Wayne's antisocial behavior in school, in jail and even at Bridgewater State Hospital where he was held for observation. This pattern of behavior, according to Dr. Annunziato, had nothing to do with any psychotic disorder, rather, it was a "characterological disorder." This disorder was also listed in *DSM-III*, but it did not constitute a mental disease or defect. The hallmark of characterological disorder was difficulty in getting along with others, leading to frequent conflicts in society.

During the cross-examination defense attorney Eisenberg and Dr. Annunziato got in an argument about Wayne's "suicidal ideation" after he ditched school and took his mother's car to Oregon. "Didn't you read the reports?" Eisenberg wanted to know, "Didn't you consider them significant? You'd interview a cab driver, but not consider the report of a trained mental health professional?"

"Well," replied Annunziato, "I didn't find that report credible."

Eisenberg howled, "You've read Dr. Plakun's resume, you know how long he's been in the field, *and you didn't find his report credible?*"

"Well," said Dr. Annunziato, "Wayne didn't commit suicide, did he?"

At one point Eisenberg waved *DSM-III-R* in the air, challenging Annunziato on something, and Doc A. replied, "I haven't memorized that book, I'm glad to say..."

So it went, down to the last witnesses, the final arguments, the excruciating wait for a verdict, and then the jury's decision that Wayne Lo would spend the rest of his life in prison.

Certainly, Annie and I were satisfied with the outcome of the trial, and certainly District Attorneys Downing and Capeless must have been happy that their strategy had succeeded. They had pitted the evidence of Wayne Lo's words and deeds against the opinions of the psychiatrists and their test results, and in the end, it was Wayne's deeds that had swayed the jury. If Wayne Lo could lie and deceive to cover his actions, he must have known they were wrong. If he had the ability to recognize their wrongness, he had the ability to make them conform to the law.

But things were less satisfactory from my 1997 perspective.

I realized that the two sides in the case had not been arguing about whether Wayne was what we'd call "crazy." All those weeks in the courtroom they had been trying to show that Wayne did or did not meet a single, precise legal standard. All the testimony from both sides had been given solely to support or reject the contention that Wayne Lo met the definitions of responsibility, as defined in our state's criminal code. Unfortunately, it was exactly this narrow legalism that prevented me from learning what I needed.

Regardless of who won in the legal arena, it was clear that *something* had gone wrong with Wayne. In human, rather than legal terms, you'd have to be crazy to do what he did. For a short while after completing my review, I entertained the suspicion that, before the shootings, Wayne had gone to the library and studied textbooks, maybe even *DSM-III*, and that he was faking insanity to avoid punishment. A little further reflection convinced me he'd have to be crazy to have done even that.

In 1997, I needed, more than anything, to know what had gone on with this kid. Was he a twisted, lying sociopath or was he disabled by a mental disease? How had his dysfunction, whatever it was, come on him? Was there even a difference, outside the legal arena, between the two states?

It was discouraging to realize that I still had a long road to travel, but almost immediately my fertile mind came up with a plan. I adjusted the harness where my flanks were beginning to chafe, lowered my head, and started pulling. Again.

❧22
JEREMY

In the spring of 1997 I had set up a meeting with Jeremy Roberts in New York City. He was the boy on the fringe of Wayne Lo's group who had made the warning telephone call to Trinka Robinson on the night of the murders, and he was the one person, of all of Wayne's friends, that I thought I should talk with. Aside from being the only person in the entire affair who'd actually tried to do anything before the shooting started, Jeremy was linked to all three areas of my investigation: the college, the gun and Wayne Lo. Our meeting was scheduled for 11:30 A.M., but I arrived in the city a few hours early. I had a book auction to preview, and I wanted to spend time with my son.

Brooks was in his second year of college by then, and flourishing. In a way, Galen had helped get him there.

Just two months after his brother's murder, one of Brooks' high school classmates stood up at lunchtime in the cafeteria, pulled out a handgun and shot himself in the head. Brooks was standing just a few feet away. They buried the poor boy right next to Galen. It took Brooks years before he could go down to the graveyard without getting furious.

He told us he'd had it with high school. The memories of Galen were still everywhere, and now this absurd and stupid tragedy was smeared all over everything. He didn't know where he'd go. He didn't care. He just knew he didn't want to go back.

We got him into a private school for his junior and senior years. It was a good school, but rather pretentious, heavy on the arts and music. French was mandatory. It actually called itself an "ecole." Acceptance at this ecole was an uphill battle for Brooks. He didn't speak French and wasn't artsy or musical, but he started taking language lessons over the summer, and learned enough to convince school officials, somewhat against their will, to accept him.

He proved adroit at navigating the politics of the situation. He cleaved to his supporters among the faculty, and tried to ignore his detractors. As for the artsy component, Brooks, the ex-high school football player, was temporarily at a loss. The idea of drawing made him blush, and he never, to my knowledge, picked up a musical instrument of any kind. However, he had a legacy from Galen, a Minolta 35 mm. camera. Galen had bought it with his own money the year before he died. This was Brooks' answer to the art requirement in the curriculum. He decided he'd take pictures with Galen's camera. That camera was a talisman for Brooks. It had been Galen's eye, and now it would be his. Over the years it would become his tool for dealing the horrible mystery of his brother's death.

There was no darkroom at the school, but Brooks showed initiative, something all the faculty was forced to regard favorably. He cleaned up an old pottery studio and converted it to a photo lab, borrowing and stealing what he needed to get the place operational. There were no photography teachers, so he read what was available, and absorbed everything he could from faculty members.

In the spring of Brooks' junior year, his class took its annual trip to France. When the class returned, Brooks stayed on in Europe for another six weeks. After he got back he showed us the photographs he'd taken on that trip. They weren't snapshots. They were fresh, live images of a world he had inhabited. They were marvelous. Annie and I realized, to our joy and surprise, that our son a gift.

Then it was time for Brooks to go to college. He and I made one memorable trip down the Eastern Macro-Metro Corridor, visiting colleges along the way, but he didn't like any of them. When we arrived at the campus of one institution, Brooks eyed the white pillars of Frat House Row and told me, "Don't even stop the car." I didn't. The tidy world of ivy walls seemed constraining to the young photographer who'd just spent his first summer alone in Europe.

In the winter of his senior year he offered to drive a friend to Manhattan for an interview at NYU. The friend was a gifted musician who was scarcely able to make his way in the world. Brooks got the boy to his interview, and on the way out, snatched up a handful of NYU brochures.

He learned from this material that NYU had a photography school. He applied for admittance to this place, and he and I went to his interview early that spring. The head of the department interviewed Brooks, then he called me in and we all talked. He said he liked Brooks a lot, but the situation was not hopeful. The school only accepted a few students out of hundreds of applicants, almost all of whom were better prepared than Brooks. What he liked, he said, was that Brooks had taught himself to take pictures. All these other kids had been formally trained. He said that Brooks seemed to have some natural ability, but he doubted this would be sufficient to convince the admissions board to accept him.

Brooks asked this man what kind of work the other applicants had submitted. He got up and took us into the next room, where there were hundreds of portfolios lined up in bins along the wall. He opened a few at random. Where Brooks' photos were poorly printed and mounted on cardboard, each of these seemed technically perfect. But, where Brooks' work transmitted an individual's vision of the world, each of these other portfolios seemed hopelessly narcissistic and self-referential. The other applicants were caught in a common teenage problem that Brooks had somehow managed to avoid.

That spring, Brooks was admitted to photography school at NYU. He'd been getting As and Bs since then, and he was still using Galen's camera.

Brooks and I went up to the auction gallery and looked at the books and then we went to a coffee shop around the corner. We caught up on family affairs and his progress at school. I reminded him who Jeremy Roberts was and explained why I wanted to talk to him. There was a big window in the coffee shop that looked out onto the street and, just as I was getting ready to leave, a strange idea came into my head. I knew that Jeremy was doing graduate work at the New School in Manhattan, and I knew that our old friend Lulu Savage, with whom Brooks shared an apartment, was an undergraduate at the same school. I said to Brooks, "Here's what we'll do. You stay here and keep an eye on the street. I'll walk past this window with Jeremy so you can see what he looks like. Then if he turns out to be a creep, you I.D. him for Lulu. She can get up close to him and slit his throat, just like in the movies."

Brooks gave me a disgusted smirk. "You're sick."

Perhaps I was. Perhaps the whole business had finally gotten to me. Perhaps my long and constant exposure to the grisly facts of my own son's murder had so desensitized me that I could joke about another murder and put Brooks and Lulu right in the middle of it. Or perhaps something in Jeremy Roberts' manner had made me sense that he might be uncooperative. Perhaps I was just nervous and was making stupid jokes to relieve the tension. I said stupid things all the time.

At any rate Brooks was not so upset that he forgot to ask me for a little walking-around money before I left. He pocketed the three twenties I slid into his palm, and stationed himself inconspicuously near the window.

This interview had been a difficult one to arrange. After I had decided to try to talk with Jeremy Roberts, I spent several days composing a letter to him, explaining my need to learn about Galen's murder, and asking delicately if we might meet. I told him I understood that he was in an ambiguous position. He had been a friend of Wayne's. On the other hand, of all the people involved in the tragedy he was the only one who'd done anything to try to remedy the situation. I made it clear that I bore him no ill will and that I understood the complexity of his situation.

The letter came back to me with "No Forwarding Address" stamped on it. I called our lawyer, but all he could furnish was the same outdated address. I asked, "What happens when our lawsuit comes to trial and we want Jeremy Roberts to testify and nobody knows where he lives?" There was a long pause, then the lawyer said, "This is one of the problems with having the trial delayed."

It took a couple of weeks of detective work to trace Jeremy Roberts from Simon's Rock to Long Island, to Paris, to Long Island again, to Florida and finally back to New York City. While I was doing this work, I kept thinking of what our lawyer had said, and about the possibility that there might be a dozen people like Jeremy Roberts to track down. Five years was a long time, especially for kids.

Once I had located Jeremy, it took another few weeks to call him. I'd had this same difficulty with each of the important calls I'd made in the course of my investigation. The difficulty appeared to lie in determining the optimum time for the call to be made. I'd start to call, and then put the phone back down thinking, "No, ten o'clock (or whenever) is a bad time." Of course this was a wholly internal calculation and it took no real account of any factor that might actually have determined an optimum time, if such a calculation had even been possible. What I think was really happening was that each new contact required an enormous amount of psychic energy. Whether I wanted to or not, I had to stop and gather my resources between each phase.

Eventually, I got through to him. I attempted to recapitulate my letter, but this was awkward in the immediacy of a real conversation. Jeremy said he thought he could understand the therapeutic value of my quest, but that speaking to me would be difficult for him. His association with Wayne had led to traumatic events, and his father had died the same year as our criminal trial. He hadn't thought about that whole dark period for a while, and it would be hard to go back to it. I told him I respected that difficulty. I said I'd be away on business for a couple of weeks and I suggested he think about my request while I was gone. He promised he would do that.

When I returned from my travels I telephoned him again. This time he said he supposed he could talk with me, but he wanted to know why we couldn't just do it over the phone? Again, my explanation was awkward. I told him it wasn't as if I had five specific questions to ask. I didn't really know what I wanted to ask him. I just wanted to meet him, to talk, and see where things went. I tried to make the prospect of a meeting easy and unthreatening.

He gave his grudging assent and we agreed to meet for lunch on a certain date. I then suggested that I pick him up at his apartment, and asked, innocently enough, "Were do you live?"

"Why do you want to know that?"

I let his question go unanswered, and told him I'd meet him in front of the auction gallery, but in the week that followed, and all the way down to New York on the appointed day, it kept running through my mind. Why did I want to know where he lived? So I could meet him, of course, and take him to lunch. Not so I could harass him. Not so I could ambush him or murder him. The kid was paranoid; perhaps not without reason. Maybe he was picking up the vestiges of my Clint and Lee persona. Perhaps this scared him and made him uptight about my visit. That, in turn, made me uptight, and I suspect was part of the reason I got into that sick riff about him with Brooks.

Jeremy Roberts was tall, pale and soft-featured. He was polite and helpful, but he seemed nervous throughout our lunch. His hands moved ceaselessly as we talked; to his hair, to his mouth, fiddling with his sleeves, turning the fork over and over at its place on the table. He never relaxed. Consequently, though I asked my questions and he answered them, we never had a real conversation. Maybe he was chronically ill at ease. Maybe I was less charming than I imagined myself.

To give him his due, he had a very tricky thing to communicate to me. He had tried explaining it to strangers before and he had been misunderstood, with unpleasant consequences. It was a very subtle matter and he made it clear that it was the key to my understanding everything else regarding Wayne Lo and his friends at Simon's Rock. Jeremy had to concentrate mightily to drag it back up and deliver it to me in anything like its true form. He was working too hard at this to relax and let it flow.

What he wanted to communicate to me had to do with a peculiar way he and his friends related. It was all about making jokes. Not telling jokes, but joking, in a very convoluted and ironical way, about what was going on around them. It was aimed at mitigating the unpleasant aspects of their surroundings, and it attempted to do so by satire and mockery. The joking was not just a private thing. It was often played out in public, in front of the very people it satirized. This separated them from the other kids, but in so doing, joined their little gang closer together.

The tricky part in relating this had to do with the subject matter of their jokes. Because the humor was so ingrown, it was very easy for an outsider to misconstrue. So they might and often did joke about, for example, killing people. But it wouldn't really be about killing people at all. You might joke about shooting someone, but it was just a way of saying that the situation was difficult. You could talk like a tough guy, about blowing people away, but it was self-mockery. Blowing people away was an absurdity, the most absurd possible thing to talk about, and so talking about it was a joke, and the joke provided relief. Could I possibly understand what he meant? He sat there over his onion soup, regarding me earnestly.

I was stuck. The only way to convince him I really understood would have been to tell him that I'd just finished joking with Brooks about slitting his throat. I didn't think this would set Jeremy Roberts at ease.

Instead I told him I understood very well what he was talking about, and he in turn continued to regard me with suspicion. When the cops had questioned him, and later on the witness stand at the criminal trial, this sort of humor had been thrown back in his face. He and his friends had talked about killing people? It was, he'd replied, only a joke. "A joke?" the DA had thundered, "You mean you thought killing people was *funny*?" Attempts to explain himself only led to stupid, unwarranted conclusions.

For the same reasons, the motives that people had ascribed to his group infuriated Jeremy Roberts. The idea that he and his friends were part of a cult was beneath Jeremy's scorn. They did not consider themselves violent, and they were not Nazis. (I gathered, however, that if a Nazi affectation would get a rise out of their fellow students, they'd try it.) On the night of the murders the police had actually barged into their dorm rooms, shining flashlights in their eyes, looking for weapons, questioning them about their Nazi cult activities. Couldn't these people understand the degree to which it had been a joke, a put-on? Could anybody be stupid enough to imagine they went around saying "Heil Hitler!" to each other? If anything, their outrageously conservative assertions, their refusal to endorse prevalent political attitudes, their demonstrative and public watching of (God forbid) the Rush Limbaugh TV show, were sane and sensible reactions to the faddish, politically correct conformity that surrounded them.

He gave me an example of how pervasive and extreme this political correctness had become on campus. His example involved an incident that had taken place in the first semester of his freshman year, and it centered around another figure I knew to be in Wayne Lo's circle, Eddie Caruso. Caruso was later expelled from Simon's Rock for other reasons, but this particular incident had such bad repercussions that he was under a cloud for the rest of his stay at the college. He was scorned by the community and finally had to write a public letter of apology. His sin was as follows:

After dinner one night, during the period reserved for public announcements, a feminist activist had gotten up and told the student body that there would be a meeting on a particular issue of interest to women, and that absolutely no men would be invited. Jeremy and his pals thought that she was so howlingly self-absorbed and humorless that, as a prank, they egged Eddie Caruso into standing up and announcing that there would also be a men's meeting that evening, and that the only women invited would be the ones who jumped out of the cake.

It was a stupid thing to have said. The word "sophomoric" comes to mind. Caruso's announcement might have occasioned a raised eyebrow at the University of Iowa or a chorus of groans at Yale. But so deeply had this little community drifted into self-seriousness, that Eddie Caruso's attempt at college humor made him a pariah for months.

That, explained Jeremy, was the context in which their harsh, right-wing humor originated, and that context accounted for some of its peculiarities. The kids in his group were conservative in a literal sense. They didn't approve of phoniness. Genuine craziness was OK, but not phoniness. There was, for instance, one kid they hung out with sometimes, a guy named Keith, and he was the wildest of them all. He was a body builder gone soft, a big jock, maybe gay, genuinely scary looking. In this little society of people trying so hard to be different, Keith, in his straightforward gay body-building way, was the most different of all. That was OK, but the kids who went to great lengths to seem weird, and were really straight underneath, that was not OK. Their radicalism was phony and this was what Jeremy and his friends objected to. Hence the "Conservative" stance. It was a reaction, a defiance.

Jeremy told me that he came to Simon's Rock from a "typical eastern

prep school background" hoping to escape the cliques and social pet-
tiness that had made his high school life unpleasant. Instead, conditions
were just as bad at Simon's Rock. Underneath all the colored hair and
piercings and loudly trumpeted radical politics, there was just as much
petty social bullshit. There was a sort of fascism of political correctness,
much of it centering on gender issues. Jeremy and his friends saw this
as mindless conformity and demonstrated against it.

Looking at that earnest, pale face in its wreath of soft black hair, I
decided that Holden Caulfield could have said a lot of what Jeremy
Roberts was saying. Jeremy was thoughtful and sensitive. He was somewhat alienated and he had problems with authority. Millions of ado-
lescents had preceded him in this. The gritty, ironical "killing" aspect
to the humor might be a recent innovation, but then, how many drive-
by shootings took place in Holden Caulfield's world?

I knew about the political correctness problem because I recalled the
adjustments Galen had to make to accommodate it during his career at
Simon's Rock. The first I'd heard of it was in the spring of 1991, midway
through his first semester on campus. I picked him up for spring break,
and on the way home, just for the fun of it, we stopped at Mt. Holyoke,
parked the car, and hiked up to the old hotel at the top of the mountain.
As we walked we talked, of course, and Galen told me all about the
feminist guerillas who had taken over social life on campus, and the
difficulty he had in coming to terms with them. His problem was how
to accommodate the demands of his newly politicized women friends.
Partly, they were ridiculous, and merited ridicule. Partly, they were serious. What they were talking about merited respect. Mostly they were
real people and Galen wanted to figure out how to relate to them. So,
he had schooled himself in the proper texts. Like learning some fraternity
code word, he could now say the correct thing, the thing that would
enable him to escape another harangue, another long debate. If they

accepted him, he could talk about other things with them, not just the same stuff everybody was saying over and over. He found the situation frustrating at first, then interesting. It had been a problem to solve, and he had solved it.

I have a particularly vivid recollection of this conversation, because it threaded through bare trees and over boulders, as we climbed, in a way that reminded me of Galen's difficulty in discovering the proper course of action. He was quite proud of himself. He was learning about the world and how to find his way through it. I was even prouder of him. He was growing up, and growing up well.

We emerged from those misty woods to the summit of Mt. Holyoke, with the whole Connecticut River Valley spread out at our feet. There was a thin overcast and all the colors were gray, black, and brown. The river had picked up a brilliant silver tone from the late afternoon sky, and it seemed alive as it wound its way through the fields and hamlets beneath us, down toward Springfield, Hartford, New Haven and the ocean.

Galen and I stood on the veranda of the old hotel and looked down at the river. The mountain was deserted. We were right back at the beginning of the world once again.

"I married a girl from down the river, you know."

"Oh?"

"Your mother is from Wethersfield, just south of Hartford, behind Springfield there, where the river disappears over the horizon. And I was born upstream a bit, and to the east, along the Miller River, more of a stream, actually. It empties into the Connecticut."

We talked for a while about the geography of our lives, the paths we made over the planet through time, how each was distinct, like a signature. Someday, I told him, he could bring his kids here and they could read their family history in that river.

"Just like a book." he chuckled.

"Exactly." I replied.

It had been a fine moment with Galen, but of greater use in this particular moment, it gave me some insight into what Jeremy was trying to describe. Raised on MTV's version of cutting-edge culture, and right at their most intense period of sexual questioning, this age group took naturally to gender-bending and the politicization of sexual identity. Among Galen's crowd before college there had been some hetero-homo switching, loudly announced and little pursued. In the Simon's Rock environment this sort of thing must have blossomed.

"Do you think that all this behavior, the macho stuff and the in-your-face humor, might have been a reaction, on Wayne's part, a way of not really dealing with those issues that the other kids were picking up?"

"It might have been."

"Did he ever go out on dates or have girlfriends at school?"

"No."

"What do you think his reaction was to women?"

"Oh, I think they scared him."

I thought they scared him too. As our talk continued, I began to think a lot of things scared Wayne, and that hanging out with these "tough" guys was a help in dealing with his fears. Jeremy told me that Wayne was very quiet when he first arrived on campus, very subdued, and that he only opened up as the year went on, after he realized he could trust his new friends. Jeremy emphasized that Wayne was physically quite small, and very sensitive about his size. He spent a lot of time working out in the weight room, and he played sports, particularly basketball, hard, with an intensity that was sometimes inappropriate for the circumstances. Jeremy told me he was quite surprised when it came out at the criminal trial that Wayne was an expert violinist. Wayne never talked to his pals about the violin or about his musical studies. Jeremy thought this went right back to that tough guy thing. Wayne didn't want his friends to know he did anything as sissified as playing the violin.

These matters, however, were secondary to Jeremy's major theme, the one he'd been so carefully laying before me, about their particular kind of humor and Wayne's reaction to it. Wayne was insecure and he compensated by acting tough, which his friends knew was a pose. He was as sensitive, intelligent and funny as they were. So they would rib him. Jeremy smiled, recalling it, "We'd be like, 'How tough *are* you, Wayne?' And he'd say, 'I'm *tough*'... It was just ridiculous."

The key thing, the core thing, was that everybody knew they were just joking. It was the glue that kept them together.

Then, without any of them becoming aware of a change, Wayne started taking it all seriously. As they realized later, to their horror, all the macho talk and the sick humor had gotten mixed up in Wayne's head and crossed over into reality.

"He really believed that stuff." Jeremy told me, "This is a terrible thing to say, but it was almost as if Wayne did those shootings to impress his friends."

The group centered around Kevin Wolak and Wayne Lo. Jeremy spent time with Wolak and Lo too, but as he said, "I had other friends, other places to go." Wayne and Kevin were the ones who kept company exclusively with each other. Eddie Caruso had been a part of it too, before his expulsion, but he'd also had other friends. In fact, Jeremy told me, Eddie had been a friend of Galen's. He'd been to the funeral service and wept with the other kids.

This caught me by surprise. Based on everything I'd heard previously I thought Eddie Caruso was simply one of the Bad Guys, one of Wayne Lo's group. The image of him as Galen's friend, weeping at the funeral, came in at a sufficiently oblique angle to get under my investigative shell. I was exposed for a moment, and it hurt. I caught a whiff of that old, inconsolable grief, and it killed my appetite for lunch.

Socially, everyone on campus was labeled by where they sat in the dining hall. Jeremy told me that the Wolak-Lo gang all sat at the same table, and that they maintained a menacing aspect. Other students were not welcome to join them. This confirmed what I remembered from the criminal trial and from my conversations with students and college staff. To Jeremy, this dining hall behavior had been just a goof. Andrew Jillings, the Residence Director, had noted it and dismissed it as a juvenile behavior of little consequence. Carly White, a friend of Galen's from the theater group on campus had found it disturbing, very objectionable. Their clannish, menacing aspect elicited a range of responses, but it did succeed in eliciting a response, which must have been an important consideration in maintaining it.

Mention of their nasty dining hall behavior reminded me to ask Jeremy if Wayne's behavior or personality had seemed to deteriorate in any way before the shootings. Had Wayne, in his interactions with his friends, conformed to the profile police and psychologists had sketched at the criminal trial? Had Jeremy noticed any change in Wayne from his first to his second years at Simon's Rock?

According to Jeremy Roberts, Wayne Lo had not appeared to deteriorate at all. If anything, he had become more sociable. Jeremy had entered Simon's Rock at the same time as Wayne, but had made friends with Kevin first. Wayne had initially been very shy and very unsure. He did not relate well to the other students. As freshman year went on, and the Lo-Wolak friendship solidified, Wayne became more relaxed and more approachable. Jeremy's own friendship with Wayne had really come into being during sophomore year, in the months preceding the shootings. Quite the opposite of any deterioration in social functioning, Jeremy reported that Wayne had seemed to improve as a friend. He became more open, more confident. He exhibited more of his sense of humor. The awful thing about this was that no one had a clue as to what was going on in Wayne's head. Or, if Wayne was giving clues, they were disregarded or lost in the general tone of the banter. I imagined them barking, Marine Corps style, "How tough *are* you, Wayne?" in jest, and Wayne responding in earnest, "I'm *tough!*"

We talked about Kevin and his friendship with Wayne. According to Jeremy, Kevin Wolak was perhaps the most truly conservative member of their group. At the heart of his political affectation was a strong sense of morality, and a rigid concepts of right and wrong. According to Jeremy Roberts, Kevin's realization of the unwitting part he had played in Wayne's crime and the possibility that he might have taken steps to prevent it, had nearly destroyed him.

This was, literally, a difficult thing for Jeremy to say. We were talking about guilt. We were talking about Jeremy's close friend, and by implication, Jeremy's own guilt. He had great respect for what he saw to be the truth of the situation and, out of respect for its complexity, he was trying hard not to impute unwarranted character or motives to Kevin. Unhappily, though he shared Leon Botstein's intellectual acuity, he did not possess Botstein's verbal abilities. Jeremy's talk sidled into unrelated issues and mumbled apologies for being so nervous. (He seemed more troubled than nervous.) After quite a bit of this shattered discourse, I was finally able to gather that Kevin Wolak was to this day carrying a heavy load of guilt for whatever part he imagined he played in the murders.

Jeremy told me that he and Kevin had been in Wayne's room on the morning of the shootings, when he'd come back with the ammunition and gun parts from Classic Arms. Wayne had started to open the package, but the residence director had come around and they'd left the room. Jeremy's account of what happened after that followed the version we heard at the criminal trial. Wayne came late to his afternoon exam and left it after only an hour. He excitedly told his friends he had gotten "gun stuff." Wayne told them essentially the same story he told Bernie Rodgers, that the "gun stuff" was for his father. When relating this to Kevin and Jeremy, however, he fudged in an odd sort of way, telling

them, "That stuff is for my Dad's gun at home ... but maybe it's not."
Then, at the dining hall that night, Wayne was acting so strangely that
Jeremy realized he might really have a gun, and that he really might
use it. When Wayne told Jeremy that he was tired of living, Jeremy knew
something was wrong, and that was when he'd made the warning phone
call. He'd tried campus security first, but had only gotten an answering
machine. Afraid to leave a message in case his suspicions were ground-
less, he called Trinka Robinson at her dorm.

According to Jeremy, Wayne had called Kevin at his dorm just before
the shootings began, not to say that he had a gun, but to say a strange
sort of goodbye.

"It was, 'I love you, man.' or something like that."

So, this was what Wayne had been doing in his room after the dorm
meeting with Floyd, just before he left with his gun. Floyd, or Ba Win
or Andrew Jillings might have burst into that room and found Wayne
on the telephone, saying goodbye to his only friend. It sounded like
another contingency with which Kevin could torture himself. He'd been
the last person Wayne had spoken to, just before the shooting. Could
he have stopped it?

Kevin was not dealing well with his guilt. Jeremy reported that, after
the shootings Kevin had turned his own SKS in to the police. He told
Jeremy he never wanted to have anything to do with guns again. He
didn't even know if he could have any more Asian friends. Things had
just seemed to get progressively worse for him. Jeremy had finally lost
touch with him. They hadn't communicated since last summer. He had
been on anti-depressant drugs, Jeremy knew that much. Once, Kevin
told him he'd been visiting a girl and Wayne called her from prison!
She gave the phone to Kevin and, "It freaked him out. He couldn't talk."

If there had been any doubt before, I understood now that, more
than being an accomplice in the shootings, Kevin Wolak was one of its
victims.

I asked Jeremy how he was handling all this. Did he feel any of Kevin's lingering guilt?

He told me he did not. He said it had been a terrible thing, that he, and everyone associated with Wayne carried a terrible weight for not realizing how far astray Wayne had drifted. Jeremy himself had finally come to the realization that as bad as it was, it had happened, and there was nothing he could do to make it not happen. He knew he had never intended anyone harm, and that he had tried hardest to do something about the situation, based on the information he had at the time, so finally he was able just to let it go, not to forget about it, but to put that burden down and turn his attention to other matters.

The only emotion that lingered around the incident for Jeremy was anger. He told me that after the shootings took place everyone went home on an extended holiday break. Toward the end of this period, Bernie Rodgers called Jeremy and his parents in to "discuss his future." Bernie told the Roberts that there had been "many complaints from parents" about Jeremy's presence on campus. Bernie said that if Jeremy were to return to the college he might "interfere with the healing process." It was finally decided that Jeremy should not return to Simon's Rock College. Jeremy said that Bernie had tried to make this seem like a joint decision, made in Jeremy's best interests, but that in fact Bernie had already made up his mind and the meeting was just a formality. Jeremy had wanted to return to Simon's Rock. He did not feel that he was exclusively identified with Wayne Lo's group, and at this difficult time, he did not want to be sent off by himself. He felt he got jobbed by Bernie Rodgers.

Interestingly, at the time of this meeting Jeremy still had not told Bernie that he was the one who'd made the warning telephone call. Throughout the two-hour conversation that would decide his future at Simon's Rock College, Jeremy Roberts had kept his silence about the fact that he had warned Trinka Robinson. Was he ashamed he hadn't done more? Did he think his knowledge of the gun would implicate him more deeply in Wayne's actions? Had the police told him not to disclose this key testimony?

I reached back for this next question, and I lost it. Suddenly there were no more questions in me. I was exhausted. We sat in uncomfortable silence for a time, then I signaled the waitress that we were through, gave her my credit card, and forgot to sign the slip. Jeremy had finally stopped fidgeting. He looked pale and blank. It had been a tiring session for both of us.

As we staggered into the sunlight I told Jeremy that he seemed to have gotten through the trauma pretty well, and that I was glad of it. I thanked him for making the effort to recall this painful subject and told him the information he'd given me, particularly about Eddie Caruso and Kevin Wolak, had been most helpful to my understanding.

Jeremy apologized again for being nervous. I told him he didn't need to apologize, and that he certainly did not need to feel ill at ease. He replied that he always felt ill at ease when discussing this subject.

"Everyone I've talked to about this has found a way to turn it around on me."

He turned abruptly at Twentieth Street and disappeared into the crowd. It was the last I saw of my wary informant, but not the last time I thought of him.

❧23
A NARROW MADNESS

At some point in my ramblings through the book stalls of New England I found a copy of the *Diagnostic and Statistical Manual of Mental Disorders* (third edition, revised). This was the famous *DSM-III-R* that had been waved, quoted and thumped at Wayne Lo's criminal trial. I don't remember where I was when I found it. Bookshops, to a hardworking book scout, can be like saloons to a man on a bender. After a while all the saloons turn into one big saloon. Nor can I recall exactly when I found it, except that it was a used book by the time it came my way, meaning it had probably been supplanted by *DSM-IV*.

I do, however, have a clear recollection of what it felt like to discover the book. It was in a box of paperbacks, and the yellow lettering jumped out at me from the blue background of the cover. *DSM-III-R*! I paused, trying to recall what meaning that designation held for me, and then it all came back in a rush, knocking me from the comfort of my book scouting routine into the painful days of Wayne Lo's criminal trial. Here it was, the "premier diagnostic instrument," a big, fat paperback, six hundred pages long. It would be my key to the knowledge of the shrinks, and it only cost me ten dollars.

I took it home and put it on my desk, where it sat, untouched, for a year or more, until a process of elimination brought me back to it.

In the years since Galen's death I had come to believe that Wayne Lo was not just a nasty kid with an attitude problem. In order to have done what he did, in the manner he did it, I believed he had to be truly sick. Now I needed to find out, if I could, what that meant.

My dealings with the Massachusetts Department of Corrections had convinced me that trying to go through official channels to obtain permission to interview Wayne Lo would be too much of a distracting battle. After speaking with Jeremy Roberts I doubted that more such conversations, as interesting as they might be in other ways, would add significantly to my store of knowledge. I had studied the testimony of his friends from the criminal trial, and read the depositions they'd given our lawyers in preparation for the civil trial, and I felt I'd absorbed what they had to say. Similarly, the testimony of police officers and prosecution witnesses had little new to offer me because almost all of it was intended to prove that Wayne had planned and committed murder with full knowledge that he was doing something wrong. The inference was that he was a selfish, bad person who deserved to be locked up in jail for the rest of his life. While this may have been true, it was not the kind of truth I was seeking.

Thus I was led to doctors Gaw, Plakun and Schouten, and to the book they'd used to validate the testimony they'd given us. However, this was a consciously ironic evolution. I did not believe in psychiatrists. I did not use them and I did not trust them. There was a very specific reason for my mistrust.

My younger sister, Wendy, had been a schizophrenic. The disease had first manifested itself in her high school years, and my parents and I followed her from one doctor to the next, with occasional stops at institutions, ranging from tony, private residential facilities with pleasant grounds and lots of family therapy, to state institutions, where a psychic fog of prescription drugs hung heavy in the hallways. By the time she reached her late twenties, her insurance had run out. She was in a state of terror and near-constant torture from a disease that only seemed to be getting worse. She was facing the prospect of a lifetime in and out of state hospitals, and, probably worse from her perspective, a lifetime of burdening her family with her violent, frightening disease. In the spring of 1977 she purchased a handgun and shot herself in the heart.

She had been a caring, courageous person, and a good friend. As much as I loved and missed her, I had some idea of how greatly she suffered and I was not unsympathetic with her final decision. I was, however, completely out of sympathy with the mental health professionals who had treated her through the 1960s and 1970s. They seemed to me no more than a bunch of high-priced phonies. It was OK to hire them to talk to, if you couldn't do that with your own friends, but for anything more serious, they were useless.

Now, in 1997, I needed them.

At least, I needed clarification on what some of their number had said about Wayne Lo. In particular, it was the diagnoses of Gaw and Plakun that I thought needed elucidation. Ronald Schouten's testimony, and his place in the trial, seemed more understandable to me.

Schouten's diagnosis of "Disorder Not Elsewhere Classified," though perhaps elicited by Wayne's lawyers for tactical purposes, was comprehensible enough. He contended that the sane, rational part of the mind could act in the service of a delusion caused by mental disease. Thus, according to Dr. Schouten and the defense, Wayne could plan. He could hide his actions. He could appear normal and functional and still be in the thrall of a deep-seated madness, referred to by all three psychiatrists as a "delusional system."

If Schouten had identified a key factor in the working of this madness, Gaw and Plakun thought the madness had a particular type. Gaw had diagnosed delusional disorder, and Plakun, schizophrenia. Type suggested form, and form implied an etiology and a prognosis, and this was the kind of information I thought I was after. What made Wayne crazy? In what way, exactly, was he crazy? Where had the craziness come from? What course would it take through the rest of his life?

I tracked down Plakun and Gaw, found telephone numbers for their offices and left uncomfortable, lengthy messages on their answering machines (like lawyers, these guys never answered cold calls) trying to explain myself and what I needed from them.

Both men returned my calls promptly. Both were sympathetic and understanding. Both were willing to help, but both told me they'd have to get clearance from Wayne's lawyers before they could speak with me.

I'd been expecting difficulties of this sort. Months before, at the beginning of my Wayne Lo investigation, I had called Stuart Eisenberg, Wayne's defense lawyer, and was surprised to find him friendly to me and responsive to my inquiries.

He told me that he hoped I understood his place in the legal process, and that I would not confuse his legal defense of Wayne Lo with a lack of sympathy for what we had suffered. I assured him that by now I had come to understand precisely these things, and that Annie and I bore him no ill-will. In fact, I said, the only people with whom I was still angry, aside from Wayne Lo, were the college and their insurance company. I told him that I thought their delaying tactics regarding our civil suit were scurrilous. Eisenberg brought me up short.

"That's not true," he told me, matter-of-factly, "The college didn't delay your civil trial, nor did their insurance company. I was the one who filed the brief preventing Wayne from being deposed until after his appeal had been heard. Your lawyers were very unhappy with me, but my first duty was to my client."

Here was an unlooked-for piece of information! It had been Stuart Eisenberg who had sent our civil suit spinning off into years of uncertainty. All the energy I'd put into my moral outrage at Simon's Rock College and the legal staff of Great American Insurance Company had been misplaced. Once again, I'd been wrong.

This was not all Stuart Eisenberg had to tell me. As my friends at the DA's office had warned, my access to Wayne Lo, in any sense, was controlled by his lawyers. This included any plans I might have to speak with Wayne's parents or his psychiatrists. Eisenberg told me that, if I ever did locate any of these people, they would need clearance from him to talk to me. He told me that he would not make a decision on any such matters until they actually occurred. He felt badly about this, he said. He was sympathetic to my endeavor, but his client's interests had to come first.

Stuart Eisenberg proved to be a man of his word. Within a week of contacting the psychiatrists, I got a conference call from him and his associate, Janet Kenton-Walker. They told me that Gaw and Plakun had called them, and that, against their better judgment, they were going to allow me to speak with these men. They wanted me to understand that this was an extraordinary circumstance. Normally, they would be completely protective of their client and any request such as mine would be denied. But they told me they had great respect for what my family and I had been through, and they approved of what I was doing now. Therefore they were allowing me access to the psychiatrists, with the strict proviso that I confine my questions to what was already a matter of public record.

I thanked the lawyers for their consideration, and I reminded them that since my civil trial could not proceed until after Wayne's appeal had been heard, it was against my interests to do anything that would jeopardize this process. I had a real incentive to stay within the boundaries they had outlined, and I assured them that I would do so. As soon as they hung up, I called doctors Plakun and Gaw and made appointments to visit them and discuss the testimony they had given at the criminal trial.

Then, in hopes that it would give me some idea of what the psychiatrists were talking about, I dove to the bottom of the pile on my desk and pulled out *DSM-III-R*.

The variety of ways in which the human mind could malfunction was awe-inspiring. *DSM-III-R* listed, in bold faced capitals, about forty categories of mental disorders, ranging from developmental disorders, through psychoactive substance-induced disorders, to the classic schizophrenia, delusional, post-traumatic and multiple personality disorders, as well as sexual, sleep and factitious disorders. Each of these headings had a number code, and each numbered classification was followed by half a dozen or more sub-classifications, in plain type, also numbered.

If this seemed an excessively rigid approach to something as fluid as the human psyche, the authors and editors of *DSM-III-R* (and there were 431 listed contributors to this massive effort) approached their work with a certain humility. These were, they cautioned, only guidelines for making diagnoses. "The purpose of *DSM-III-R*," they wrote, "is to provide clear descriptions of diagnostic categories in order to enable clinicians and investigators to diagnose, communicate about, study and treat the various mental disorders."

So far, so good. Communicating about, and studying Wayne's mental disorder was just what I had in mind. I opened to the chapter about schizophrenia.

In the introductory paragraphs I learned about the onset of this disease in early adult life, its recurrence and the accompanying deterioration in social and occupational functioning. There followed a seven-page discussion. I read through this information, and I thought about Wendy and I thought about Wayne Lo. Initially, it seemed odd that two such vastly different people might be suffering from the same mental disease, but there were symptoms specific to each of them. For example, in the "Content of Thought" category I found "delusions that are often ... bizarre (i.e. involving a phenomenon that in the person's culture would be regarded as totally implausible)..." These might be Wayne's commands from God. Wendy had complained of terrifying auditory hallucinations, and I found those listed, as well as a symptom that had affected her perhaps more than any other, "The sense of self that gives the normal person a feeling of individuality, uniqueness, and self-direction is frequently disturbed in schizophrenia. This is sometimes referred to as a loss of ego boundaries, and frequently is evidenced by extreme perplexity about one's own identity and the meaning of existence." I could recall Wendy describing exactly these symptoms to me. The fit was uncanny.

I read on, with closer attention, thinking now of Wayne. I found much that might apply to him: the delusions, the flat affect, the social isolation, and the magical thinking. There was also a requirement for a "Prodromal phase: A clear deterioration in functioning before the active phase ..." This prodromal phase required the presence of certain symptoms. In Wayne's case, "social isolation" and "unusual perceptual experiences" seemed the most likely.

I thought about Wendy, and I thought about Wayne. I wondered if Wendy's experience hadn't prepared me, in some way, to envision Wayne Lo. Because of her, I could understand mental illness as a real and grave disability, not just as a personal weakness. If I allowed for the difference in backgrounds between them, and in their personal natures, and in the support systems that surrounded them, it was not impossible to imagine them suffering the same general sort of impairment. The great unbridgeable difference was how this impairment had played out in their lives.

Then I moved into Gaw's diagnosis of delusional (paranoid) disorder, which happened to be the next chapter in the book. I learned that the essential feature of this disorder is the presence of a "persistent, nonbizarre delusion." So, in a sense, Gaw was at odds with Plakun from the outset. This had been apparent to me even during the criminal trial, and now as then, I ascribed it to differences in personality or perception of the two doctors. To Gaw, perhaps, a command from God was not necessarily bizarre.

Regarding Dr. Gaw's diagnosis of Wayne's delusional disorder as

Grandiose, the book had this to say. "Grandiose delusions usually take the form of the person's being convinced that he or she possesses some great, but unrecognized talent or insight ... Grandiose delusions may have a religious content." Another common characteristic of people with delusional disorder was the appearance of normal behavior, "when their delusional ideas are not being discussed or acted upon." Immigration was included as a "predisposing factor."

Most of the criteria listed in this chapter fit Wayne to a T.

DSM-III-R was a huge book. The discussions of schizophrenia and delusional disorder had occupied sixteen pages, parts of which I had not fully understood. However, I had gotten some sense of the purpose and use of this tome. It might not help me know how or why Wayne Lo had gone mad. But if Dr. Erik Plakun and I were discussing "295.34, paranoid schizophrenia, chronic with acute exacerbation," there would be little disagreement about which symptoms needed to be present.

I read the same sections the next day, and again the day after that. I waited a few days and read them once more. Then I sat at my desk and stared out the window and thought again about Wendy and Wayne Lo. It was time, I guessed, to go see the shrinks.

The Bedford VA Hospital was a sprawling expanse of rolling lawns and big trees dominated at its high end by a cluster of multistoried brick buildings. There was a sense of age to the place, and I could imagine nurses in white uniforms pushing doughboys in wheelchairs, or shell-shocked grunts standing smoking in tight groups under trees on the lawn. Dr. Albert Gaw did not fit into this. A short, dark-haired man of Asian origin, dressed in a cheap suit and clashing shirt, he managed to project a presence at once businesslike and gently humorous.

His office was in a residential facility at the rear of the complex. Following his instructions I had parked my van in lot 9, entered through the rear of the building, and taken the stairway to the second floor. Here

I encountered a locked metal door with a small wire-reinforced window that was in sharp contrast to the gentle green ambiance of the rest of the hospital. This was where the crazy people lived. A receptionist in an office directly across the hallway saw my face at the window and let me in. She had no sooner finished telling me that Dr. Gaw was making his rounds, than he cruised around the corner with an intern in tow, smiled at me, nodded, shook my hand and took me to his office.

I sat in a chair opposite his cluttered gray desk and recited a more polished version of the message I had left on his answering machine. Frustration at the delay of our civil lawsuit, I told him, had driven me to undertake my own investigation of Galen's death. I had looked into the college's role in the shootings, and I had researched the murder weapon and its origins. Now I was trying to gain some understanding of Wayne Lo. Gaw smiled and nodded, hands folded on the desktop. I felt at ease with him. He was a man who had heard many things. We got down to business.

He told me that my interpretation of *DSM-III-R* placed undue emphasis on the bizarre or non-bizarre nature of an hallucination. Certainly Wayne was delusional, but the important thing was the content of Wayne's delusion. The most significant thing about Wayne's dysfunction was that it operated only in an area involving religious beliefs.

Wayne believed that he had experienced, and subsequently carried out, a command from God, and that this had been his sole purpose in life. Clearly, the ideas of purpose and its religious dimension were not bizarre. What was important in Dr. Gaw's analysis was that everything else about Wayne seemed relatively normal. He told me he'd had to try several lines of questioning until he got onto the religious theme, but that once Wayne got going on it, the whole command from God narrative was delivered with absolute conviction.

According to Wayne, the command had come into his body directly, like an electrical charge, on several distinct occasions. The examples that

Gaw had used at the trial, of magical thinking and delusions of reference, were reported to him by Wayne during the same interviews, and with the same degree of conviction. The remarkable thing, Gaw stressed, was that the delusions were limited to the narrow area of these religious beliefs. Perhaps, during the acute phase, the madness had spilled over and taken control of his other actions, resulting in the shootings, but for the most part, Wayne exhibited relatively normal behavior.

I asked Dr. Gaw how Wayne could have been that crazy and that functional at the same time. Gaw looked at me dead-level and replied, "There are people far crazier who are still perfectly functional." He told me a story of two patients he'd had on his ward years ago, who only went crazy at Christmas time. "One thought he was Jesus." Gaw related with a smile, "And the other thought he was the Virgin Mary. So we had our own Christmas Pageant on the ward each year."

I asked him why he thought that Dr. Plakun had diagnosed schizophrenia. Gaw replied that the possibility had occurred to him too, but that ultimately he had rejected it. He reminded me that Plakun had first examined Wayne immediately after the shootings, whereas he had not been called in until the next month and had continued to interview Wayne throughout the next year, so perhaps the timing had some effect on the appearance of the symptoms. The sentence stopped there, and he waited patiently for the next question. No second-guessing colleagues for this guy.

The prognosis for this kind of disorder, untreated, (as Wayne would be untreated in jail) was very poor. Wayne was still in the grip of his command-from-God delusion, and Dr. Gaw doubted there would be a recovery. Again, he stressed that the craziness was only in one specific area. For the rest, Wayne might appear functional, or even normal to his jailers or visitors.

Causes? Nobody knew. There was some indication of an abnormally high level of copper in Wayne's body. Perhaps someday they'd discover a correlation between copper level and this type of disturbance. But there was nothing conclusive yet. Certainly the stresses of immigration, of the pressures put on him by his parents, of pressures at school—these were all contributory factors—but no one cause could be singled out.

In the end, all he could do as a clinician was to describe the disorder.

Before long I realized I was out of questions to ask about the material he had covered at the trial. I felt we could have sat and talked all day about Wayne, in some speculative fashion, but I was very conscious of the restraints the lawyers had put on our conversation. The interview lurched to a stop.

He asked me how I was doing. I told him this felt like a heavy thing I'd been carrying for a long time, but that now I was almost ready to put it down. He smiled, nodded. I thanked him for taking the time to talk with me. We shook hands, smiling, and I walked back down the stairs and across the lawn to the parking lot, still carrying my heavy thing, thinking, oddly, of the intelligent and industrious crows gawing away in my back yard each morning, and of a narrow madness.

A week later Dr. Erik Plakun and I met in the reception area at Austen-Riggs Center in Stockbridge, Massachusetts. Austen-Riggs was located kitty-corner from the famous Red Lion Inn at the center of this quaint New England village, just two miles down the road from the Norman Rockwell Museum, an idyllic setting.

I was happy to see that Dr. Plakun had gained weight in the comfortable surround of this high-class facility. A second chin was bulging beneath his close-cropped beard, and his torso filled the loose collarless blouse he wore. I was glad that he'd gained weight because I didn't like him. I hadn't liked him at the trial and I could see immediately on meeting him now, that I still did not like him. There was a self-contained certainty to him that got my back up. In my own mean-spiritedness I rejoiced, momentarily, that he might be struggling with his weight.

He motioned me into his office, just a few doors down the hall, and told me to have a seat. There was a chair in front of the desk so I sat in it, remembering from my experience with Dr. Gaw that he would sit at the desk.

"No." he told me, "That's my chair."

I apologized and, in acute distress, moved to the chair across from his. The fucking desk was three times the size of Gaw's, and made of real wood instead of gray metal, and this pompous porkchop wasn't even sitting at it! Who did he think he was, kicking me out of his chair like that?

My heart was pounding. I flew to the top of the room and looked down on us both.

If I didn't like the way this guy comported himself, so what? His manner was what it was. If I chose to interpret it in a negative fashion, that was my problem, not his. In fact, he was volunteering his time and knowledge to help me out, and either I could lighten up and avail myself of this help, or sit there like a jerk thinking *he* was a jerk.

Once I got that straightened out, Erik Plakun had a lot to tell me.

The main question I had for him regarded the duration of Wayne's illness. According to *DSM-III-R*, one of the major diagnostic criteria called for continuous signs of the disturbance for at least six months. Wayne had not seemed to exhibit any symptoms until shortly before the shootings. How did his behavior conform to the diagnostic requirements?

Plakun reminded me that he had examined Wayne over a period of many months, and that his diagnosis at the trial had been made after observing Wayne throughout this period. Wayne's delusional belief in the command hallucination had not diminished or disappeared during the time between the shootings and the criminal trial. Hence, the six-month criterion was easily met.

My next question related to this. Two of the other criteria for diagnosis of schizophrenia called for a "Prodromal phase" in which there is a clear deterioration of functioning before the active phase begins. Again, according to the testimony of his friends, and to the chronology developed at the trial, I did not see much evidence of this deterioration.

Dr. Plakun explained that, in fact, there had been a decrease of sorts in Wayne's functioning. The Thanksgiving incident and the arguments with Floyd, the controversial AIDS paper, and the rumored harassment of other students were all evidence of this. He also reminded me about the testimony several witnesses had given at the criminal trial regarding a test Wayne had taken on the afternoon of the shootings. His answer to the essay question had started normally, then deteriorated into a crazed rant about his perfection. Wayne had ultimately come to feel as if he were the final arbiter of what was true and right, and that no one else was competent to judge his work. Furthermore, in Plakun's estimation, Wayne had been a sneaky sort. He did not tell anyone, even his mother, about the onset of the command hallucinations, and it was possible there were other symptoms, or other occurrences of the hallucinations that he was hiding.

As a final part of the answer to my question, Plakun talked about the kind of situation Wayne was in with his friends, the kind of militant, oppositional humor they engaged in, and how this might have masked Wayne's symptoms. When Wayne talked about shooting people his friends disregarded him or thought he was just joking, as they were. They'd talk about blowing people away, about shooting people in the dining hall, and Kevin Wolak, for instance, would be kidding, relieving some internal pressure, voicing his discontent in a harmless manner, while Wayne, unbeknownst to anybody, would be deadly serious.

This was fascinating to me, particularly in how it echoed Jeremy Roberts' statements. Supposing all Wayne's friends, for their own social reasons, had talked and acted crazy? Symptoms that might have been obvious in another context might pass unnoticed. I thought once again of their banter. "How tough *are* you, Wayne?"

I reminded Dr. Plakun of the "transgression, punishment, purification" cycle he'd discussed at the trial, and asked him how it related to his diagnosis of schizophrenia. His explanation began in a rather strange way. He told me that in the old days, a hundred years ago, before they had tools like *DSM,* there were more informal and anecdotal ways of making diagnoses. It was said that you could always tell you were talking to a paranoid schizophrenic if their words made the hairs on the back of your neck stand up. Plakun said that some of the things Wayne told him elicited that reaction in him.

The "transgression, punishment, purification" cycle, he continued, had not been intended as a diagnosis of Wayne's disease, but rather as a model of a way in which the disease might function, or as a paradigm of Wayne's behavior that fed into the disease. Wayne's parents had been heavy disciplinarians and Wayne had come to expect that when he did wrong, he would be punished. As a result of this punishment the score would be settled and things would be back to normal. While his behavior in the shootings followed this pattern, the roles had changed. The transgressors were now the people at the college, not Wayne himself. The shooting, the punishment, was a means to purification, but now, rather than being the one who was punished, Wayne was the punisher. He was taking on the role that had formerly belonged his parents. In this sense the shootings had been an initiation to manhood.

Plakun's analysis rocked me in its twisted, intuitive correctness. Galen's and Ñacuñán's murders had been, for Wayne Lo, a rite of passage.

It was at this moment, sitting in a shrink's office of all places, that I came to the nub of it.

I realized with a pang that Wayne was indeed truly, deeply crazy. He was as afflicted with his disability as Wendy had been with hers. After three decades of living with my sister and her illness, I had been unable to penetrate its mystery. Now, after only a few months of relatively cursory research, how could I presume that I would understand anything about Wayne's madness? He was insane. There was, as his father had reported at the trial, "a different soul inside." It was a terrible mystery, a holy mystery; one I could not hope to solve. As of that moment, I was content to stop trying.

I had assumed my anger for Wayne Lo was so deep and potentially destructive that it could only be approached in the most delicate manner; that, in essence, I would spend the rest of my life sidling up to it, nibbling away at it; that it would be my own dark burden until I died. Now I saw the matter differently, and my inability to understand became its own kind of understanding.

As he continued to speak of Wayne's illness, Plakun, like Gaw, stressed the fact that it seemed to occupy only a narrow part of his psyche. Plakun used the example of an infection that might make your whole hand swell up, as opposed to a boil, which would contain the infection in one location. Wayne's illness was analogous to the boil, and it occupied only the area of religious thinking.

I told him what Dr. Gaw had said about the illness and its extent, and he concurred. It was quite plausible to both of these men that Wayne could seem functional in most respects and still be delusional in a narrow area.

Plakun also agreed with Gaw regarding the cause of the disease. No one knew. It was as simple as that. One could discover contributing factors, and indeed, many were mentioned in *DSM-III-R* and much had been made of these at the criminal trial, but science was still a long way from isolating the organic and psychological components of this disease.

As for a prognosis, treatment was possible, perhaps. But in Wayne's case, there was an interesting wrinkle. Motivation played a big part in treatment, as it did in any aspect of recovery. The patient has to want to get better. As long as Wayne believed he was God's instrument, he could feel that he'd done the right thing. He could show complete dis-interest in the criminal trial because he believed his actions had been judged on a higher level and that his fate had already been decided by God. He would show no remorse for the murders he'd committed because he believed that he'd done what he was supposed to have done. If he recovered sufficiently to see that this had been a delusion, he would be faced with the gravity and the wrongness of his acts, and this would be very difficult for him to accept. In this instance, Wayne had no motive to get better. Given that he wasn't receiving any treatment in prison, the prognosis didn't seem good.

Then, as it had with Dr. Gaw, our talk reached the limits of what the lawyers had allowed and stopped. There was a pause, and Plakun made ready to say something. I thought he was going to tell me he was sorry about Galen, or ask me how I was feeling, but he did neither.

Instead, he told me he'd heard that Wayne was exceedingly angry at his defense lawyers for not doing more research into the lives of the people he'd murdered.

Wayne was convinced that such research would prove why these people had been chosen by God to die, and that his actions on December 14, 1992, would thus be vindicated.

24
LO!

One of my reasons for telephoning Stuart Eisenberg had been to initiate the long process of establishing communication with Wayne Lo's parents. I recalled that Wayne's lawyers had let it be known to our lawyers that the Los had expressed their regrets for what had happened, and had stated their willingness to help us, if they could. I still cherished the fantasy of using them to gain access to Wayne, so I asked Eisenberg if, within the constraints of the current legal situation, there was anything he could do to help me talk with them.

Stuart Eisenberg answered this question with startling, unlawyerlike alacrity.

Mr. and Mrs. Lo, he told me, had suffered greatly since the shootings. Part of their suffering was caused by the intensity of their need to apologize to the Gibsons, and was compounded by their hesitation to do so. They were afraid to contact us. They felt it would be presumptuous and improper. They felt that any overture should come from the Gibsons. So they had waited, since the murders, for us to call. Mr. and Mrs. Lo would like very much to speak with us. It was something they had badly needed to do for years.

Having said this, he reminded me again that his primary job was to defend Wayne Lo against the criminal charges brought by the Commonwealth of Massachusetts. This forced him to ask me, and he hoped I understood his reasons for asking, if my desire to speak with the Los was in any way related to my lawsuit or to any criminal or civil action against his client. I assured him that my call was in no way related to

305

any legal action; that it was strictly motivated by my own desire to understand what had happened.

In that case, he said, he would relay my request to the Los. He was certain they would accept, but he would advise them that before calling me they should spend a couple of days considering their decision and its possible ramifications. Then he told me that he admired me for making this call. He knew the courage it must have required, and he could only speculate as to the amount of effort it must have taken to overcome my own pain and reach out to the Los. The respect that he felt for me and my family moved him to confess something that had been bothering him, and he hoped I would take it in the spirit in which it was intended.

Toward the end of the criminal trial, he said, he had passed Annie and me in the hallway outside the courtroom. In an effort to, "perhaps put a human face on what we were doing" he had stopped and introduced himself to us. He told me that after he had done this, he saw from the look in Annie's eyes that, far from bringing her any relief, he had only added to her pain. He sincerely regretted this, and he had felt badly about it ever since. He hoped I would accept his apology, no less heartfelt for having been tendered all these years later.

I told him that no apology was necessary; that Annie and I both had come to understand his necessary role in the proceedings, and then, I think, I thanked him and hung up. I was getting rattled.

Eisenberg hadn't really listened to what I'd said, or I hadn't explained it well enough. He was making assumptions about me and my family, and I was allowing him to proceed, uncorrected. His expression of admiration for what I considered to be my rather manipulative use of him and the Los was disconcerting to me. However there was a deeper cause of my uneasiness, and it had nothing to do with how either of us interpreted the content of our telephone call.

I was getting rattled because suddenly our conversation had deviated from the cold, clean world of relentless investigation. As long as I was in my fact-finding mode I was safe from the emotional turmoil surrounding Galen's murder. It was my haven, and from there I could deal with the hurt and confusion little by little, as and when I chose. Stuart Eisenberg had gone instinctively and immediately to the "feeling" component of the situation. He had talked about the Los' pain and his pain. He had insinuated my family into the process as well, and he was assuming that we were trying to make contact with the Los to let them know that we forgave them for whatever role they imagined they had played in Galen's murder. In fact, our family didn't think about the Los very often. We had never assumed they were responsible for anything, and when we considered them at all, it was with pity, knowing they had suffered a hurt that, if possible, was worse than our own.

Implicit in all his assumptions about our motives was the understanding that recovering from the death of a loved one involved heavy commerce in pain and suffering. This was messy business, quite unlike the clean, focused, hard-nosed investigating I had been doing, and Eisenberg was dragging it all up before me. I could analyze the trajectory of the bullet that passed through my son's body with barely a ripple of emotion, but a few minutes on the telephone with this man, talking about his own emotions and the emotions of Wayne Lo's parents nearly did me in. It was a strange displacement.

There was one other factor adding to my confusion. While writing my report of Wayne Lo's criminal trial I had characterized Stuart Eisenberg as a droning rat, an unctuous weasel, and worse. These calumnies provided me with vast relief, as well as an occasional chuckle. I needed someone real and graspable to be angry at and Wayne Lo would not do. At the time of the trial he represented a bottomless well of rage and pain that, if I ever entered it, might consume me. So the defense lawyer and his colleague Janet Kenton-Walker were my daily targets, and I had been much satisfied with them in their role. Now Eisenberg was ruining that. He was being helpful, empathetic, and honest.

Things had started rolling, though, and however uncomfortable I felt, the press of events was not going to stop. I thought, too, that despite the welter of emotions that were surfacing, my original plan might still be preserved. Perhaps this troubling contact with the lawyer would ultimately work to my advantage. Through his good offices I could establish a relationship with the Los. I could gain their confidence sufficiently to have them let me visit them at their home in Billings, Montana. Once there I could interview Wayne's friends and teachers and perhaps gather more facts about whatever had caused his disintegration. I could see the Los in their own environment, see how they related to one another and to their surviving son Ryan. I could visit and perhaps even dine at their restaurant, the Great Wall. Then, ultimately, Mr. and Mrs. Lo and I would walk into Wayne Lo's jail, arms linked and heads held high, and Stephanie Connolly and her cronies at the Department of Corrections would writhe in impotent rage.

I was still thinking about my own agenda, and not about the realities of the situation. Therefore I got what I deserved when, two days later, the Los actually called me up, and that whole agenda came untracked.

The phone rang, and it was Mr. Lo himself. There followed a few seconds in which it felt as if my head were spinning on my shoulders. Then some other part of me took over. I heard myself assuring Mr. and Mrs. Lo that I understood what they'd been through. I heard my own voice saying to them over and over again, "We've felt bad long enough. We don't need to feel bad anymore. We'll meet, and we'll talk, and then we can begin trying to feel good again."

I had the odd sensation of listening to myself talking with them. The listening part of me, naturally enough, was scrambling to keep up with the rapidly changing situation. The talking part was out there on its own, saying attentive things, kind things, even wise things.

I heard them out. I heard their sorrow and guilt and their confusion and pain, and Mr. and Mrs. Lo did the same for me. I described to them how I had needed to come to my own understanding of things, and how I had gotten on the path that prompted my call, and why I needed to speak with them as badly as they needed to speak with me. They did not listen with suspicion. They thanked me for my efforts.

Even as I talked with them, I was realizing that, somehow, in the course of all my digging after facts, I had changed. As it had with Annie, this transformation occurred in a secret place, secret even from myself. Perhaps the business of healing was so important that it kept my conscious mind from getting in there and mucking it up. Perhaps the healing actually was work that my body, my whole organism, did. While my mind struggled to "understand," the rest of me went quietly about its business, which, after all, was life.

In any event, the shock of suddenly being in conversation with the Los brought all these unnoticed gains to the fore. It was the cresting of a wave, and I was riding it, feeling good about myself and about them too. I could hear how badly they'd suffered, and out of my own suffering I understood how I could help them and I saw how they could help me.

So, as the wave crested, I said to them, "We will talk about these things. We will visit together soon and spend however long it takes to talk about everything. If it's all right with you, I will come and visit you in Montana, and we'll talk."

To which Mr. Lo responded, "No, no. We come visit you!"

And the wave crashed.

I had never even remotely considered the possibility of the Los coming here. In my fantasy, I would go to Montana alone. I would case out the town, and meet with these alien people under vast western skies. It was more of my Clint and Lee baloney. The idea of them coming here, of them in my house, of them meeting my family, was too real, too human to fit into any of my Hollywood scenarios.

However, it turned out that Mr. and Mrs. Lo had already made plans to come east and visit Wayne in jail. They'd been working on the details of this trip for a year, and it was scheduled to take place in just a few weeks. They were so happy that my call had come right at the perfect time! They were going to stay out east for a week, and they would certainly have a chance to come up to Gloucester and visit with me and my wife.

With his simple, "We come visit you!" Mr. Lo completed a process that had begun in secret, right after Galen's death, and had been forwarded by such diverse characters as Leon Botstein, Theresa Beavers and Stuart Eisenberg. My hard-boiled cover was useless to me now. Everything was out in the open. Annie and Celia and Brooks and Galen and I were involved in a real-life event with Mr. and Mrs. Lo and Wayne, and his younger brother Ryan, and something else was on the agenda besides getting the "facts."

So it came to pass that C. W. and Lin Lin Lo and Annie and I spent a couple of days together in the spring of 1997. Their visit was preceded in our home by short tempers and jangled nerves. We dropped things. We stumbled and barked. We were distracted. We kept telling ourselves it was no big deal, but of course, it was.

I was concerned about having drawn Annie into this without consulting her first, but she reacted to the news of the impending visit with her usual lovely calm. This business with the Los was my trip, but she certainly felt badly for them. If she could help make them feel better, that would be a good thing to do.

So, one Saturday afternoon, Mr. Lo stuck his head around the corner of the hedge in front of our house, where Celia and her friends were jumping on the trampoline, and inquired if this might be the Gibson residence. Celia led him and Mrs. Lo into my office, where I was wrapping a book.

"Dad," she called, "You have visitors."

We sat in the kitchen and I made them coffee and we got down to work. We'd come too far to hesitate now. First we got rid of the "Mr." and "Mrs." I was Greg. He was C. W. and she was Lin Lin. I explained that Anne Marie was at work now, but would be joining us for dinner.

They were good-looking people, a little younger than me, short in stature, fastidious, erect and eager. Lin Lin, very slender in her trim business suit, was quiet at first, concentrating hard to contain emotions that were on the verge of overwhelming her. C. W. wore a blue blazer and khakis. He had a little more meat on him, and a manner that, under other circumstances, would have been convivial if not garrulous. It was obvious that he liked relating to people, liked telling stories. It was easy to imagine him hosting at the Great Wall restaurant in Billings, Montana.

Their speech omitted some verbs and rounded some consonants. Over the telephone it had sounded cliché, and they were apologetic about it. In person their syntax and enunciation had quite a different effect. It conveyed a certain efficiency and determination, as if all the words and sounds Americans used weren't really necessary to get from one end of a sentence to the other to arrive at meaning.

The formal declarations were made. The Los told me they were very sorry for what had happened to my son. They had suffered greatly in the past few years, and much of their suffering was caused by how badly they felt for us. They thanked me for calling them, and for this chance to meet so that they could personally apologize.

I thanked them for their condolences and said their apology was not necessary. I told them that we never considered them at fault and that they should not consider themselves so. We recognized that they were decent, honorable people who had been the victims of a great misfortune. Because of what we had experienced we could understand what they had been through. We had much in common, and we should proceed on this basis, not on the basis of our differences.

I told them what I had told Stuart Eisenberg: that my frustration over the legal situation had motivated me to try to find out on my own what had happened to Galen. I had finished with the college and the gun, and now I was trying to do what would probably be an impossible thing—I was trying to understand about Wayne. I told the Los I would be glad to help them however I could, but that I needed their help too. I needed them to help me with Wayne.

Lin Lin nodded gravely. C. W. said, "O.K. I help you with this. I tell you what I think and what I believe is true. But I tell you, Greg, this is only *my* truth, not the *truth*."

It was a touching and eloquent disclaimer.

We all began to relax after that. Inside the boundaries of our lives, the conversation wandered, in a free-associative manner. I'd say something and it would remind them of something else, not necessarily related to what had just been said, but so important it could no longer go unsaid. We compared our joys and sorrows with dignity and compassion, and in a curious inversion, we exchanged specific information with the eagerness of kids swapping baseball cards.

This was the form of our conversation all that Saturday and Sunday. Their story, in any narrative sense, didn't take shape until much had been said, and the long series of images and impressions had begun to accumulate. The full meaning of their narrative, and the meaning of their visit, did not appear until after we'd parted company. It is still evolving.

Sitting at our kitchen table over coffee, C. W. told me how, after the shootings, none of his Chinese friends called him. In the Chinese culture one did not do such a thing. All his American friends though, had come over right away, to help with Ryan and to clean and bring food. He liked the American way better, he said, and if anything bad happened to any friend of his in the future, he would go to that friend, not stay away.

He said he guessed it was hard for me to call him. I told him it hadn't been hard, that the time had simply come. Well, he replied, it may not have been hard for me to call him, but it was hard for them to come here. That shocked me for a moment, as I suddenly became aware of the difficulty of their situation, needing so badly to talk to us, yet not having any idea of what they were getting into, coming to my house. I looked at him, somewhat slack-jawed. He was smiling, pleased to see the realization wake in me. "Yes," he repeated, "Very hard for us, you know."

It went on like that. We talked about ourselves, about the terrible thing we had in common, and about our differences too. They told me about their life in Billings, and about how Wayne had been in those days. I gave them the history of our still-deferred lawsuit, and the results of the Beavers' Workmen's Compensation hearing, about which they knew nothing. Suddenly it was late afternoon. Celia had left for her job bussing tables at a local restaurant, Annie would be coming home from her job in an hour or so, and I was feeling the effect of our meeting.

So were Lin Lin and C. W. We agreed, with a laugh, that this sort of thing was hard work indeed, and went outside for a breath of air. It was a gloomy afternoon, chilly and gray, just on the edge of drizzling. We ambled down the front walk to the edge of the street, and then Lin Lin asked if we could ... if we could drive or walk ... The sentence would not come out. I knew immediately that she wanted to see Galen's grave and could not say the actual words. I was filled with great affection for her. She began to weep. I wanted to hug her but was too shy. Instead I touched her shoulder and said yes, Galen's grave was just down the street. We could easily walk there.

When we arrived I told them this was a peaceful place for us, that it was nice having it near our house, and that we came here often. Our children had grown up playing here and now it was even more a part of our lives. At the edge of the grave, Lin Lin tried to explain to me the concept of shame that they carried about what had happened. I gathered that it was not just personal disgrace, or a reflection on their race or country of origin, but something deeper and more precise, a stain on all the Los everywhere, forever. Whatever it was, exactly, in their culture, they were carrying the weight of it, and no kind words from me, or anyone, would lighten their burden.

After our walk I drove them to their motel so they could rest a bit. When Annie came home from work, we had a drink and I filled her in on the details of my afternoon. Then we drove back to the Los' motel, picked them up and took them out to dinner. Annie fit right in. As the talk started up again, the four of us chattering excitedly, C. W. and Lin Lin felt at once like our closest friends and important dignitaries from far away.

It had started to rain. The restaurant we had planned on was full and could not seat us. The next one was full as well, and as we ranged farther from home our outing took on an existential character. It was Saturday night, and we were trying to walk into the best places without reservations. What were we thinking? What did it matter, with such important things to discuss? Finally we found a roadhouse three towns away. Not too bright, and not too crowded, it was perfect. C. W. surprised me and ordered the prime rib. Lin Lin ate light.

The talk was broader with all four of us in it, and as the food and drink warmed us we swapped stories and made table-pounding points. The laughter was surprising and wonderful, and the crying felt good too. Our only boundary was pain, or more precisely, fear of the other person's pain. They didn't talk too much about Galen because our pain hurt them. For the same reason it was hard for us to ask about Wayne, but we kept pushing, gently. Details from the afternoon's conversation fit in with things they were saying at dinner, and their story began to take shape.

They'd been doing pretty well in Taipei. He'd been a career man in the Taiwanese Air Force and she'd taught Suzuki violin. She had a sister over here, in Chicago, and they'd both had a taste of American life back in 1983 when he'd been attached to the Taiwanese embassy in Washington.

C. W. figured he could have made General in the Air Force if he'd served out his entire career, but something had happened to him along the way. He thought perhaps it was because of all the traveling he'd done. Somehow he began to see too much. He'd never believed in what the government of Communist China had been saying, but when he got a global perspective, he found that he could no longer believe his own government, either. Then he knew his days in the Air Force were numbered. He could not be an effective soldier if he didn't believe in the people he worked for.

They thought about staying in Taipei, but the future seemed cloudy for that place. C. W. knew that the United States was where they had to go. The U.S. offered the best future for their children.

They'd first mentioned this when we were sitting in the kitchen, and they'd repeated it several times. I was impressed by how much he and Lin Lin still believed in the future, and how much they still believed in the United States. I thought about the anglicized names they'd given their children, and about the risks they'd taken, giving up established jobs and coming here. Their whole lives had been planned around the future they could provide for Ryan and Wayne. If they ever saw the irony in this, they ignored it now.

Lin Lin had come over and investigated the possibilities in the United States while C. W. closed out his Air Force career in Taiwan. It seemed there were several options for them over here. One friend had a fish business in the Chinese community in Los Angeles. Another friend had a Chinese restaurant in Great Falls, North Dakota. Lin Lin visited her sister in Chicago, then the fish dealer in LA, then the restaurant in North Dakota. She liked the restaurant best. She went home and conferred with her husband and they both rejected the LA option. They felt Los

Angeles was too crowded. After the density of Taipei, they wanted to experience the open spaces America had to offer. Also, in Los Angeles, it was a cloistered Chinese community. If they were coming to America, they wanted to mix with Americans, not with other Chinese. They wanted to learn to be real Americans, and Montana seemed like the place to do it. In 1986 C. W. left his pension for his mother, took whatever grubstake he had accumulated, and they came over here.

We were driving home from dinner by then. The rain had gotten heavier, and as we wound along the dark country road through Ipswich and Essex into Gloucester, wipers clicking away, C. W. amused us by recounting all the statistical information pertaining to the five major cities in Montana. It was something of a virtuoso performance. He got us laughing, but it was also clear that these people hadn't just hopped on the plane for America. They'd done their homework. In one sense, they knew more about Billings than the locals did.

In quite another, though, they knew nothing. This was a handicap against which he and Lin Lin struggled still. Lin Lin told us how bewildering it had been on that first trip to Chicago, just to go into the post office and mail a letter. Everything was so different than it had been in Taiwan. Finally, Joyce, her sister, had just dropped her in front of the post office and driven off to find a parking place. It was, said Lin Lin, the only way she could have learned to do it herself.

Our culture, our language, all the transparent things we took for granted, all the subtle ways in which we were Americans, were the very things they struggled so hard to master. On top of this difficulty, and even more pressing, was the fact that they had to learn the restaurant business from scratch, and learn it fast. C. W. and Lin Lin had come over alone and worked at the friend's restaurant until they knew enough about the operation to start one of their own. Meanwhile they'd decided to settle in Billings. Eventually, they found a good location there and sent for the children. Wayne took his brother Ryan on the airplane, alone, from Taipei to Chicago, where the sister lived, then on to Billings. Wayne was twelve and Ryan was eight.

If there was a new perspective to be gained from the Los, this was it. I had pictured Wayne Lo at first as a narcissistic killer, then as a mentally ill young man, bent somehow, by the unhealthy aspects of our culture. C. W. and Lin Lin Lo introduced another element into my conception of their son.

Everything I understood about Wayne was now underscored with a sense of the enormous distance between Taiwan and America, geographically, culturally and in every possible way. For example, Lin Lin told us how important age and respect were in her culture and how confusing it had been to unlearn these things over here. Because Joyce was her older sister, Lin Lin still called her "Sister," never "Joyce," whereas Joyce called Lin Lin by her given name. When Wayne first got to college he called all his professors "Sir." They asked him if he was being sarcastic.

So, just as the confusion of puberty was coming upon him, Wayne's parents had left him, and then he had been dropped into an alien culture. At the same time, he was expected to shoulder tremendous responsibilities. He was, in large measure, his brother's keeper. While C. W. and Lin Lin worked long hours at the restaurant, Wayne was home taking care of Ryan. Since all this struggle was intended to be for their advancement, for their futures, both boys were expected to perform to the highest standards. Music lessons were a constant, and nothing but the best grades were expected in school. When he got to high school, Wayne was transferred to the most advanced academic environment Billings had to offer. There was, as Stuart Eisenberg had tried to underscore at the trial, a vast amount of pressure on the boy.

This did not excuse anything. Many immigrants from many cultures faced similar pressures. Not many bought guns and shot people. After hearing the Los however, it was easier to believe that the pressures were part of the cause of the "disability or defect" that had overcome Wayne. This was essentially the view the Los took. Something terrible had happened to Wayne. Our culture called it mental illness and believed that such stresses as Wayne had undergone were in part responsible for it. In a way, they had already done what I was trying to do. They had created a version of events that they could live with, one that was necessary for their survival. In their version, the pressures built up inside Wayne and then something broke in him. He heard commands from God.

This was one of the first things C. W. told me about when we were sitting in the kitchen. He said he'd specifically asked his son if he had been commanded by God, and that Wayne had explained the experience of this command by telling him a sort of UFO parable. (Charmingly, C. W. pronounced them "oofoes.") No one believed in UFOs, Wayne said, but if you had been abducted by one, you couldn't help but believe in them after that. The experience of being commanded by God was the same. He had never even believed in God, but when God had come to him he had been powerless to resist, powerless to conceive any other reality than that which had issued the command.

This had stolen from them the Wayne they knew, the son they loved. Now there was some kind of automaton in his place. Lin Lin told us it was as if Wayne's life had stopped on the day of the shootings. Now, when they visited him (Lin Lin had been once since the trial. C. W. tried to go twice a year), he would recall events in past family history in Billings or Taiwan, but he never referred to the murders or to the specifics of his life in prison. The same was true of his few letters and phone calls. If he spoke about present conditions at all, it was as a little boy would speak to his mother, telling her he had a cold or that there had been a snow storm in Massachusetts. Lin Lin and C. W. kept hoping that he would wake up one day, and realize what he'd done, but they did not know when, or if, this would happen.

Like us, the Los were angry with the people at Simon's Rock College.

They felt the administration had failed them, had failed their son. "Why they no call us?" Lin Lin asked, over and over. They heard, later, other students' accounts of Wayne's antisocial behavior. If there were problems with Wayne's teacher about the AIDS paper, or fights with Floyd Robinson, the residence director, why hadn't the school called them? All the school's promotional materials promised that the children would be closely supervised. Why hadn't anyone noticed that things were going wrong with Wayne? If anyone noticed, why hadn't they called?

They'd gotten the same overture from Simon's Rock that Galen had received in the mail. Wayne, who was certainly getting bored in Central Catholic High School, had been attracted. Lin Lin studied the brochure. She believed what it said. Lin Lin's friends had told her there were many good private schools in the east. She and C. W. did more research. They bought the book on colleges put out by *Newsweek*. Simon's Rock was ranked number one among small schools of its kind. Lin Lin told us she thought Simon's Rock College was a small, elite prep school on the East Coast. This was a woman who, just a few years earlier, had learned how to mail a letter in our country.

There was the usual application procedure. Test scores, grades and recommendations were forwarded, there was a telephone interview, and Wayne was accepted. There was no campus visit. Wayne simply got on a plane in the fall of 1991. When he arrived on campus he was probably overwhelmed by another wave of culture shock. The distance between Billings, Montana, and Simon's Rock College was, in some ways, nearly as great as the leap from Taiwan to the United States. The wild clothing and grooming habits, the orthodoxy of liberalism, the secular humanism and the intellectualism were all a far cry from what had been the norm at Central Catholic High in Billings, Montana.

Lin Lin told us that Wayne also felt very insecure about his language skills. He'd just started the Writing and Thinking Workshop which was part of the week-long indoctrination process for new students, and he became painfully aware of his deficiencies in English. Having been in this country for only for six years, his understanding lacked the richness and depth that even the slowest of his fellow students possessed. It was difficult for him, but he seemed to be progressing. The first year his reports from school said he needed to express himself more. The second year, in the fall semester, the reports said that Wayne was doing better.

That was why Lin Lin had been so confused. They said he was doing better. If he was having trouble, why hadn't they told her? It was so hard to understand. Wayne had always been outspoken at home. If there was any grievance, he would demand that it be aired. Even when he had done wrong, C. W. said, he was forthright. He would hold out his hand and say, "Punish me." (This was recollected by C. W. with a certain fondness, and I could imagine recounting anecdotes about Galen in a similar fashion. I also heard in it the seeds of Dr. Plakun's "transgression, punishment, purification" theory.)

After the murders they'd been treated shabbily by college officials. The telephone call from Bernie Rodgers on the night of the murders had been blunt, hard, cold. There had been no follow-up, no official expression of sympathy for the agony the Los obviously were suffering. One lady in an office where Wayne had worked, and one Chinese professor on campus, wrote to them once; but then all letters stopped. The Los were convinced that the college had stopped them.

There had been no official word at all from the college after the shootings, and since they'd been witnesses at the criminal trial, they'd been cloistered, and not allowed to attend the proceedings. They were shocked, five years after the event, at some of the things we told them. They hadn't known, for example, about the misgivings Wayne's high school teacher, Gary Guadreau, had expressed regarding Wayne's mental state. They hadn't known that Sister Barbara, the high school guidance counselor, also had knowledge that Wayne seemed to be having psychological difficulties. Neither Guadreau nor Sister Barbara had said anything about their concerns to Simon's Rock or to Mr. and Mrs. Lo.

"We see these people in the market, on the street, all the time. Why they no tell us?"

It was painful, for them and for us, but we needed to rehearse these common frustrations together, and so we did. Between the four of us we reconstructed the sequence of events, and enumerated the many places where persons in authority could have altered the outcome, but did not. "Why they no tell us?" Over and over.

I have, in my mind, a picture of C. W. at the table, when things were getting their heaviest, bullheadedly, stupidly, insisting that the future was all that mattered, and me almost getting angry at him for not realizing the complexity of the situation, then understanding that he *had* to say what he was saying. A few minutes earlier when I'd asked Lin Lin if she still taught Suzuki, she told me she'd tried to teach for one year but that the preparation for each lesson took too much time away from the restaurant. I asked her if she still played the violin for her own pleasure. She shook her head no.

"It was a big change in your life to come here," I said.

"It was a big change in my life to come here," she replied, softly, with a devastating wistfulness.

Not that it was all morose. Lin Lin and C. W. were, in their way, lovely people who had lead interesting lives. Stories got told. Jokes got made. After dinner we stopped at Celia's restaurant to pick her up from work, and C. W. told us how odd it was that fourteen-year-old children made the best bus people. One could train a fourteen-year-old in just the right way, but eighteen-year-olds had too many preconceptions. Their behaviors were too formed. They could never be trained quite as well in the most efficient way to clean and set a table. Celia, he told us, was at her prime for this line of work. Looking her over with a professional restaurateur's eye, he guessed that she had a fine career as a busgirl ahead of her.

321

The restaurant adjacent to the Los' motel served a good brunch, and it was there that we finished our talk the next morning. Knowing that our time together was nearing an end, we concentrated on the harder things, questions about Wayne and his life in prison. This yielded one particularly memorable image.

They told us they stayed in a motel in Randolph, Massachusetts, and drove daily to Norfolk to see their son. I didn't understand if they were allowed to sit with him together or had to go in singly, but their visit did not take place through a glass or screen partition, as the movies had led me to imagine. According to the visiting rules of this particular facility, they sat in a room with Wayne, on chairs, side by side, like at a wake.

Wayne would respond to questions, or be silent, or recall something that had happened in his childhood. While he sat there he rocked, slowly, back and forth, almost as if he were nodding, but using the whole of his torso, from the hips up. Lin Lin demonstrated in her chair at our breakfast table, a slow, stiff bob, as her upper body moved six inches forward, then returned to vertical.

After she'd demonstrated this, she told us, "One day I ask him, 'Wayne, why you do that?' He tell me, 'Mom, lots of times people talk. They have nothing to say, they just need to talk. So I move like this because it looks like I listen to them, and then I don't have to listen.' Then I ask him, 'Do you listen to me?' and he say, 'Sometimes ...' So I tell him, 'Well you stop that, Wayne. You no need to move like that when I talk.' So he stop, for a few minutes maybe, and then he start again."

And she showed us again, despite herself, rocking back and forth in her chair.

Then it was time to leave and we gathered in the motel parking lot and wept and hugged. We climbed in our van and they stood on the stairway leading back into the motel and waved goodbye to us as we drove away. They seemed exceedingly sweet standing there waving like that, as if we were leaving their house after a long and pleasant visit. Annie and I were suffused with a feeling of the absolute rightn ss of our meeting.

We drove home through Rockport, comparing our impressions about Mr. and Mrs. Lo and what they'd had to say. A mile or so out of town the road angled up and opened to a view of the ocean. I looked out at the Atlantic, misty and gray, and it struck me suddenly that whatever had taken our boy from us was far crueler in taking the Los' boy from them and leaving his animate body behind.

It was not Galen, always so much with us, but this other, stolen, rocking creature who truly was the Gone Boy.

⁊₅25
LA VITA NUOVA

I can talk all I want about the work I did in secret from myself, and about my healing and all the rest, but I spent months after the Lo's visit feeling like I'd been walloped, as I struggled to encompass the new information they had provided.

Finally, toward the end of the summer of 1997, I began to realize that what I thought of as "the story" had in some way been completed by their visit to our house, and that the activity of gathering the materials of this story, my "walkabout," was also over.

This was not a rational calculation. It was as instinctive and directed-from-within as any of the other impulses that had guided me over the past few years. I could think of many more people to talk to, and of more parts of the story to be investigated, but the urge to do this was gone. Lin Lin and C. W. Lo had elicited something in me. Maybe it was empathy or compassion, or maybe there was no precise word for it. Whatever it was, they had drawn it out, and it had repaired something deep in my being. The need that had driven me was satisfied.

It felt strange. I suppose I could say I was "at peace," that being one of the nominal destinations of an adventure such as mine, but that wasn't quite the truth. I still had my edgy, angry demands of the world, and my drunk's cynicism, balanced by the mighty blessing of the joy life gave me. None of the things that made me who I was had changed, yet something was different.

Frequently, in the difficult parts of my walkabout, I had consoled myself by thinking about how, when it was over, I could return to my old life as a bookseller full time, and what a pleasure that would be. Now that "it was over," whatever that meant, the one thing I saw was that there would be no returning to my old life, as a bookseller or anything else.

When that telephone woke me from a fitful sleep on the night of December 14, 1992, while Dean Bernard Rodgers was telling me there'd been a terrible accident and my son was dead, and while I was sputtering and gasping, a part of me had already figured the whole thing out. All I could see, and this mental image was so strong it overrode whatever visuals were before me at that moment, was an irregular, white, cylindrical "Y," rather like a forked stick of wood that had been stripped of its bark. Now, nearly five years later, my own experience gave concrete meaning to that vision.

One branch of the Y, the left one, had begun withering even as I first saw it. That was my old life, the life I would have led if Galen had not died. The other branch was this new life. My walkabout had been a journey to get me here, and it had been a success. Now that I was here, I felt a tremendous nostalgia for that old place, but I could no more reclaim that life than I could return Galen to the living. I was "at peace," but it was merely the peace of a man who'd managed to do what he was supposed to have done. Now, there was the matter of this new life to attend to.

I knew that the first thing I needed was a vantage point, a place from which I could see the terrain I had covered, and look ahead in hopes of divining what lay before me. I had a good idea of where to go to do this, but before I could get there, my new life turned around and delivered me a jolt. It was not entirely a bad jolt, more like a healthy Zen slap.

At the moment I least expected it, the money thing reared its ugly head.

It turned out that Howard Thomas, the kick-ass, big city lawyer, had been right all along. He was the one with the wounded son who'd gotten in a dispute with the college over unpaid tuition, their attitude, and the way they'd behaved on the night of the murders. When I visited him in his Park Avenue office during my walkabout, it had been his contention that our civil trial was not being delayed by Wayne Lo's criminal appeal or by any concern over his fifth amendment rights. These were just "window dressing." According to Howard Thomas, we'd get some action on this case when the primary insurer and the secondary insurer settled their arguments with each other over who was going to cover how much. Now, just at the end of my walkabout, they had apparently done that, because our lawyer called to report that the insurance companies were ready to talk about settling the case.

We'd already had one mediation session with the insurance people, and it had been a farce. In our lawyer's estimation, this first failed session may have been a part of the insurance company's strategy. The primary insurer, Great American, had offered us $250,000 and a free education for Brooks and Celia at Simon's Rock, or any Massachusetts state college. They would not budge from this position and negotiations had collapsed. In hindsight, it seemed possible that they had tendered their absurd offer to make a trial seem immanent and thus to enhance their leverage over the secondary insurer.

Now, our lawyer was calling to inform us of all this, but also to ask how much money we wanted. He would, of course, try to get as much as he could from them, but to carry the bargaining to a successful conclusion, he needed his marching orders from us. What was the minimum amount with which we'd be satisfied? How much did we want in our pockets?

Momentarily, Annie, Celia, Brooks and I were thrown back into that old, awful pickle. How much is a dead Galen worth? Once again, we traveled the loop of absurdity and rage. But we'd been cooking the problem over the years, processing it with whatever chemistry healing provides, and we had it pretty well distilled. The answer had its roots in that split between God's Will and mundane event. At bottom, the mystery of Galen's loss could only be "understood" through ceaseless meditation on God's Will. This money stuff was an approach to the problem from the mundane side, just a part of this benighted world, markers we moved around as substitutes for our business with God. It was lawyers' work, clay. It was, comparatively, a snap.

The lawyer had already counseled us to forget about the $X million settlement for the spilled cup of coffee. That was in no sense a measure. Of all the thousands and thousands of civil cases heard each year, only the whacko ones made the national news. They were aberrations. Our case was not a $Y million case. It was probably not even a $Z million case, though who knew? There were measures for these things, but they were vague, and there were many variables. So, years before, at our bogus mediation session, we'd had to come up with a number for a settlement amount, and after some excruciating calculation, we decided on that number, then lessened it by a slight amount as a gesture of good faith. Was this what Galen was worth? It had nothing to do with Galen. But it would pay our bills and leave Annie and me a modest amount to put away for the future, and then we could get on with our lives.

Although that first mediation session may only have been a ploy by Great American Insurance Co., it had not been a wasted exercise for us. We'd had to learn to deal with the absurdity of the money side of the issue. Now that it was back in our laps again, we knew better what to do. We took the old amount, removed the good faith deduction, and added the interest that had accumulated over the years.

Interestingly, the lawyer was specific about asking us to name the figure we wanted. I took that to mean he could then bargain with his share of the remainder if necessary. I took it to mean that this was indeed a negotiation in earnest, and that we'd chosen the right lawyer to represent us.

I waited through the weekend, increasingly sure the settlement would be made, and increasingly excited about an influx of cash. Now Annie and I could get that little place in Ireland we'd been dreaming about. We could pay all the bills, repair the house, put the kids through college, have a nest-egg for later in life. I could pump more cash into my business and move it up to the next level. That money, the dollars we'd earned with our pain and suffering, would not be spent in vain. Finally, we'd have enough to think of creating a meaningful memorial to Galen ... a scholarship fund? A new building on the Simon's Rock campus? Who knew? Suddenly there were too many things to do with the money. The amount we'd demanded was not enough. No amount would ever be enough.

It was a wonderful teaching.

So, too, was the exercise of reversing all the fantasizing. The lawyer called the next day to report that this, like the last, had been a futile session, nothing but posturing by the insurance people. Negotiations had never even started. I gave back the house in Ireland, unpaid all our bills and the college educations for Brooks and Celia, withdrew the money from my business and undid, for the time being, the memorial to Galen.

Then I got back to where I'd been before this money nonsense had interrupted me. I needed that vantage point, and I was sure I knew where it was. I was going to take Stephanie Connolly at her word. I was going to drive down Route 1A to Norfolk, Massachusetts, and see that panorama of MCI Norfolk and Bay State Correctional Facility, as Ms. Connolly had promised, all in one view. Was it finality that I needed, the "closure" that grief people are always talking about? I didn't know, but I was certain that would be the place to go to see whatever it was that I needed to see. I was going to go take a look at Wayne Lo's jail.

As it happened, I'd just gotten a call from a book dealer in Connecticut who was selling a scholarly library for a client. There were about thirty cartons of literature, art, archaeology, classical antiquity, and philosophy. Was I interested? I assured this gentleman that each of these subject areas was a particular specialty of mine, and that I would be at his doorstep late the next morning to make an offer on the lot. In fact, being a specialist in nautical books, I didn't know much about any of those subjects, but they sounded interesting. Perhaps I could drive a deal. More importantly, Norfolk, Massachusetts, was on the way. I could stop there, look at the prison, and get some insight on my new life before continuing to Connecticut.

Accordingly, I slid out of the house early next morning, underneath rush-hour traffic, and drove through sleeping New England toward the place where they kept Wayne Lo. The situation was exactly the way I'd imagined it. The morning was grey and chilly. The autumn colors were muted. Tree-lined roads opened on church steeples, towns. Walpole and Norfolk were just waking up, getting ready for work.

I saw the sign for MCI-Norfolk on the outskirts of town, drove less than a mile down a rural road, and found the place. There was no missing it. I pulled into the visitor's parking lot across the street, with my van facing the prison complex, and looked.

I looked hard and long. But my new life was not to be seen. All there was, was a wall. A big white stupid wall. Behind it were piled-up ugly institutional brick buildings, with lines of lower roofs just visible over the top of the wall, a stone building at the front gate, barbed wire icing, and stumpy corner guard towers. The vibe was bad, very bad. Wayne was in there somewhere, but he was lost in that morass of human sickness and misery. There was nothing to see here but dysfunction and plain old fucked-up evil.

I headed back up Route 1A and got on the interstate southbound, pushed the needle up to a steady seventy-five miles per hour, turned on the music, and chuckled, despite myself. What a nasty place! What a foolish notion. I might as well have gone out in my back yard and stared at the cesspool for enlightenment.

Well, it was too bad about that damned money. Worse, still, because if we'd settled the case I could've gone and talked to Bernie Rodgers and Ba Win, and they wouldn't have had any lawyer reasons for evading me, and I wouldn't have been afraid of tainting any witnesses. I would have told Ba Win I understood his actions on the night of the shootings, and that I forgave him. I would have told Bernie that I did not understand his refusal to take any responsibility for what had happened to my son, and that I needed his help to try to forgive him, or at least to put him behind me, and what did he have to say for himself? I was fairly certain that Ba Win would accept my forgiveness, and that Bernie Rodgers would remain in denial, but none of that mattered as much as my being able to confront these men, and tell them what was in my heart. It would be the final stop on my long journey.

Now that chance was gone, but it would come around again. We'd settle the case on the courthouse steps, or we'd have that trial, and then I'd have my words with Bernie and Ba Win, and be clean of the last shred of this bloody mess. One way or another, I'd finish my business. I wouldn't forget. I wasn't going anywhere.

Just moving down the Eastern Macro-Metro corridor on my way to the next chancy book deal, listening to the music, thinking about the deal, thinking about life, looking at it laid out all around me, seeing it, just for a moment, fresh as the first man who ever walked this earth.

❦26
HIBERNATING STOATS

Sometimes our lives seem to proceed as if according to a plan.

Several weeks after my drive past Wayne Lo's prison, our lawyer called and told us that the insurance companies representing Simon's Rock College had offered a settlement. It met our demands, he said, and aside from a nondisclosure clause regarding the amount, it placed no restrictions on what I could say about my experiences. We accepted their proposal. Brief articles announcing the settlement appeared in Massachusetts newspapers, and the world forgot about us again. I waited a few weeks to get my wits about me, and then I went back to Simon's Rock College and had my conversations with Ba Win and Bernie Rodgers.

I said to the provost and the dean, each in private, exactly what I had planned to say to them.

Ba Win thanked me for my understanding and forgiveness. He said he needed it. I did forgive him, and that felt good.

Bernie Rodgers regretted intensely what had happened on December 14. He had no explanation for why he had not kept in contact with us immediately after the shootings. He did not know why he had failed to keep us informed about the case as it unfolded. There were so many things he wished he had done differently. But at the time, he did what he thought best.

We were sitting in the same room, in the same places we'd been sitting five years ago, and despite all he'd been through, Bernie Rodgers still had not progressed beyond denial and regret. It was, unfortunately, just as I'd anticipated, and it left both of us in a predicament.

Before I could forgive this man, I needed him to accept some responsibility, however slight, for Galen's death. He needed this too, only he didn't know it. I couldn't tell him what to do, because then the acknowledgment wouldn't be his.

I let him go on about his regrets and his decisions, but we never came any closer. He was too ready to defend himself, point by point, and after five years his defenses were strong and well-prepared. He didn't see that he was trapped behind them.

"If you did everything as well as you could, why am I still angry at you?"

"I don't know."

"Has it ever occurred to you that there's something else to this situation, something you've missed?"

"I don't know what you mean."

"I need your help, Bernie, and whether you know it or not, you need mine. I need for you to look in your heart—not now, but some time in the future—and see if you can discover something that might have gone unsaid, something that might help us both, because we're joined together in this business."

"I don't know if I can help you."

"Neither do I. But I'm damned certain you can't help either of us if you don't try."

"I'll try."

There was no more to be said. I rose, shook his hand, and left. As soon as I was out the door I could feel his relief behind me, as strong as if he'd muttered at my back, "I'm glad that's over!"

Of course, it wasn't over. It would never be over. It wouldn't even change until something in that poor Man of Words changed, and he wasn't likely to change. This made me sad for a moment, and then I realized I'd just have to accept him for who he was and move on.

I could do that.

I went for a walk in the cemetery.

It should have been a solemn and elegiac walk, but the whole thing with Bernie had been such an anti-climax that I couldn't get in the mood. By the time I'd confronted him, I'd already moved beyond him. So, if I'd have stood over Galen's grave and told him that I'd finally settled the score and that now he could rest in peace, he would have given me the razzberry. Instead, I stood over Galen's grave and looked at the lawn.

The summer after he'd died, I got in the habit of going down there, having a beer and watering the flowers. It was very peaceful. I liked the idea of watering the daisies I'd be pushing up some day. After a while, though, I began to notice how healthy and green my neighbor's lawn was. I began fertilizing the lawn on our plot, and watering it daily, lest the sun should dry it out. I was determined that this guy was not going to have a better lawn than Galen's and mine. People would see me out there on my hands and knees over Galen's grave, and sort of, you know, avert their eyes from this poor man whose grief had overcome him. But grief hadn't overcome me. I was pulling crabgrass. Somebody told me that my lawn rival was related to a mortician, and that the mortician was supplying him with professional cemetery lawn-care products. So, I was tremendously satisfied when, in the third year, my lawn pulled even with his. Then he got dysfunctional, for whatever reason, and gave up on the lawn. I started watering it for him, whenever I could, but it finally croaked, cut off from those professional lawn-care products.

Now, standing here in the patchy snow, comparing the scraggly tufts that covered his plot with the thick, even pelt on ours, I did not feel the satisfaction of having triumphed. I missed the contest.

That was what much of it had been for me: with the college, with all those people I'd battled. The struggle had kept me together, a single thread of purpose in my life. It had kept me from winding up in a detox ward, or from jumping off a bridge, or from shooting someone myself, while I healed. And now I had the story of what had happened to Galen, and with it, by some miracle, my life.

I looked at the lawn and I thought about the blood on Galen's hands where he'd clapped them on the wound to keep his life in. Some crazy kid and a gun. Galen would never come back and Wayne would never get better. No one was ever better for having a gun. I was not a better person for having survived. Celia, whose every Christmas was now a funeral. Brooks, his mentor and boon companion slaughtered for no reason on earth. Poor dear Anne Marie. No one's life ever got better because of a gun.

Better was what it was all about, for sure. But better would be very difficult. That would be the rest of my life. To take the energy this horrible thing had released, and turn it around somehow, and send it back out there, clean, so the world might be a better place for it, not worse; for Brooks and Celia and for their children, and on—that would be the job, a matter of "restoring the church to its original state," as Galen had said. It wasn't about getting better; it wasn't about making ourselves better. It was about making *it* better, somehow.

It was about taking that terrible energy, inside, till it filled you, teeming, endless blades of grass alive, a thousand conversations at once, and opening some other part of you and back out it would go. Up! A prayer. That was the thing. It would be clean as a prayer. That was the job for us, eh, Galen?

Suddenly there was a noise. It was the oddest damned noise, a sort of cooing, gurgling yodel, coming from the oak tree just a few yards away, next to the plot with the scraggly lawn. I looked up in the bare branches, but there were no birds.

It didn't sound like a bird, anyway. I walked across my turf and my neighbor's turf to the tree. It was a good, healthy, gnarly old oak, three feet in diameter, and in it, at about chest height, around the other side of the tree from the graves, was a hole the size of my wrist, with fresh scratch marks around the edges of it. And from that hole the sound came again, chuckles and a moan. What could it be? Chipmunks? Squirrels? Martens? Fishers? Weasels? Stoats and ferrets in the trunk and branch lines like subway commuters? Ptarmigans? Adders? Marmots?

If, at that moment, you'd gone up a hundred years, or out to wherever Galen was, where that prayer was bound, and looked down, you'd have seen a man and a tree alone in a field, the man staring through his tears, transfixed, into a hole in the tree, whose massive, sustaining roots went down under the man's grave, and his wife's, and their first-born son's, and cradled them, as a mother might tenderly cradle her children, as the world had cradled him, on more than one occasion, in the course of his eventful journey through it.

AFTERWORD

When *Gone Boy* was first published, I thought that finally my seven-year journey was at an end. The book, I imagined, would have its own life. It would speak for me and my family. It would say for us the things that we held closest to our hearts, and it would answer all the questions people might have about an experience such as ours. It would leave us free to begin our lives anew. As it happened, I was wrong.

I'd gotten quite used to being wrong, so this was no great burden for me. In fact, as the months went by, it became yet another source of joy. In the course of lectures and readings and talk shows that the publisher arranged for me, the story contained in the book seemed to resonate and grow, until finally it overflowed the rather artificial boundaries of its front and back covers and found its place in the world. At readings, or via email or letters, more and more people came forward with their own reactions to the Simon's Rock shootings. Many had suffered similar losses. Many were involved with gun control or victims issues. A surprising number were themselves parents of murdered children, some in places like Littleton, many on anonymous city streets. Some knew people who had been involved with the college or who had been present that night. A few even provided new information about the murders.

Some of this information proved to be important for legal reasons. Bruce and Theresa Beavers were still pursuing civil suits against Simon's Rock and Bard Colleges, and a few of the facts that came to light after *Gone Boy*'s publication were helpful in the prosecution of their lawsuits.

It felt good that the book could be of use in this way, and it felt even better when the emails and letters from Galen's college classmates began pouring in. These were students who'd been on campus the night of

339

the shootings. Without exception their letters told me that reading *Gone Boy* helped them understand and accept what they'd had to endure since that horrific night. The book helped these kids bear what they would always carry with them. Each one of them shared their loving memories of Galen, and nearly all of them thanked me for talking about things the grownups would never acknowledge or discuss. If there was ever a question in my mind about the validity of what I had written, these letters answered it.

Once, after a reading, I was approached by a young lady, a friend of Galen's, who had been in the library when the shootings happened. We talked for a while, and it was clear to me she had survived and overcome the trauma of that terrible event. Behind her was an older woman, who, it was equally clear to me, had something heavy on her mind. She told me that the young woman I'd just spoken with was her daughter, and that Galen had saved her life. When that student had burst into the library with his report of an accident down the road, her daughter had been headed for the door. Galen grabbed her and said, "You wait here. I'll check it out." I felt an incredible burst of pride in Galen, my karmic champ! But imagine what this woman must have been carrying for those seven years; the terrible knowledge that her daughter had survived in place of my son. I could imagine the anguish she felt at needing to tell me and not wanting to tell me. And I could imagine what a loss it might have been, for both of us, if she had not found the courage to speak with me that night. Thus the rippling circles initiated by a single act of gun violence.

Some months after the book first appeared I was approached by a former employee of the college. Her name was Sharon Flitterman-King, and she had taken an interest in Wayne Lo and in his case, She'd been corresponding with him, and had even visited him. She asked me if I would care to receive a letter from Wayne. I replied that if he was ready to acknowledge the terrible cost of his actions to our family, the other victims, and his own family, I would consider hearing from him. Otherwise I had no interest in anything he might have to say.

To my surprise I got a letter from Wayne shortly thereafter. He told me that he had come to realize the enormity of what he'd done, and its tremendous cost. He said he was not writing me in hopes of changing my mind about him. Indeed, he expected I should hate him for what he'd done. He felt it was right that he should be in jail for the rest of his life, and he had no desire to change any of that. He was writing, he said, simply to let me know that he accepted full responsibility for his crimes. He regretted them more than words could say. He wanted me to know that he was sorry for what he'd done.

It was a moving letter, but I mistrusted it. It seemed too sudden, too profound a switch from his crazy insistence the he had been on a "Mission from God." Confused, I telephoned his father, C. W. Lo. Lin Lin and C. W. Lo were devout Christians, and their fondest hope for their imprisoned son was that he might someday break through his denial, accept the wrongness of what he'd done, and begin the process of atonement. When we'd talked years before they had despaired of it ever happening.

Mr. Lo told me that he and his wife had visited Wayne a year ago, and at that point nothing had changed. He was still in denial about his crime. He did not talk about the shootings. This year, however, he and his younger son Ryan had gone to see Wayne in prison, and everything was different. Wayne was talking about what he'd done and was willing, even eager, to accept responsibility for it. I asked him what had changed between this year and last. C. W. Lo told me, "Greg, he read your book."

There could not have been a more unexpected consequence of my earnest labors.

So Wayne and I embarked on a correspondence which continues to this day. We've covered a lot of ground and we'll cover a lot more. We've got all the time in the world. One of the most memorable things he's told me has to do with the gun. He said that when he thought he was on his Mission from God, the ease with which he was able to obtain the gun and ammunition seemed like a blessing, as if God was paving the way for him. Now he realizes it was the greatest curse in his life.

This underlines what to me is the most profound tragedy of all. When this kid was so addled that he thought God was talking to him, it was still a simple matter for him to obtain a semiautomatic rifle and 200 rounds of ammunition. It was a simple matter for him to carry them onto a college campus, and it was a simple matter for him to use them. Apparently we like it this way in America, because if we didn't, we'd change it. This is a tragedy that far surpasses my own family's suffering, and the suffering of any individual victim of gun violence. I consider it a great shame on our nation.

Perhaps Wayne Lo and I will find a way to work together at getting this message across to people. I think it would be a powerful one, coming from us both, and it might save the life of some future Galen. Or some future Wayne.

Gloucester, Massachusetts
April 2000

ACKNOWLEDGMENTS

Kenny Turan and John Brown got me started on this project, and saw me through it. There would have been no book without them. I am also greatly indebted to my patient and generous readers: Nick Kazan, Joe Burns, Gerritt Lansing, Joe DeGrazia, Jean Kaiser, Rudy Rucker, Barry Feldman, Bill Feiss, Meg Tipper, Sue Chady, Lou Schneider, Lewellyn Howland III and Anthony Weller.

For research assistance, my thanks to Sarah Carson, and to the tireless legal geniuses, Neil Rossman and Paul Denver, of Rossman, Rossman & Eschelbacher, and Ted Miller of Kodansha America. Also, Liz Keegan, Gerry Downing, David Capeless and Sgt. Steve DelNegro for advice and assistance on aspects of the criminal case.

Thanks again to the already-thanked Howland and Weller, who guided me through the world of agents and publishers with sound counsel and an enthusiasm that made the whole adventure fun. Thanks, too, to Kathy Robbins and Susan Protter for their unselfish efforts.

Neeti Madan, of Sterling Lord Literistic, Inc., and Deborah Baker, of Kodansha America, believed in this project and made it real. Thank you!

And of course, Anne Marie, Celia, Broox and Galen.